SHOPPING THE WILD

Now that you're at the beach on weekends, take advantage of the clams and beach plums. . . . Since you're going skiing, take a little time off the slopes, hunt down the maples, and cook up maple syrup like you've never tasted. . . . Spring and fall days in the country are extra-special with wild strawberry jam and dandelion coffee. . . .

EATING FROM THE WILD points out the edible treasures all around you. Inspired by Yankee know-how and culinary wit, here is the one book you'll take with you — wherever you go.

D1453357

EATING
from the
WILD

**Dr. Anne Marie Stewart
and
Leon Kronoff**

BALLANTINE BOOKS · NEW YORK

To
our parents

SBN 345-24419-2-175

First Printing: December, 1975

Printed in the United States of America

BALLANTINE BOOKS
A Division of Random House, Inc.
201 East 50th Street, New York, N.Y. 10022
Simultaneously published by
Ballantine Books of Canada, Ltd., Toronto, Canada

Acknowledgments

We wish to thank Mr. Bob Rhodes and Miss Selma Kristel of the Windham College Library for providing such a fine reference library and for helping to obtain books on interlibrary loan. We are also grateful to Mrs. Annetta Castle of the Massachusetts Horticultural Society, who found and lent us some useful volumes on colonial life and customs. Others who located material for us were Mrs. Phyllis Lynch, Mrs. Anna Splaine, Dr. Richard Carter, Mr. Bruce Hamerslough, and Dr. Clarke Johnson.

Perhaps the most interesting and delightful part of writing this book was meeting and listening to the tales of our fellow Vermonters, who fascinated us and moved us with their lore and love of nature. Mrs. Mable Kent of Dummerston freely shared her impressive knowledge of field botany with us. Mr. and Mrs. Fred Wilkins of East Jamaica provided us with wild nuts, shared some old family recipes and demonstrated to us the great versatility of the common apple. For Mrs. Josephine Petelle of Derby Line, living on wild foods was often a necessity, as she and her farmer husband struggled to raise a family of eight children. She told of family berry-picking outings, drying apples for winter, catching and salting down barrels of fish, making homemade honey and putting up jars of wild and home-grown fruits and vegetables. Mr. John Walker and Mr. Leon Hall of Wilmington, both retired farmers, quietly told us of their yearly cycle of activities. bringing to mind an earlier time when life was hard but slow and rich. Mr. George Daniels of Royalton, somewhat skeptically toured us through his family woods, philosophizing, testing our knowledge of wild plants and giving us ideas for homemade wines that once put into effect should keep us happy and busy for a long time.

We thank Dr. Arthur H. Westing and Dr. Charles Tseng of the Windham College Biology Department for critically reading parts of the manuscript. Mrs. Dorothy Bugbee, who typed the manuscript, offered several helpful suggestions and was always a pleasant co-worker.

Finally, we are grateful to Dolores and David Ahern, who first suggested that we attempt this book, and to our families whose assistance and encouragement helped it become a reality.

Contents

SUMMER

AUTUMN

WINTER

The Choice Life

Although many people voice the desire to break away from store-bought foods and wish to venture back to nature for some of their nutrients, they are faced with a basic dilemma of our civilization: they know much about being good consumers but know little about living without depending on money or middlemen. In this field guide we try to lead the reader into the wild and help him locate, identify, collect and cook some of nature's delicious offerings.

The wild-food forager is faced with the very real problems of determining when and where to search for edible animals and plants. Then, in the case of plants particularly, he must identify the organism or risk gathering an inedible or poisonous species. In this field guide we have tried to lessen these problems by dividing the book into four units—Spring, Summer, Autumn and Winter. In general, we have presented the organisms in the season and the order in which they are most readily available. For each animal or plant featured there is a short history of its use as a food. Its habitat and range are given as well as a description and directions for collection and preparation. In addition, we have pointed out edible species that could be confused with inedible or poisonous ones.

As aids for identification of the broad spectrum of edible animals and plants discussed here, we have included an illustrated glossary as well as labeled drawings of each of the edible organisms. All illustrations were drawn from living or freshly collected specimens.

Our recipes tend to be simple and inexpensive. They mainly contain ingredients that can be gathered in the wild and those that can be homegrown. We have included many American Indian dishes particularly suited for camping outdoors. Our philosophy concerning food belongs to no single school of thought; we buy as few processed foods as possible. We try to live off the land, which offers us in each season its own specialties that cost no money but are as free as each sunrise and sunset. We raise our own organically grown vegetables, fruit, beef and poultry, supplementing these foods with wild fruits, vegetables, as well as fish and shellfish, which we gather all the year round.

We customarily keep on hand the following staples:

Flour—whole wheat, unbleached white, cattail pollen, elder flowers (dried), acorn meal, cornmeal

Oil—olive, sesame, soybean, corn

Vinegar—paper birch, maple, cider, red and white wine, strawberry

Salt—algal salt, sea salt

Pepper—pepper or, in season, poor man's pepper

Sweeteners—maple sugar, maple syrup, honey, raw sugar

Seasonings—wild leek leaves, mint leaves, bayberry leaves, sweet fern leaves, sea lettuce leaves, dulse leaves, wild carrot seeds, ground calamus root, garlic bulbs, vegetable bouillon cubes

Coffee—chicory root, dandelion root

Tea—sweet goldenrod leaves and blossoms, mint leaves, white clover blossoms, raspberry leaves, wintergreen leaves, sassafras root, twigs and leaves, witch hazel twigs and leaves

Pudding materials—Irish moss, various dried berries

Nuts—butternuts, black walnuts, hickory nuts, beech nuts, hazelnuts, acorns

We advise beginners to start with some of the more familiar wild foods, such as the dandelion, strawberry and apple. Then, as experience is gained in locating and identifying edible organisms, one can progress to the lesser-known ones. Foraging and fishing can be relaxing, healthful and inexpensive activities. We hope that more and more people will begin to discover the pleasure of turning back to nature and finding the primitive in themselves.

Dummerston, Vermont
June 30, 1973

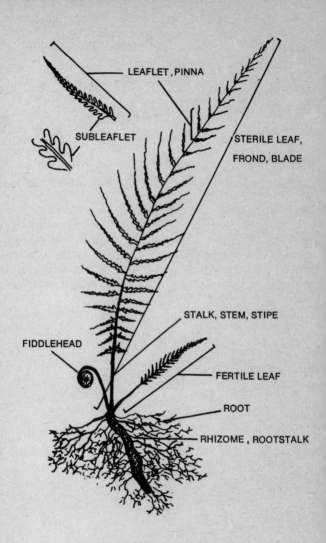

FERN PLANT (SPOROPHYTE)

Key Identifying Characteristics

Ferns

These are distinguished by the general morphology of the sterile and fertile fronds (leaves), rhizome (underground stem), and roots, as well as by habitat.

The fertile leaves of the fern plant (sporophyte) produce spores in spore cases (sporangia). The ripened spores fall to the ground and germinate into tiny, heart-shaped plants (gametophytes) which produce eggs and sperm. The fertilized egg of a gametophyte develops into a large, leafy fern plant sporophyte.

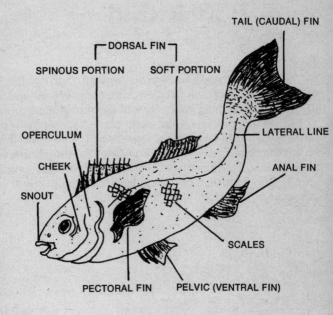

TAIL (CAUDAL) FIN

DORSAL FIN

SPINOUS PORTION   SOFT PORTION

OPERCULUM

CHEEK

SNOUT

LATERAL LINE

ANAL FIN

SCALES

PECTORAL FIN   PELVIC (VENTRAL FIN)

BONY FISH

Fish

Pattern of scales, fin structure (particularly that of the dorsal fins), teeth, body size, morphology and, in some cases, color. The operculum (see illustration) covers the gills and there are 2 sets of paired fins—the pectorals and pelvics—which correspond to our arms and legs, respectively. The dorsal, anal, and tail fins are unpaired. In some cases the dorsal fin is divided into an anterior spinous, and posterior soft portion.

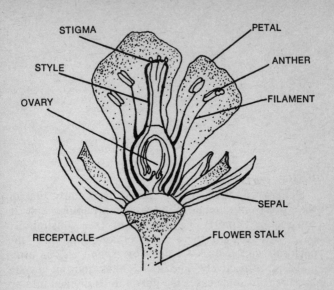

FLOWER PARTS

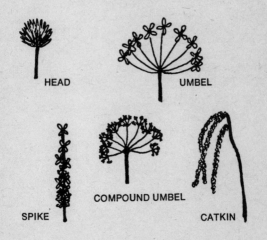

SOME TYPES OF FLOWER CLUSTERS

Flower Parts

The anther produces pollen grains, each of which can produce a pollen tube that grows down to the ovary, where fertilization takes place. The fruit is the ripened ovary with its contained seeds. The various kinds of fruit, such as berries, legumes, nuts, and samaras, are classified by botanists primarily on the basis of structure.

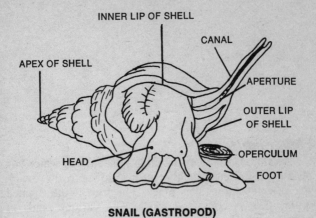

SNAIL (GASTROPOD)

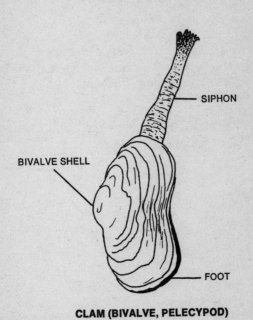

CLAM (BIVALVE, PELECYPOD)

Snail (*Gastropods*)

Varieties are identified through variations in shell size, morphology, color and habitat.

Mussels and Clams (*Bivalves, Pelecypods*)

Generally, these are distinguished from one another by size, morphology, color, and habitat.

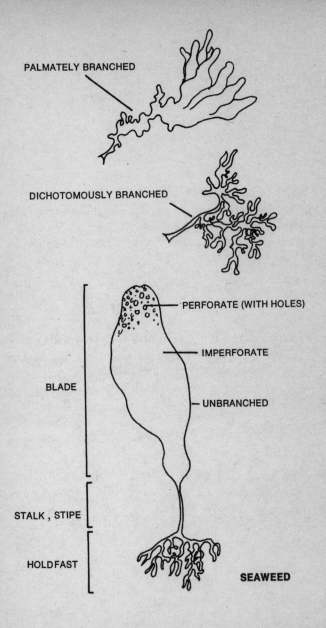

PALMATELY BRANCHED

DICHOTOMOUSLY BRANCHED

PERFORATE (WITH HOLES)

IMPERFORATE

UNBRANCHED

BLADE

STALK , STIPE

HOLDFAST

SEAWEED

Seaweeds

Differentiated by general morphology of the blade, stem, and holdfast (see illustration), as well as by coloration and habitat.

Twigs and Leaves

Leaves are generally described on the basis of their arrangement on the twig, on whether they are simple or compound, and by shape.

(OVERLEAF)

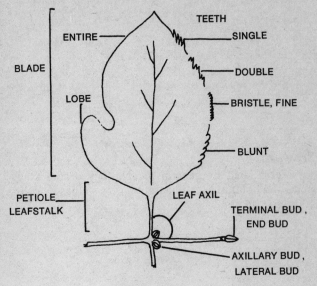

SIMPLE LEAF

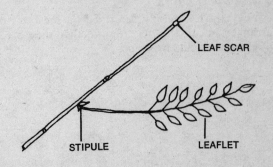

COMPOUND LEAF

TWIG AND LEAF TERMINOLOGY

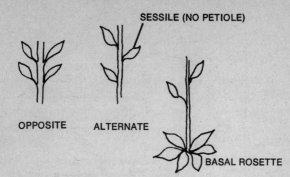

SESSILE (NO PETIOLE)

OPPOSITE   ALTERNATE

BASAL ROSETTE

LEAF ARRANGEMENT

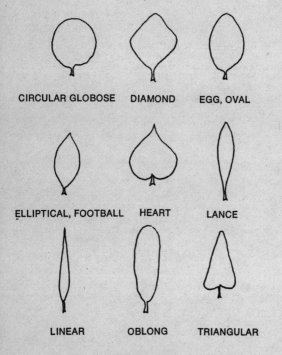

CIRCULAR GLOBOSE   DIAMOND   EGG, OVAL

ELLIPTICAL, FOOTBALL   HEART   LANCE

LINEAR   OBLONG   TRIANGULAR

LEAF SHAPE

Spring

Dandelion

The Common Garden Dandelion
(*Taraxacum officinale*)

History

In Europe, the dandelion has been used as a medicine, as a potherb and as a salad green for several hundred years. The common garden dandelion was probably brought to this country by the first settlers. Indeed, it is probable that dandelion seeds were carried by the pilgrims on the Mayflower (Solbrig 1971). For some unknown reason, subsequent generations of Americans discontinued the use of dandelion as a foodstuff, but today it is having a bit of a comeback.

Habitat and Range

Dandelions are perennial or biennial herbs. Several species are found in the temperate and cold regions of the northern hemisphere as well as in the colder regions of the southern hemisphere. The common garden dandelion (*T. officinale*) was introduced from Europe and is now naturalized in the United States. It is found in lawns, grasslands, and open ground.

Description

The dandelion is a rosette-leaved plant with one central taproot, bright yellow flower heads, and a downy seed ball containing many "silky" tufted seeds. If the plant grows in a relatively open area and is not trampled

3

upon, it grows relatively upright in the shape of an up-side-down bowl. However, if it is subjected to trampling by man or animals, such as in a lawn, the leaves grow somewhat parallel to the ground, forming a flattened rosette. The leaves are the edible dandelion greens.

The taproot is a food-storage organ similar to a carrot or beet and can grow up to 10 inches in length and an inch in width. The root contains a white viscous liquid (the "milk"), which imparts a bitter taste to the uncooked root. Fortunately, this bitterness is lost when the root is boiled or baked.

The yellow flowers are produced in the spring and fall and are borne at the top of a hollow stemlike structure called "the scape." Usually the flower remains open for only a day and then closes. Often it and the scape lie prostrate on the ground for a few days. Then the scape becomes erect again and the leaves surrounding the flower open and expose the downy, white ball of seeds.

Most people probably think they can identify a dandelion plant when they see one, but this might not always be the case. There are several species that resemble dandelion, but they can be readily distinguished from it by their hairy leaves and/or branched flower stems as opposed to the smooth leaves and unbranched flower stems of the dandelion.

Collection and Preparation

The dandelion is a favorite plant of the forager because it is ubiquitous, adaptable, hardy and highly nutritious. Chances are that you, like most Americans, are prejudiced against dandelions. You were raised with the belief that the dandelion was a noxious weed, a pest and a bane to the home owner with a lawn. Granted, some of these assertions are true. Your mother probably dutifully shopped in a shiny supermarket, spending your father's money to provide her family with nutritious greens such as spinach and lettuce. Meanwhile, she ignored the nutritious, delicious and free dandelion

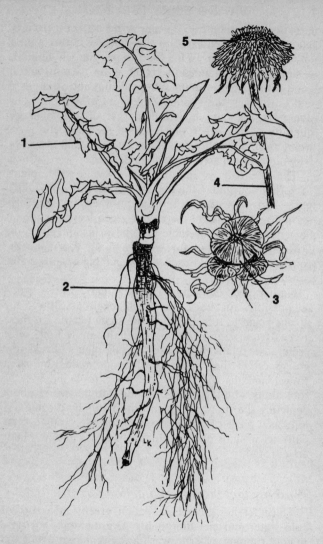

Common Garden Dandelion. 1, Green leaves of a newly sprouted plant—raw or cooked vegetable. 2, White tap root—cooked vegetable or coffee substitute. 3, Flower buds—cooked vegetable. 4, Hollow scape. 5, Yellow flower head—wine.

growing all around her. To show you how she erred by ignoring the dandelion, go to a library and peruse a book on human nutrition. In the food charts you will find that a single cup of dandelion greens is an extraordinarily good source of iron, potassium, calcium and vitamins A and C. In fact, the vitamin A content of a cup of dandelion greens rates higher than that of a comparable quantity of any other vegetable on the food chart. No wonder our forebears used them for medicinal purposes. Now, how about trying some dandelions?

The dandelion is one of the many wild edible plants to sprout soon after the melting of the snow. Its edible parts can be gathered throughout the year. In early spring one can collect the tender green leaves or the fat flower sprouts for vegetables; in midspring and in fall the flowers are collected for wine; and all year long the roots can be dug and used as a vegetable or as a coffee substitute.

Gather your dandelion greens as early in the spring as possible, for once the plants begin to flower the greens begin to turn bitter. While some people eat these greens from spring right up until the snow falls, most prefer the relatively sweeter spring plants. Break the greens off at the rootstalk with your hands, or use a trowel and dig the plant up by the root and use the root along with the greens as food. Do not worry about depleting the supply of dandelion plants by digging. As long as a piece of the root remains in the ground, it repairs its wounds and eventually two to five new plants arise from it.

Washing and Storing Dandelion Greens

Place freshly picked dandelion greens in a sink of cold water and mix thoroughly. Do not soak, but rinse in cold running water to wash away remaining sand and grit. All freshly cut greens should be used immediately because vitamins are lost in storage. If you do have extra greens, wrap them in a clean towel and store in the refrigerator.

Dandelion Salad
(for 4)

1 lb fresh dandelion leaves*

Oil and Vinegar Dressing
(for 4)

½ tsp salt   ⅓ cup olive oil
½ tsp pepper   1 tsp sugar
½ cup wine vinegar

Beat all the ingredients together in a medium-size bowl, pour over the dandelion when ready to eat, mix thoroughly, and enjoy.

Lemon and Oil Dressing
(for 4)

2 fresh lemons   ½ cup olive oil
2 tbsp raw sugar   salt and pepper to taste

Take the two lemons and squeeze the juice into a medium-size bowl, add sugar and dissolve. Add the oil, salt and pepper, and beat the mixture thoroughly. Pour over greens, and enjoy the tangy freshness.

For that little extra taste, slice fresh onion rings and add them to the salad. For even more flavor, sprinkle toasted sesame seeds on the greens.

Dandelion and Cucumber Salad

Add the desired amount of chopped cucumber and yogurt to your dandelion greens.

* One can mix iceberg or romaine lettuce and dandelion greens half and half with a pleasing result.

Boiled Dandelion Flower Heads
(for 4)

3 cups fresh, opened dande-   4 tbsp water
   lion flowers or flower   salt and pepper to taste
   buds   butter to taste

Bring the salted water to a boil. Add the flowers, cover and cook over medium heat for 5 minutes. Remove from heat, stir flowers, cover and let stand for 2 minutes. Serve with butter and condiments.

Boiled Dandelion Roots
(for 4)

3 doz medium-size dande-   ½ cup water
   lion roots (about 4 inches   salt and pepper to taste
   long)   butter to taste

Wash the roots thoroughly and remove root hairs. Salt the water and bring to a boil. Add the roots, lower heat, cover and simmer for 20 minutes or until they are soft but not mushy. Serve, adding butter and condiments to taste.

This is a sweet and palatable vegetable that can be obtained year round, but is at its best when the roots are dug in winter.

Baked Dandelion Roots
(for 4)

3 doz large dandelion roots

Wash the roots thoroughly, remove root hairs and place in a preheated moderate oven (375°F). Bake for 30 minutes. Serve.

These roots taste just like baked potatoes. Eat the "jackets" and all; they are a delicious surprise.

Dandelion as a Coffee Substitute

To Prepare the Roots

Dig out several dozen large dandelion roots and wash them thoroughly in lukewarm water. Dry them in a moderate oven for about 2 hours or until they are dark brown in color and quite brittle. Cool, break them into pieces and crush to a powder. Store in a covered jar.

To Prepare the Coffee

Take one teaspoon of the powdered root per cup of water. Steep 15 minutes. Sweeten, if desired, and serve. Perhaps a better use of powdered dandelion root is as an adulterant to ordinary instant coffee. Take ⅓ teaspoon of powdered root plus ½ teaspoon of instant coffee and steep in a cup of water. The result is an espresso-type drink that we find preferable to either plain dandelion coffee or instant coffee.

Dandelion Wine

1 gal water	2 lemons
3 qt dandelion flowers	1 lb white raisins
3 lb raw sugar	1 pkg yeast*
4 oranges	1 slice dark bread (toasted)

For a smooth, pleasant wine, it is important that the flowers be picked while fully opened. Plan to gather your flowers in the middle of a warm, sunny day. You should then start to make your wine immediately.

---

* We used baking yeast but you might prefer an all-purpose wine yeast.

Bring the water to a boil in a large pot or kettle. Have the yellow flower heads in a large crock and pour the hot water over them. Cover the crock and steep for three days in a cool room (about 60°F). Do not exceed the time, because the infusion might spoil.

Pour the infusion back into a pot, add the rinds of the lemons and oranges (save the juice), and boil for 15 minutes. Pour this mixture into the crock through a fine sieve lined with cheesecloth. Add the sugar to the mixture and stir until dissolved. Strain in the juice of the oranges and lemons. Sprinkle the yeast onto the bread. When the liquid is cool add the yeast, bread and raisins. Cover the crock and let stand and ferment for two weeks in a cool room. During that period, uncover and stir every other day. When the solids have settled to the bottom and the supernatant is clear, siphon the wine off into clean bottles. Stopper and store for four months in a cool, dark corner of the cellar.

Spring-made wine will be ready for Halloween, while wine made in autumn will bring you Christmas cheer. However, dandelion wine is much finer when it is allowed to age two or three years.

Note. A useful way to siphon is to take your siphon hose and tie it to a stick. The bottom end of the hose should be at least 3 inches above the stick. In this way you will be able to stay clear of the sediment. Also, one can use old wine bottles and recork them. If you do not have any corks, they can be purchased at a hardware store.

Burdock

The Common Burdock (*Arctium minus*)
The Great Burdock (*Arctium lappa*)

History

Burdocks are weed plants of the Old World that were brought here by the settlers, who used them for food and medicinal purposes. The roots, leaves and flower stalks were consumed as cooked vegetables and the candied flower stalk was a popular confection. The root of the great burdock was used in Europe as an antiscorbutic and the roots, leaves or seeds were used in decoctions that were drunk to treat skin ailments. In America, an extract prepared from the seeds was a favorite medicine that was applied externally to treat chronic skin disorders. The use of these plants is not common here today, but in Hawaii and parts of Asia they are still consumed as a foodstuff.

The Iroquois Indians learned to use the great burdock as a food plant, cooking the leaves as a potherb and using the elongate roots in soups. Quantities of burdock root were also collected and dried by the fire for winter use, when they were soaked in water and then boiled to make a soup.

Habitat and Range

The common burdock (*A. minus*) is found throughout most of the United States and southern Canada, while the great burdock (*A. lappa*) is in most of the northern United States and adjacent parts of Canada both species are "naturalized" from Europe. Favorite habitats of these plants are roadsides, waste places and around old buildings.

Description

Burdocks are stout biennial herbs that have a long, slender taproot; large, alternate leaves; round heads of purple (sometimes white) flowers; and brown fruits, which are borne in the familiar burrs. The large, heart-shaped basal leaves grow to a foot or more in length and have a soft down on the underside, while the upper leaves are smaller, more egg-shaped and less hairy. Burdock roots grow 1 to 3 feet in length and to an inch in width.

The common burdock grows to a height of 5 feet and the petioles (leaf stalks) of the lower leaves are mostly hollow, while the great burdock can reach a height of 10 feet and has mostly solid petioles.

Collection and Preparation

In the spring, when you find an old rooted stalk bearing "sticky burrs," you are in an area that is likely to have sprouting burdock plants.

The downy leaves emerge early in the spring and can be harvested with the first wild vegetables; later in the spring, the flower stalks can be picked, peeled of their rind, cooked and eaten. The long taproot of these biennials can be harvested from midsummer of their first year to late spring of their second year. These roots are rich in starch and when eaten raw have a flavor resembling raw carrots.

Boiled Burdock Roots
(for 2)

8 burdock roots	1 tbsp butter
2 cups water	salt and pepper to taste

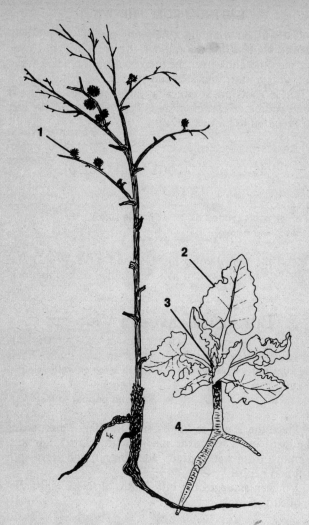

Common Burdock. 1, Dead burdock with brown burs at the end of second year. 2, Sprouting burdock in the spring of its second year showing the heart-shaped basal leaves—cooked vegetable. 3, Area from which the flower stalk will emerge—cooked vegetable or confection. 4, White tap root—cooked vegetable or confection.

Cut washed roots into inch-long pieces and place in boiling water (do not remove the tasty rind). Cover the pan and cook over medium heat until tender. Serve hot with butter, and salt and pepper.

These roots are a sweet-tasting vegetable, and are a good source of carbohydrates. Peeled flower stalks can be prepared in the same way.

Burdock Root Confection
(a tasty sweet)

burdock roots (boiled as described above)   maple sugar

Roll the boiled roots in sugar and serve. Peeled and boiled flower stalks can also be candied in this manner.

Burdock Leaves in Vinegar
(for 2)

1½ cups burdock leaves*   3 tbsp birch or white wine
½ cup water   vinegar
                                              salt and pepper to taste

Place the leaves in lightly salted boiling water, cover the pan and cook over medium heat for 5 minutes. Remove from water, drain, add vinegar, and serve with salt and pepper.

Vinegar assuages the bitter taste of this bright-green cooked vegetable.

* Use very young leaves not more than 3 inches in length.

Docks

(*Rumex*—various species)

History

The docks are cosmopolitan weeds that are represented in the United States by several native plants as well as by some European species that were inadvertently brought into this country. All the docks are edible, and various tribes of our western Indians utilized the roots, stems, leaves or seeds of some native species. In addition, the Iroquois Indians and some western tribes ate the leaves and seeds of the curled dock (*Rumex crispus*), a European "import" that has become a common weed here.

The vitamin-C-rich dock plants have an ancient history as antiscorbutics. It is believed by some scholars that the herb that cured the soldiers of Julius Caesar from the afflictions of scurvy in the Rhine country was the root of the great water dock (*R. aquaticus*). Decoctions of the roots or leaves of several other dock species are also old herb remedies for scurvy and skin disorders.

Habitat and Range

These cosmopolitan weeds are distributed throughout the United States. The various species occupy diverse habitats from swamps, waste areas and fields to rocky beaches and saline soils.

Description

Docks are characterized by their long, mainly basal, usually lance-shaped leaves and their tall stout stalk

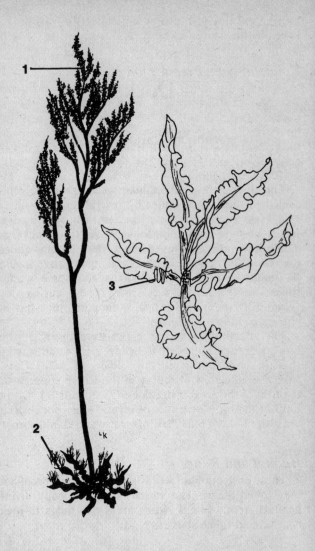

Curled Dock. 1, Mature plant with winged, brown fruit —grind for cereal and bread. 2, Basal leaves (not edible when mature). 3, Sprouting basal leaves— cooked vegetable.

bearing the tiny green to purple clusters of flowers followed by the winged brown fruits.

Collection and Preparation

In summer and autumn, dock plants are very noticeable and can be readily identified by their elongate basal leaves and tall, brown fruit stalk. However, by late winter or early spring the leaves will be dead and the fruit stalks will, in all probability, be lying on the ground. At these times of the year, search along roadsides or old buildings for the prostrate brown stalks. The new dock leaves will sprout adjacent to the base of these stalks and can be collected when they first sprout in the spring until the time they become too strong in taste. In addition to the spring crop, docks again sprout tender, young leaves in the autumn; these can be gathered for as long as the plants continue to produce them.

Dock Greens
(for 2)

1½ cups young dock leaves   1 tbsp butter, if desired
⅓ cup water   salt and pepper to taste

Add the leaves to the salted boiling water, cover the pan and cook over medium heat for 5 minutes. Stir in the butter and serve with the juice and condiments.

This vegetable has a flavor resembling that of beet greens. It is rich in vitamins A and C.

Wild Leek

(*Allium tricoccum*)

History

The wild leek is a native species of the northeastern United States and southeastern Canada. Its culinary qualities were appreciated by the colonists and some Indians. Leeks were widely used by the Iroquois as a food and medicinal plant and were eaten by Indians of Minnesota and Wisconsin. The bulbs were consumed raw or dried and were also employed as a seasoning.

Perhaps the earliest written record dealing with this native plant is that of Hariot who mentioned them in his account of the fated English colony that was established in Roanoke, Virginia from 1585–86. "There are also Leekes differing little from ours in England that grow in many places of the countrey, of which, when we came in places where, wee gathered and eate many, but the naturall inhabitants neuer" (Hariot 1893).

Habitat and Range

The wild leek grows in rich woods of the northeast from New Brunswick to Minnesota and south to Tennessee and North Carolina.

Description

Wild leeks are low-growing plants that form colonies that sprout with the earliest spring greens. At that time of year, the leek beds produce patches of green that contrast sharply with the brown of their surroundings. Up close, the plants can be identified by their onion-like odor as well as by their two (sometimes three) lance-shaped, green leaves and the small, white underground bulb loosely attached to a few other bulbs. The leaves are tapered at both ends and grow to about 3 inches in width and 9 inches in length (counting the sturdy reddish-purple petiole). The bulbs grow to about 2 inches in length and ½ inch in diameter. Usually the leaves have died back by the time the erect flower stem appears with its umbellate cluster of whitish flowers in June or July.

Collection and Preparation

Early in spring, search for the green patches of leeks in open wooded areas and along fields and roadsides bordering rich woods. Our favorite collecting spot is a woodland maple-sugar lot.

Both the aerial and underground parts of the plant are edible. The leaves have a pleasantly mild onion-like taste. The bulbs are mild early in spring but develop a stronger flavor by the time the flower stalk has sprouted. Remember, take only what you need; do not decimate the beds.

Leek and Dandelion Salad
(for 2)

2 cups dandelion greens
6 leek leaves (chopped) or
   4 leek bulbs (sliced)
⅓ cup olive oil

¼ cup birch or white wine
   vinegar
salt and pepper to taste

Toss all ingredients together and serve immediately.

Dried Wild Leek

Set oven at 250°F. Thoroughly wash leek leaves in water and set on an absorbent towel to drain. Place

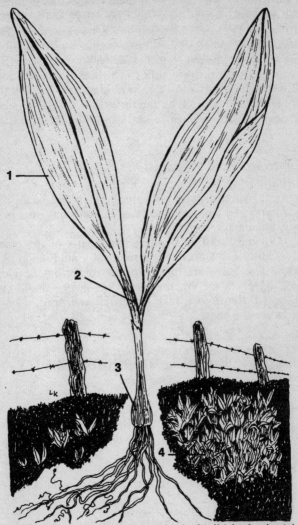

Wild Leek. 1, Lance-shaped leaf of wild leek plant in early spring—raw and cooked vegetable, condiment or soup. 2, Region from which the flower stalk will emerge. 3, White bulb—raw or cooked vegetable. 4, Group of leek plants in early spring showing habit of growth.

individual leaves on a sheet pan and dry in the oven for an hour or until the leaves are crisp. Remove from oven and cool. Crumble the leaves with your hand and store in clean, covered containers. Use as a garnish or flavoring for soups, salads, egg dishes, etc.

Leek bulbs can be dried for winter by hanging bunches of them in a dry room. These are particularly good in soups.

Leek Soup
(for 4)

1 lg handful fresh leek
   leaves (coarsely chopped)
4 tbsp butter
1 cup water

3 tbsp unbleached white
   flour
2 cups milk
salt and pepper to taste

Heat two tablespoonfuls of butter in a pot, add the leaves and sauté over medium heat for 3 to 4 minutes. Add the water and simmer over low heat. In another skillet melt butter, stir in the flour and add one cup of milk. Blend. Then stir in the other cup of milk. Add this sauce to the leeks, stir and simmer until ready to serve (approximately 10 minutes).

Macaroni or boiled potatoes make a pleasant addition to this soup.

Wild Leek Omelette
(for 1)

2 eggs
1 tsp dried leek leaves or
   2 fresh leaves (chopped)

salt

Beat eggs in a bowl, add a dash of salt, then add the

leek leaves. Pour into a hot, greased skillet and sauté until the omelette appears firm; during this process move skillet in a rotary motion. Roll the omelette and cook to desired firmness.

Nettles

(*Urtica*—several species)

History

Today the common stinging nettle (*Urtica dioica*) is considered to be an obnoxious weed, but only a couple of generations ago it and related species were used in parts of Europe for an impressive number of purposes. The young plant tops and leaves were cooked as an early spring vegetable. In Germany, during World War I, thousands of acres were planted with nettles whose fibers were used for military clothing. The stalks of these nitrogen-rich plants were dried and chopped for cattle and horse fodder or powdered and added to poultry feed. A green dye was extracted from the aerial parts of the plant and a yellow dye was made from the roots. The plants were also used in a variety of herbal remedies whose curative powers must have been due in part to their high amount of nitrogen and vitamins A and C.

As far as we can ascertain, nettles were never popular with Americans, but the Iroquois Indians are recorded to have used the cooked tops as a springtime food.

Habitat and Range

The nettles are represented by about fifty species in both hemispheres. In the United States there are several

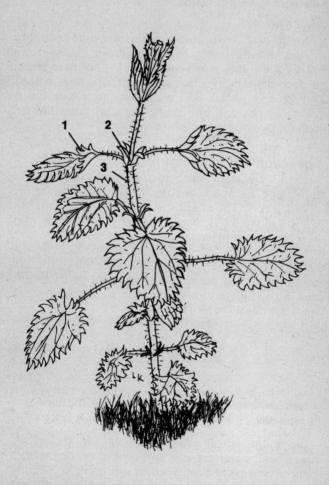

Common Stinging Nettle. 1, Young nettle plant with bristly, opposite, toothed leaves—cooked vegetable. 2, Region from which the flowers will emerge. 3, Bristly stem—cooked vegetable.

species, some native, some introduced. These are found throughout the country in waste places, along road-sides and in moist areas.

Description

Nettles are herbs that contain many tiny stinging bristles on the stems, petioles and leaf blades (one variety sometimes grows no bristles). They have heart-to lance-shaped leaves that are simple, opposite, toothed and strongly ribbed. The plants can grow to about 6 feet in height, and bear numerous tiny, green flowers in the axils of the upper leaves.

Collection and Preparation

Nettles are among the earliest greens to sprout in the spring and are noticeable because of their prominently ribbed leaves. The conclusive test for nettles is to run a finger along the stem or leaves; if you are stung, you have the correct plant.

Collect nettles in early spring before they flower. Hold the plant with a gloved hand and with your other hand, cut off the young leaves and tops of the plants with a pair of scissors. Place them in a collander and wash thoroughly before using.

Nettle Greens
(for 4)

4 cups fresh nettle greens	1 tbsp butter, if desired
¼ cup water	salt and pepper to taste

Bring the salted water to a boil, add the greens, lower heat, cover the pan and cook 5 to 10 minutes. Longer cooking of young nettles will result in a mushy vegetable. Drain and serve with butter and salt and pepper.

Although this is a dish rich in protein and vitamins A and C, it is not one of our favorite vegetables.

Plantain

English Plantain, Rib Grass
(*Plantago lanceolata*)
Seaside Plantain, Goose-tongue
(*Plantago maritima*)

History

Among the several edible species of plantain that grow in the northeastern United States, we recommend English plantain (*Plantago lanceolata*) and seaside plantain (*P. maritima*) for their superior flavor, large size, and abundance.

English plantain, or rib grass, is a common weed plant intimately associated with man for centuries. It has been often said that wherever on the globe the English flag traveled, English plantain soon became established in the area. Such was the case with this plant in the New World, where it became established in the colonies and now grows throughout the United States.

The English made a tea with the fresh leaves of English plantain and also utilized the young leaves as a salad green and potherb. The mucilaginous seeds were widely collected and used for canary food. This plantain along with the common plantain (*P. major*), was also widely used in England as a medicinal herb. It might interest campers to know that these plantains were used to alleviate the pain of burns, by applying a moist preparation of the leaves to the afflicted area and the fresh leaves were rubbed on the skin to assuage the pain from insect bites or the sting of a nettle plant. Beyond all these uses, we consider the English plantain to be the finest tasting of all the cooked spring greens.

Seaside plantain is a circumboreal species of maritime areas, which grows abundantly on our northeast coast. In Wales it has been cultivated for sheep fodder, and in parts of eastern Maine and Nova Scotia it is used as a summer vegetable.

Habitat and Range

Plantago is a cosmopolitan genus represented by over 200 species that grow throughout most of the world.

English plantain is a European species that has become naturalized throughout the United States and southern Canada, where it proliferates on roadsides, lawns and waste places. Seaside plantain is found on coastal rocks, beaches and salt marshes throughout the colder regions of the Northern Hemisphere. On the Atlantic coast it ranges as far south as New Jersey.

Description

English plantain is a low-growing plant with fibrous roots, a rosette of green leaves and a few elongate stalks that bear a rust-colored, conical flower spike at their tip. Tiny white flowers are borne on the spike. The lance-shaped leaves are ribbed and taper at both ends; they can be upright or flattened and grow to a length of 10 inches. The flower stalk is about twice the length of the leaves.

In general, seaside plantain resembles English plantain, but the leaves of this maritime species are more linear in shape and are very fleshy; the flowers can be greenish and are borne on a more elongate spike.

Collection and Preparation

English plantain is among the first edible wild greens available in the spring, with seaside plantain ripening a little later in the season. Pluck the younger, more tender leaves and wash them thoroughly before using.

English Plantain. 1, Rust colored flower spike. 2, Lance-shaped leaves—cooked vegetable and soup. 3, Fibrous roots.

Plantain Greens
(for 2)

2 cups fresh plantain leaves
⅓ cup water

1 tbsp butter, if desired
salt and pepper to taste

Bring the salted water to a boil, add the leaves, cover, and cook over medium heat for 5 minutes. Stir in the butter and serve with the juice. Add salt and pepper and enjoy the nut-like flavor of this superior-tasting vegetable.

Plantain Soup
(for 2)

2½ cups water
2 cups fresh English plantain
   leaves
¾ cup boiled diced burdock

root or potato
1 tbsp butter, if desired
salt and pepper to taste

Bring salted water to a boil, add the burdock root and plantain leaves, lower heat, cover and simmer for 10 minutes. Stir in the butter and serve hot with salt and pepper.

This is a delicious, simple-to-prepare vegetable soup.

Birches

(*Betula*—several species)

History

The twigs, bark and leaves of the black or sweet birch (*Betula lenta*) and the yellow birch (*B. alle-*

ghaniensis) have a distinctive wintergreen flavor and were used by the northeastern Indians and the colonists for gently stimulating, aromatic teas. The twigs alone were used as a flavorful chew. Oil of wintergreen can be readily obtained by steam distilling the bark and twigs of these trees. Until recently the black birch was the main commercial source of this product.

Most species of birch can be tapped just before the leaves begin to appear in the spring. The copious saccharine sap can be converted into wine or beer as has been the practice in Europe for centuries. The sap can be consumed as a fresh drink; this was a popular beverage of the eastern Indians. Some of our older Vermont neighbors tell how drinking birch sap was a part of their normal cycle of springtime activities. Mr. Leon Hall, a retired farmer from Wilmington, Vermont, related the following information to us. "In May it was fencing time and we cut and split the hardwoods for fence posts. This was the time we would 'box' a yellow birch with an axe and drink the sweet sap. You couldn't drink it fast enough, the flow was so great."

Habitat, Range, and Description

There are about 40 species of birch distributed throughout the cooler regions of the Northern Hemisphere. Most of the birches can be readily distinguished by the bark, which is marked by distinct horizontal cross streaks (lenticels). In older trees the bark separates rather readily from the tree in sheets. The leaves are simple and alternate; the flowers are borne in catkins and the fruit is a small one-seeded, winged nutlet grouped with other nutlets to form a cone-like structure. Additional features of some of our common birches are listed in the accompanying chart.

Collection and Preparation

In Vermont, birches can be tapped from about the middle of April until mid-May. Use the same techniques as employed for tapping maples on page 362.

Younger people might enjoy using birch sap in the ways described for maple sap on page 365, but it is more commonly used as the main ingredient of birch beer or vinegar.

Sweet Birch Beer
(a pleasant, mild beverage)

2 gal birch sap
  (yellow or black birch)
2 cups raw sugar or 1 cup
  honey

2 qt birch twigs
½ yeast cake
1 piece dark bread
  (toasted)

Boil sap, sugar and twigs in a large pot for 15 minutes. Allow to cool, then strain liquid through a cloth into a large crock. Spread yeast on the bread and float

TABLE 1
Habitat, Range, and Description of
Four Common Eastern Birches

Species	Habitat	Range
Black birch (*Betula lenta*)	Mature, rich, well-drained woods	Southeastern Canada south to Appalachian mountains and vicinity; southern Michigan
Yellow birch (*B. alleghaniensis*)	Moist woods	Southeastern Canada, northeastern United States and along Appalachian mountains
Paper birch (*B. papyrifera*)	Young forests	Transcontinental Canada and northern United States
Gray birch (*B. populifolia*)	Sterile soil, abandoned farms, burned-over land	Southeastern Canada, northeastern United States

bread in the liquid. Cover crock with a towel and let stand in a cool room for 10 days to 2 weeks. Use immediately or bottle.

The white birches can also be used to prepare birch beer—just omit the twigs.

If you desire birch vinegar, you can allow the sap mixture to continue to work in the crock for another 6 weeks to 2 months or you can make birch vinegar according to the recipe given below.

Birch Vinegar

5 gal birch sap (we use paper birch)

3 cups raw sugar

Mix ingredients in a large crock, place in a cool

Description

Height:
  Medium, 50–60′
Twigs:
  Wintergreen taste
	Leaves:
	  Egg-shaped, sharply toothed
	Bark:
	  Dark brown

Height:
  Medium, 60–70′
Twigs:
  Wintergreen taste
	Leaves:
	  Egg-shaped, sharply toothed
	Bark:
	  Scaly, lustrous yellow gray

Height:
  Medium, 50–70′
Twigs:
  No wintergreen taste
	Leaves:
	  Egg-shaped, sharply toothed
	Bark:
	  Lustrous creamy white, very papery

Height:
  Small, 20–30′
Twigs:
  No wintergreen taste
Leaves:
  Triangular with long, pointed tips, doubly toothed
	Bark:
	  Dull gray or white, brittle, numerous black triangular patches on trunk below branch insertion

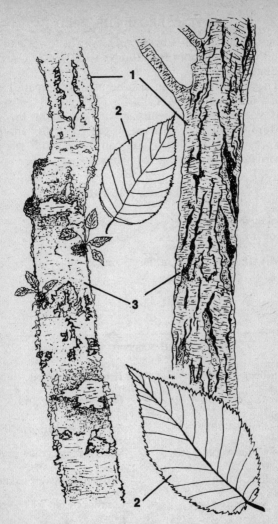

Yellow Birch (left) and **Black Birch** (right). 1, Scaly lustrous yellow-gray bark of the yellow birch compared to the bark of black birch, which is dark brown and broken into thick plates. 2, Egg-shaped, sharply toothed leaves. 3, Conspicuous lenticels (cross streaks). Sap of both birches—fresh drink, beer, or vinegar. Twigs and bark—tea and used in beer making.

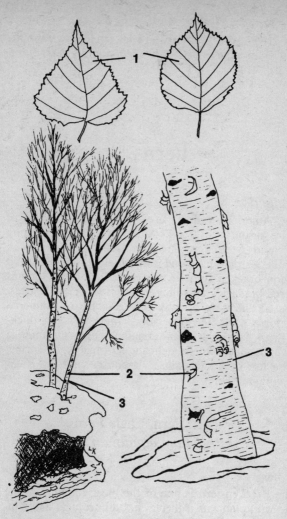

Gray Birch (left) and **Paper Birch** (right). 1, Triangular, sharply toothed leaf of gray birch compared to the egg-shaped leaf of paper birch. 2, Bark of gray birch is dull gray or white, has numerous black patches and is brittle; that of paper birch is soft, lustrous, creamy white and papery. 3, Lenticels (cross streaks). The sap of both birches—fresh drink, beer, or vinegar.

room, cover with a towel, and let stand for approximately 2 months with occasional stirring. Filter and bottle.

Ferns

Introduction

The American Indians used over twenty species of fern as a source of food. Among the most common types used were the cinnamon fern, the interrupted fern, the ostrich fern and the widely distributed and common bracken fern. In the early spring the Indians gathered the newly uncoiling fern leaves, or fiddleheads, and used them as a cooked vegetable or simmered them for a while and then added them to soups thickened with flour. For years country people in America have appreciated these delicate harbingers of spring, yet the use of fiddleheads as a source of food is far from common here.

Bracken Fern, Eagle Fern
(*Pteridium aquilinum*)

History

The Bracken fern is one of the most common of the edible wild plants as it thrives in both tropical and temperate regions. Bracken fiddleheads are diminutive, are fairly easy to clean and they taste somewhat like asparagus; they are used as a cooked vegetable in Japan, parts of Europe and in New Zealand. In addition, the bracken rhizome can be peeled and roasted. This nutritious, pungent food was particularly relished by the Indians of the northwestern United States.

Habitat and Range

Bracken is the most common of all our ferns; several varieties are found throughout the United States. These plants often grow in dense stands in dry, sandy or gravelly soils of such diverse areas as roadsides, dry open woods and recently burned clearings and pastures.

Description

It is best to locate and identify bracken fern in the summer or fall and then wait until early spring to collect the fiddleheads. Bracken is a wiry fern with hairy, cylindric stalks, often one-half inch thick at the base. The uncoiling frond (leaf) is distinctly three-forked and has a smooth, light-green spot at the angles, which soon becomes a deep purple. Spores are located in brown spore cases (sporangia) borne in clusters on the margins of the underside of leaflets.

Be sure to collect your fiddleheads when they are young and uncoiled. Older bracken fronds are tough and have been known to poison livestock fed quantities of them. Do not let this word of caution scare you, for the young, tender fiddleheads are safe to eat.

Ostrich Fern (*Matteuccia struthiopteris*)

History

Ostrich fern fiddleheads are large, easy to clean and delicious. We did not find much written information concerning the use of this fern as a foodstuff. Many older Vermonters are in the habit of eating the tender fiddleheads, just as their parents and grandparents did.

Habitat and Range

The ostrich fern is found from Newfoundland to Virginia, west to the Great Lake states, Missouri and South Dakota; in the northwest it ranges to southern Alaska. It most often grows on the rich, alluvial soil of brooksides, river and stream banks and in rich, shaded

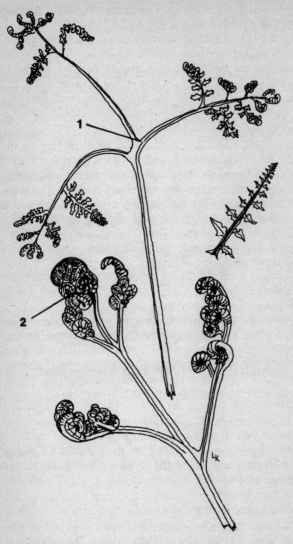

Bracken Fern. 1, Leaf that is too old for consumption (note its 3-forked arrangement which is a distinctive characteristic of this fern). 2, Fiddleheads ready for cooking—soup, cooked vegetable.

thickets and woods. Plants in these favorable habitats sometimes reach a height of 9 feet.

Description

The ostrich fern has been called the "graceful giant" and, it lives up to its name. It has a deep, creeping rootstalk called a rhizome, from which emerge the tender young fiddleheads. Some of these fiddleheads soon expand into the long (4 to 9 feet tall), graceful, green sterile fronds* that form vase-like clumps. In the midst of the green fronds emerge the shorter (1 to 2 feet tall), feather-shaped, spore-bearing, fertile fronds, which are at first green, then brown. These brown, feather-shaped fronds are the structures by which you can conclusively identify the ostrich fern year round.

Interrupted Fern (*Osmunda claytoniana*)
Cinnamon Fern (*Osmunda cinnamomea*)

History

Osmunda is a small genus of tropical and temperate areas, which is well represented by three species in the eastern United States, but is conspicuously absent in most of the western parts of this country. In early spring the East Coast Indians used to gather the young fronds of the interrupted fern (*O. claytoniana*) and used them as a cooked vegetable, while the later-appearing cinnamon fern fronds (*O. cinnamomea*) were favored as spring potherbs for soups.

Interrupted fern is too bitter for most palates, but this bitterness can be assuaged by sautéing the fiddleheads in butter for a few minutes rather than serving them as a boiled vegetable. Cinnamon fern is almost impossible to clean and is rather dry in taste, but it is a suitable emergency vegetable and can be used in soup.

---

* In this species of fern as well as in the next two ferns discussed, the spore-bearing, fertile fronds are morphologically distinct from the sterile fronds, which do not bear spores (see *Fern* in Key Identifying Characteristics.

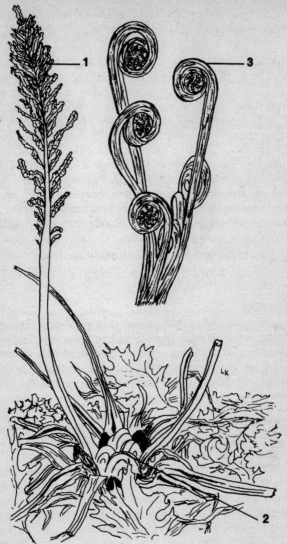

Ostrich Fern. 1, Plant in late winter showing the stiff, brown fertile leaf (of previous year's growth). 2, New fiddleheads. 3, Fiddleheads ready to be gathered for eating—cooked vegetable, soup.

Interrupted Fern (*Osmunda claytoniana*)

Habitat and Range

The interrupted fern prefers dry areas and is generally found along roadsides and at the edges of woods, but it is also found in moist areas. Its range is from Newfoundland to Manitoba, south to Arkansas, and as far east as Georgia.

Description

The sterile and fertile fronds are separate and are broadest in the middle, tapering at the apex and base. The sterile fronds grow to a height of about three feet and arch outward, while the fertile fronds are taller and more erect. Only the leaflets in the middle of the fertile frond bear spore cases, hence the name Interrupted fern. The rounded spore cases are brown in adult plants.

The fiddleheads are about ½ inch in diameter and are covered with a layer of "wool," which tends to be cinnamon colored on the dorsal surface of the stalk, but is whitish on the rest of the stalk and the fiddlehead.

Fiddleheads of fertile fronds tend to grow taller than sterile fronds. Toward the center of the fertile frond are thickened green leaflets containing round, yellow-green spore cases. These plump leaflets bulge through their wooly cover early in the season, revealing their granular-looking structure. Uncoil a fertile frond to expose the delicate leaflets at its apex and base and the plump spore-bearing leaflets in the middle.

Cinnamon Fern (*Osmunda cinnamomea*)

Habitat and Range

The cinnamon fern is found in wet areas, swamps, low woodlands, and thickets throughout southeastern

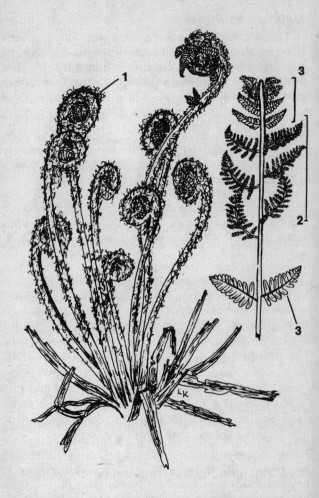

Interrupted Fern. 1, Fiddleheads—soup, sautéed vegetable. 2, Close-up of uncoiled fertile leaf with fertile leaflets bearing granulelike spore cases. 3, Smooth sterile leaflets.

Canada, the eastern United States inland to Minnesota, south to Florida and west to New Mexico, as well as tropical America.

Description

The sterile and fertile fronds are separate. The tall, green, arching, sterile fronds set off the shorter, green, then cinnamon-colored, fertile fronds. The sterile fronds grow to five feet in height. The rootstalk often forms mounds on the surface of the ground that reveal its numerous small, black, wiry roots.

Fiddleheads of this fern are about ¾ inch in diameter and are covered with a thick coat of "wool," which tends to be cinnamon colored at the top of the fiddlehead and whitish toward its base.

When a fertile frond is divested of its thick wool coat and uncoiled, the green, granular-looking leaflets are revealed. These spore-bearing leaflets extend the length of the frond and if allowed to mature, change from green to cinnamon brown.

Collection and Preparation

One of the first edible tastes of green plant life offered us by the awakening spring is the fern fiddlehead. In Vermont, as soon as the amber earth bares itself after the melting of the snow, one can forage for fiddleheads. Because the ostrich fern is our favorite, we hike to the nearest stream or riverbed to collect the desired morsels. The clumps of emerging fiddleheads are a silent confirmation of the continuity of life.

The fiddlehead is borne at the tip of an edible stalk, which should be 4 to 8 inches long before it is picked. Pluck the plant at the base of the stalk and cook the tender sections of the stalk and the fiddlehead. Remember, only the coiled or partially uncoiled fronds are tender and palatable. Never take all the fiddleheads from a single clump; take a few from several clumps until you have enough.

To prepare for cooking, remove the protective mate-

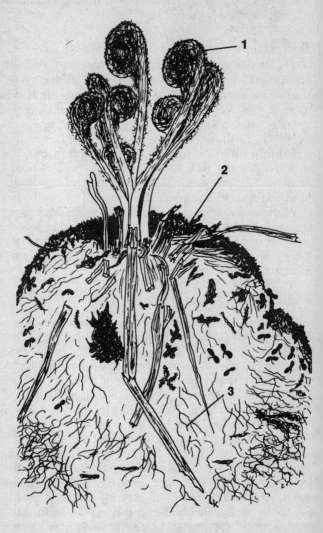

Cinnamon Fern Fiddleheads. 1, Plant in early spring showing fiddleheads—soup. 2, Typical mound formed by the rootstalk. 3, Black, wiry roots.

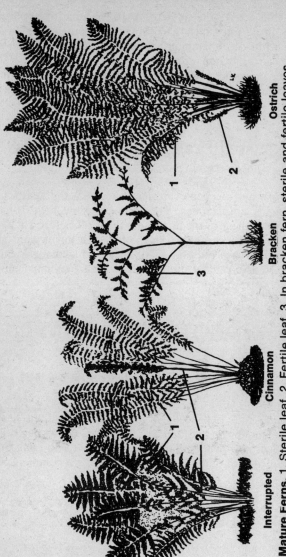

Mature Ferns. 1, Sterile leaf. 2, Fertile leaf. 3, In bracken fern, sterile and fertile leaves are not morphologically distinct.

Interrupted   Cinnamon   Bracken   Ostrich

rial that covers the fiddlehead. In the case of bracken fern, interrupted fern, and cinnamon fern, this material is a white- to cinnamon-colored woolly-like substance that can be tedious to remove. In the ostrich fern, it is a thin scale-like material that is easily peeled from the fiddlehead. Wash the fiddleheads thoroughly in cold water. Cook immediately.

Roasted Bracken Fern Rhizomes
(an emergency source of carbohydrates)

Wash and peel the rhizomes and bake the hearts in the coals until tender. They will probably have some ashes adhering to them, so peel them off before eating. If you use hickory wood in the fire, you might want to leave some ash on your food, because hickory ash can be used as a salt substituite. The Virginia Indians commonly used this ash for seasoning.

Sautéed Fiddleheads
(for 2)

2 doz fiddleheads   salt and pepper to taste
2 tbsp butter

Sauté the fiddleheads in butter over medium heat for 5 minutes or until tender. Turn once or twice. Serve with salt and pepper. There are other ways to cook interrupted fern fiddleheads, but this is the recommended way.

Buttered Fiddleheads
(for 4)

4 doz fiddleheads   1 tbsp salt
2 cups boiling water   ¼ lb butter

Place fiddleheads in the salted, boiling water, lower heat, and simmer until tender. Melt your butter and have ready to pour over the cooked fiddleheads. Serve and enjoy.

Fiddlehead Salad
(for 4)

4 doz fiddleheads	¼ cup white wine vinegar
⅓ cup olive oil	salt and pepper to taste

This can be used as a side dish or a main course for your luncheon. Cook as described above, omitting the butter. Beat vinegar and oil and pour on top. Serve hot or cold with condiments.

For a little extra garnish, chop two hard-boiled eggs, and sprinkle on top of the fiddleheads.

Fiddleheads with Hollandaise Sauce
(for 4)

4 doz fiddleheads	1 cup butter
2 cups boiling water	1 tbsp salt
4 egg yolks	2 tbsp lemon juice

Wash and cook fiddleheads as above. Place your egg yolks with ⅓ of the butter in the top of a double boiler. Keep the water hot, but do not boil. Stir the butter and egg yolks constantly with a whip. When the butter melts, add another portion, and as this melts and the mixture begins to thicken, add the remaining butter. Keep stirring at all times. As soon as the mixture is thick, remove it from the heat and add the salt and the lemon juice, stirring it constantly. Place on table and spoon out over the fiddleheads.

This is our favorite way of serving fiddleheads.

Creamed Fiddlehead Pottage
(a gourmet dish from the wild, for 4)

20 ostrich fern fiddleheads (diced); more fiddleheads will be needed if smaller ferns are used

4 slices bacon (coarsely chopped)

1 medium onion (chopped)

2 medium potatoes (diced)

2 cups water

2 cups milk

2 tbsp butter

2 tbsp unbleached white flour

sherry to taste

salt and pepper to taste

Sauté the bacon and onions in a large saucepan for 5 minutes. Add the potatoes, fiddleheads, and water; cook over medium heat until the potatoes start to soften. In another skillet, make a roux with the butter, flour, and milk. Stir until smooth. Blend the roux into the pottage and pour in the sherry to taste. Garnish with salt and pepper, and serve. The cooking time is approximately 20 minutes.

FRESHWATER ANGLING

Introduction

To most fishermen, fishing is considered a sport, to some others it is a livelihood and to a few it is an inexpensive means to obtain food. We address this section to the latter group of people.

Fishing is both an art and science, but anyone can catch edible fish with a minimum of experience and inexpensive gear. However, many people are under the mistaken impression that the only fish suitable to pursue and eat are the "glamour" fish, such as trout and large bass. Once you have done a little freshwater fishing you will see that it is a brave man who, under the scornful glances of his fellow fishermen, dares keep his catch of pumpkinseeds or bluegills rather than throwing them back or using them for bait in an attempt to catch that "big one." However, these members of the sunfish family (Centrarchidae) are fine eating and very easy to catch.

Sunfish are emphasized here because of their abundance and eagerness to nibble at worms, but a period of fishing often results in a mixed catch. For example, two hours of fishing in the Connecticut River one June evening yielded seven fish—a yellow perch,* a small largemouth bass,* a black crappie,* three pumpkinseeds; and a white bass, which is a freshwater member of the sea bass family (*Serranidae*), whose members resemble the sunfish but usually can be distinguished from them by the tall, spinous portion of the dorsal fin as opposed to the shorter, spinous, dorsal fin in the sunfish (see Fig. 15).

Habitat and Range

The Centrarchidae range throughout temperate North America and generally favor the waters of ponds, lakes, and the warmer streams and rivers where spawning begins in spring and, in some species, continues through most of the summer. With the exception of one western sunfish, all members of this family are nest builders. The males hollow out a depression in the bottom and guard the fertilized eggs and fry. Most species feed in the shallows, but when the water temperature gets too hot or too cold they migrate to deeper water.

---

* For additional information, see the section on Ice Fishing. Also, for a guide to where and when to fish in the fifty states, see the February 1972, issue of *Field and Stream* (76, no. 10: p. 68).

Description

Several species of the common sunfish (*Lepomis* spp.) are found in eastern waters. They can be easily recognized by their small size (seldom more than one pound), their short, deep, laterally compressed bodies, the small mouth with jaws about equal in size and the dorsal fin whose spinous and soft portions are confluent. Some species are brilliantly colored with blue, green and orange. Even experts sometimes find speciation of these fish difficult, because they tend to hybridize. However, this is of no concern to the fisherman because all the sunfish are delicious tasting.

Gear and Hints for Fishing Success

You will need a rod or pole, a strong line, some hooks (we use #6), a bobber such as a piece of cork and a few sinkers. Ordinary garden worms are suitable bait. Take a pail for your fish as well as some extra hooks and a sharp knife.

The catch rate for freshwater angling is generally highest in spring and tapers off in late summer, due primarily to high water temperature and low water oxygen. At that time, many fish move to deeper and colder water, and must be sought there. By autumn, fishing usually improves a little, and in winter it is excellent for some species and poor for most of the sunfish. Within certain limits, there is a positive correlation between the clarity of the water and good catches, which is probably due in part to the fact that many panfish and game fish locate food primarily by sight. Finally, the quiet fisherman with a quiet boat can expect better results than one who announces his presence with a loud voice, noisy motor, or blaring radio.

Cleaning Fish

Snip off the dorsal and ventral fins with strong,

Sunfish and Nest. The bluegill sunfish illustrates the general characteristics of the common sunfishes (*Lepomis* spp.). The whole fish can be sautéed. 1, Small mouth with jaws about equal in size. 2, Laterally compressed body. 3, Spinous portion of dorsal fin attached to 4, the soft portion of the dorsal fin.

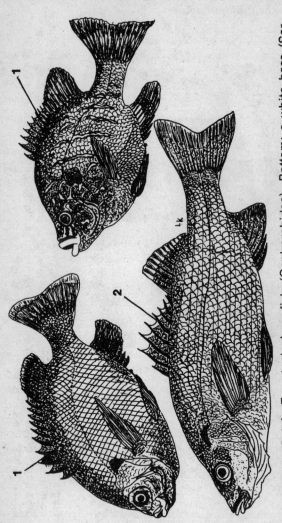

One Day's Catch. *Top:* typical sunfish (Centrarchidae). *Bottom:* a white bass (Ser- ranidae). Note that the spinous portion of the dorsal fin (1) is shorter in the sunfish than in the white bass (2).

scissors, scrape off the scales, make a longitudinal incision along the ventral surface and remove the viscera. Wash the fish thoroughly.

Sautéed Sunfish
(for 2)

4 sunfish	¼ lb butter
unbleached, white flour	½ lemon

Dip whole fish in flour and sauté in a hot, greased skillet over medium heat until golden brown. Place on a platter and pour melted butter over fish. Serve with lemon wedges.

Oriental Sauce
(a delicious topping for sautéed fish)

1 medium onion	1 vegetable bouillon cube
10 leek leaves or 1 clove garlic	1 cup water
2 cups escarole (shredded) or Chinese cabbage	4 tbsp soy sauce
	cornstarch

Sauté the onions, leek and escarole in a greased skillet for 3 minutes, stirring continuously. Add bouillon cube and water and bring to a boil. Lower heat and simmer for 5 minutes. Mix in the soy sauce, make a paste with the cornstarch and slowly stir into the mixture to desired thickness. Pour sauce over the fish and serve.

Sweet Flag

Sweet flag, Calamus, Flagroot
(*Acorus calamus*)

History

Sweet flag is a highly aromatic plant with a ginger-like odor and taste that has been sold commercially under the name of sweet flag or calamus root. However, the commercial product is not actually a root but is a rhizome, which is an underground stem. This plant was grown for centuries in Asia and exported to Europe, where the aromatic rhizome was used in perfumes and in herbal medicines, and as a food flavoring. This moisture-loving plant gradually spread throughout Europe and was early introduced into the New World, where it has proliferated in the northern and eastern United States.

The candied rhizome was a popular early American confection which was eaten and sold by Shakers and other New Englanders. Mr. John Walker of Dummerston, Vermont, an octogenarian neighbor, related to us the following story about sweet flag. "When I was a boy, it was a springtime tradition to eat sweet flag root (rhizome) which my aunt gathered from a marsh near Dwight Miller's farm. She always candied her sweet flag with maple syrup but I never learned the recipe."

Habitat and Range

Sweet flag is widespread in Europe and Asia. In the United States it grows throughout the east to Texas and Florida and ranges across the northern part of our country to Montana and Oregon. It grows in shallow waters adjoining ponds and rivers, and is found in wet meadows, marshes, and swamps.

Description

The sweet flag plant is a perennial herb with a stout, cylindrical rhizome; numerous white, worm-like roots; tall, yellow-green linear leaves that are similar to those of an iris plant; and a flower stalk that resembles the leaves but near the middle of its length has a flowering spike projecting upward and outward at about a 45° angle. This erect spike is about the same size and shape as a woman's baby finger and in spring mainly consists of numerous tiny, yellow-brown flowers, followed later in the season by dry, brown fruits. All parts of the plant have an aromatic, ginger-like odor and taste, which is most marked in the rhizome.

Note. The superficial resemblance of sweet flag to the wild irises should be of some concern to the wild-food gatherer, as the irises are highly purgative and, in addition, share the predilection of sweet flag for moist areas. To avoid confusing these plants with one another, follow the directions under Collection and Preparation of sweet flag very closely and remember, the irises do not have the aromatic ginger-like aroma.

Collection and Preparation

Sweet flag can be readily identified year-round by its flower stalk and aromatic odor. From late spring until early autumn, the green flower stalks with their unusual brown spikes are upright and visible for a distance of several feet. However, as winter approaches, many of these stalks fall to the ground and by early spring, when the rhizomes are usually collected, most of the flower stalks are prostrate.

Search along the wet ground for sweet flag. When

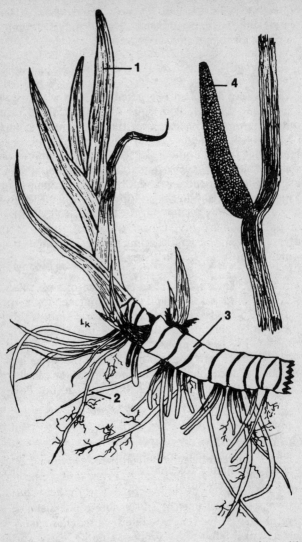

Sweet Flag. 1, Plant as it appears in early spring with linear yellow-green leaves—raw vegetable. 2, White roots—confection. 3, White rhizome—spice or confection. 4, Finger-shaped flowering spike.

you find a flower stalk with its brown spike, trace the stalk into the mud, down to the rhizome. The rhizome can be easily removed with a shovel. Calamus rhizomes are very pungent and three or four should be sufficient for a family of four. Do not take more than you will use. If you take more than one rhizome, follow the same procedure and check to ensure that all of them have the characteristic gingerlike odor. If any shoots have sprouted, note that they have a reddish-purple sheath at the base and when crushed are also very aromatic.

The new shoots, the long, thick rhizomes and the small roots, can be used for food. Wash the plant thoroughly before using.

Sweet Flag Spice
(can be used as a substitute for ginger or cinnamon)

1 or more sweet flag
  rhizomes

Wash, but do not peel the rhizome (much of the aromatic oil is in this outer cover). Cut off the numerous white roots and save for the next recipe. Cut the rhizome into thin slices, place in a baking pan, and dry in a slow oven (200°F) for an hour or so. Remove from oven, crush with a rolling pin, and pour through a fine sieve. Store in clean, covered jars.

Use this spice in recipes that call for cinnamon or ginger. A delicious topping for buttered toast can be made by mixing together one part sweet flag spice to eight parts raw sugar.

Sweet Flag Maple Candy and Candied Sweet Flag Root

(a single recipe providing two different kinds
of confections)

2 cups raw sugar
4 cups water
½ to 1 cup sweet flag roots

¼ cup maple syrup,
if desired
waxed paper

Mix the sugar with the water and bring to a boil over medium heat. Stir in the roots and maple syrup. Continue to cook until the liquid forms a ball when dropped into a glass of cold water. Remove from heat and quickly drop the viscous liquid by teaspoonfuls onto the waxed paper. Take the roots from the pan with 2 spoons or tongs and place on the waxed paper. Store the candies in clean covered jars. Slice the candied roots into inch-long pieces, and store in the same fashion.

The pungent roots are crisp and delicious; the aromatic candies are crunchy and sweet.

Candied Sweet Flag Rhizomes

(an ancient medicine)

Cooking the Rhizomes

3 sweet flag rhizomes

Remove the roots, cut the rhizomes into thin slices, and place in boiling water 30 to 40 minutes. Remove from water and drain.

Candying the Rhizomes

1½ cups raw sugar   3 sweet flag rhizomes
3 cups water   (sliced and cooked)
                                            waxed paper

Mix the sugar with the water and bring to a boil over medium heat. Add the sweet flag rhizomes and continue to boil until the syrup forms a ball when dropped into cold water. Remove the rhizomes with two spoons and place on waxed paper to cool. Store in clean covered jars.

The candied sweet flag rhizome has long been used by Asians as a cough lozenge and as a chew to relieve indigestion.

Cattail

The Broad-leaved Cattail (*Typha latifolia*)
The Narrow-leaved Cattail (*Typha angustifolia*)

History

For centuries, various parts of cattail plants have been eaten by a diverse group of people. The Iroquois Indians bruised and boiled the fresh rootstalk, or rhizome, for its syrupy gluten, which was mixed with cornmeal pudding and the dried and pulverized rhizome was prized for its sweet flour, which was used in breads and puddings. Many of our western tribes of Indians used the thickened shoots of the rhizome as a fresh or cooked vegetable. The Cossacks reportedly relished the emerging cattail stems as a vegetable. The Paiute Indians favored the cooked young male flower spikes and the natives of New Zealand used the pollen from the mature male flower spikes for bread.

It would seem that a plant which provided such a variety of dishes might have been analyzed for its nutritional value. This is the case at least for the flour extracted from the cattail rhizome (Classen 1919). Table 2, taken from Professor Classen's paper, shows that the composition of cattail flour is not that different from other commonly used types of flour. The main drawback with cattail flour is the work it takes to extract it.

Habitat and Range

Cattails of various species are found in temperate and tropical regions throughout the world. Our own broad-leaved cattail is found in freshwater marshes throughout most of the United States. The narrow-leaved cattail is most common along the East Coast,

TABLE 2

Chemical Analysis of Wheat, Wheat-flour Substitutes, and Cattail Flour

Food Source	Protein %	Fat %	Carbohy-drate %	Water %	Ash %
Spring wheat	12.50	1.00	73.83	12.00	.42
Potato (dried)	12.25	.43	74.80	6.82	4.01
Rice (polished)	8.81	.24	80.74	9.65	.36
Dasheen (peeled)	8.00	.46	77.80	7.48	4.12
Yellow corn (raw)	7.88	2.82	80.83	6.96	.82
Cassava	1.44	.29	86.45	8.21	1.60
Cattail (Washington analysis)	7.75	.65	81.41	7.35	2.84
Cattail No. 1, U. of Kans. anal.	5.71	3.71	83.81	6.77	2.37
Cattail No. 2, U. of Kans. anal.	7.22	4.91	79.09	8.78	2.48

residing in brackish marshes and in alkaline waters. Both species also grow in Eurasia.

Description

The cattails are tall plants with grass-like linear leaves several feet in length. The broad-leaved cattail is about 6 feet tall and the leaves are about ¾ inch wide, while the narrow-leaved species averages about 4 feet in height and its leaves are about ⅓ inch in width. In both types of cattail the flowers are borne at the tip of a stout cylindrical stalk with the male flowers clustered above the female flowers. The male and female flowers of the broad-leaved cattail are contiguous, but in the narrow-leaved species they are separated by a short space. The newly emerging male spike of flowers is green; then as the pollen matures, the spike becomes yellow. After pollen production, the male spike shrivels and falls off the stem. The fatter, bottle-brush-shaped female spike is also green at first but at maturity it becomes a rich rust color and then a darker brown. When the brown spike finally opens, it reveals a fluffy mass of down attached to the seeds.

The young, firm, rust-colored female spikes, resting on their cylindrical stems, are what people commonly refer to as "cattail." These are the structures which are gathered and used in dry flower arangements.

Collection and Preparation

Cattails share with the dandelion the distinction of being widespread, common, and vigorous plants from which a great variety of foods can be prepared. Cattail rhizomes can be gathered year-round and used either as a vegetable or prepared into flour. In early spring, the young, green, emerging stalks are gathered and eaten raw, pickled, or cooked. These are tasty. Later in the spring, the young, green, male flower spikes can be collected and prepared like corn on the cob, and, although they are rather dry, they have a deep, rich flavor. Finally, as the male spikes mature and

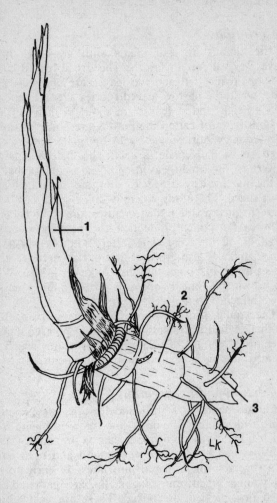

Sprouting Broad-Leaved Cattail. 1, Plant in early spring showing young leaves covering the emerging stem which can be used as a raw or cooked vegetable. 2, Rhizome—raw or cooked vegetable and source of flour. 3, Roots.

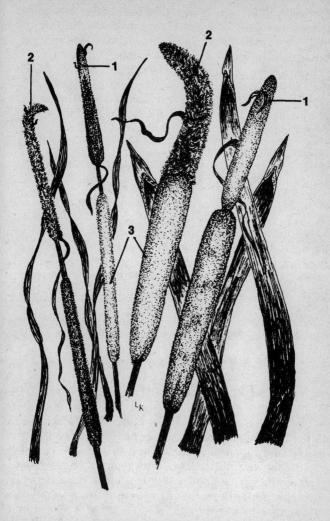

Narrow-Leaved Cattail (left) and **Broad-Leaved Cattail** (right). 1, Green, male flower spikes—cooked vegetable. 2, Older male flower spikes with yellow pollen—flour substitute. 3, Green, then brown female flower spikes—decoration and pillow stuffing.

become yellow, the pollen can be shaken into containers and used as a rich-tasting flour. Remember to leave some male flower spikes untouched to ensure that the female flowers in the swamp will be pollinated.

Perhaps the greatest virtue of cattail is that it can be used in a variety of ways that require a minimum of supplies and preparation. This should appeal to those of you living or camping in the wild. Here are a few suggestions.

Cattail Rhizome Flour
(a year-round emergency source of flour)

Dig out several dozen rhizomes; wash and peel. Dry the food-filled core in the sun for several days or in a slow oven (200°F) from 2 to 4 hours. Pulverize between stones or in a grinder and pick out the fibers by hand or by sifting. This is a good flour, especially for biscuits.

Note. See *Note* in section on Sweet flag.

Cattail Pollen Flour

Collecting the yellow pollen is rather time-consuming, as the pollen grains are as fine as baby powder and will be blown away even in the slighest breeze. We recommend that you use a large brown paper bag for the pollen; when you finish collecting, close the bag and secure the top with an elastic or string. Store your pollen in clean, screw-capped jars.

The yellow pollen is a rich-tasting and colorful addition to your pancake flour. You can mix it one to three or four with your flour and still get a very different and delicious product. We especially like to add cattail pollen to flower fritter batter.

Cattail Pollen and Fish Chowder
(a simple outdoor recipe, for 2)

1 qt water
1 lb any type fish

2 cups cattail pollen
salt and pepper to taste

Clean and wash the fish. Cut it into medium-size pieces. Place in water and bring to a boil. Add the pollen and cook until tender. Season and enjoy.

Cattail Spikes on the Cob
(for 4)

16 cattail green male flower
  spikes
2 qt water

¼ lb drawn butter
1 tbsp salt

Place the cattails in salted boiling water, cover, lower heat, and cook for 10 minutes. Drain, place in a skillet with drawn butter, and serve.

Cattail Tinder

When living outdoors gather the dried stalks and mature female spikes as needed to start your camp fire. They are very inflammable and quite easy to obtain.

Cattail Pillow

From the downy mass of seeds of the female spike, one can make an emergency outdoor pillow. If you have an old shirt sleeve, sew or tie one end and fill it with seeds and then seal the other end. It will be soft enough for any weary head.

Chicory

Chicory, Wild Endive, Succory, Witloof
(*Cichorium intybus*)

History

Chicory has had a long history of use as a food plant. The Romans knew the superior flavor of its crisp leaves and the plant has been cultivated for over 1,000 years in continental Europe, where it has been used as a vegetable, a coffee adulterant, and as a forage plant for sheep. It was brought into this country by the first settlers who cultivated it as a food plant and for its lovely blue flowers. It soon escaped from around houses and gardens and is now considered a weed.

One of the more popular products of this plant is witloof, which is a head of crisp, tender leaves produced by forcing chicory roots in the cellar during winter or by suitably preparing the soil around chicory roots in the garden. The procedure for producing this vegetable is given in the Autumn section.

Coffee adulterated with chicory root has always been more popular with Europeans than Americans, except in parts of the South. During the Civil War, chicory coffee was used here both in the North and South. In 1862 chicory seed was being sold for 15 cents an ounce by B. K. Bliss of Springfield, Massachusetts, who advertised the virtues of its roots as a coffee substitute and supplement.

Habitat and Range

Chicory is a Eurasian plant which has become a cosmopolitan weed. It is found throughout the United States along roadsides and in waste places and fields.

Description

Chicory is a perennial with elongate basal leaves that emerge in vase-like clusters from a deep taproot. These leaves resemble those of the common dandelion but tend to be thicker and are covered with many tiny, white hairs. The sparsely foliated, branching, twig-like flower stem appears in the second year and grows to a height of about 3 feet. In the axils of its diminutive upper leaves are borne blue flower heads (sometimes white or pink) that are followed by goblet-shaped fruit clusters.

Collection and Preparation

From midsummer until early autumn, older chicory plants can be readily identified by the flower stalks, with their rosettes of blue flowers. Later in the year, the plants must be distinguished by the cylindrical fruit clusters. By midspring the old flower stalks are sometimes broken and are often seen adjacent to the emerging clusters of dandelion-like leaves. If these stalks are not present, the plant might be confused with the dandelion, though this is no great problem, because the leaves of both species are edible.

The leaves can be plucked and eaten from the time they emerge in the spring until they grow too tough to chew; the roots are usually gathered from autumn until spring.

Chicory Greens and Butternuts
(an Oriental-tasting wild vegetable dish, for 2)

2 cups young chicory greens   ¼ cup chopped butternuts
⅓ cup water   1 tbsp butter (if desired)

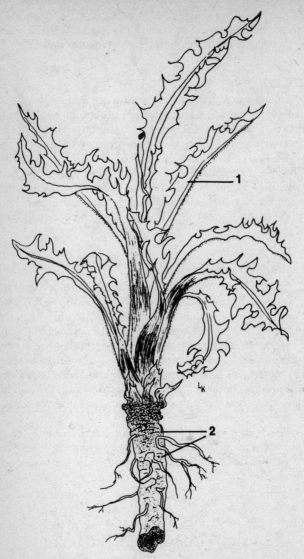

Sprouting Chicory. 1, Leaves which resemble those of dandelion but differ from them in being hairy—raw or cooked vegetable. 2, White tap root—coffee substitute or adulterant.

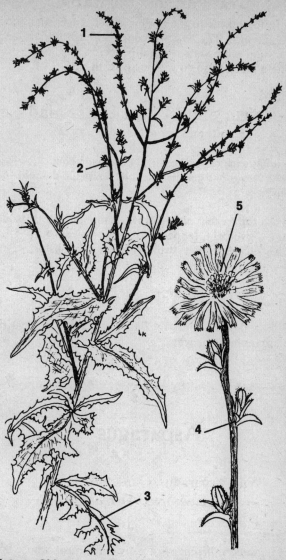

Mature Chicory. 1, Blue (sometimes white or pink) flower head. 2, Diminutive upper leaves. 3, Larger basal leaves. 4, Close-up of a bud in the axils of small leaves. 5, Flower head.

Add the leaves to the boiling water, cover and cook for 3 minutes. Do *not* overcook. Stir in the nuts and butter, and serve with salt and pepper.

These greens also go well mixed with rice.

Chicory and Violet Leaf Salad
(a nutritious springtime dish, for 2)

2 handfuls each of young violet leaves and chicory leaves

3 tbsp sour cream
violet flowers, if desired

Wash the freshly picked leaves and mix with the sour cream. Serve cold, topped with violet flowers.

This salad goes very well with fish and lobster.

Chicory-Root Coffee

Follow the procedure for dandelion coffee on page xx and use in the same way.

Asparagus

Wild Asparagus, Garden Asparagus
(*Asparagus officinalis*)

History

Asparagus officinalis is a native of Eurasia whose fine gustatory qualities have been praised by epicures since Roman times. It was first cultivated over 2,000 years ago and today is an important food crop in Europe and

America. Most of our cultivated asparagus comes from California, followed by Washington, New Jersey, Illinois, and South Carolina.

Wild asparagus is a descendant of the cultivated forms and is now found in most parts of the United States. In some areas, such as Wisconsin, wild asparagus is a common roadside weed.

Habitat and Range

Wild asparagus is found throughout the eastern United States and in other parts of the country where it has been under cultivation. It prefers sandy fields, waste places, roadsides and salt marshes.

Description

Asparagus is a perennial arising from a rhizome which looks rather like a mat of long whitish worms. Early in spring, the familiar stout asparagus stem, with its scale-like leaves and tiny branches, emerges. The young stems are the asparagus of commerce. When the stem is allowed to grow, it reaches a height of up to 6 feet; the branches elongate and reveal the filiform branchlets and the stalked, greenish-yellow, bell-shaped flowers. The fruit is a scarlet berry.

Collection and Preparation

Wild asparagus can be recognized either by the emerging "spears" or by the lacy appearing stem with its bell-like flowers followed by the round, red fruit. Gather the asparagus "spears" by slicing off the emerging stalk with a knife. Wash the vegetable thoroughly and use immediately.

Raw Asparagus

Freshly picked asparagus is so crisp and delicious that it is fine eaten raw or chopped into a salad.

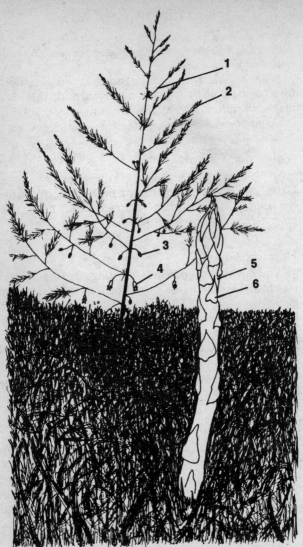

Asparagus. 1, Plant in flower, showing branches. 2, Filiform branchlets. 3, Maturing fruit which will develop into a round red berry. 4, Greenish-yellow flower. 5, Emerging "spear" or stem; the spear is the edible asparagus. 6, Scale-like leaf.

Cooked Asparagus

See the recipes for preparing fern fiddleheads on page 45 and substitute asparagus for fiddleheads.

Violets

(*Viola*—several species)

History

Since ancient times the violet has been a favorite flower. In medieval flower symbolism, the violet was the emblem of constancy, and signified the humility of Our Lord. In addition to its fragrant beauty, the violet has been appreciated as a herb and as a foodstuff by many peoples. A favorite beverage among the Romans and Persians was violet wine. In Tudor days it was the custom to employ violet leaves in salads and pottages and to prescribe that delicate people feed upon the pastes, syrups, and conserves of violets. Candied violet leaves have been a favorite confection in England for years. In this country, southern blacks have long employed the leaves of *Viola esculenta* in their soups because of their mucilaginous quality. Recently, it has been found that violet leaves have a very high vitamin A content. Moreover, the flowers and leaves of the violet are one of the best sources of vitamin C available.

Habitat and Range

Viola is a large and nearly cosmopolitan genus. In North America alone it is represented by more than four-dozen species many of which hybridize freely. With the great number of existent violet species, we can expect to find one type or another in a variety of habitats ranging from moist woods to open, dry, sandy areas. Most species flower from April through June, with a few commencing in March and some others flowering as late as August.

Description

Violets are low-growing herbs with leaves and flowers emerging directly from the rootstalk or from runners. Most species of violets have two types of flowers. The first to appear is the five-petaled usually blue or violet showy flower; this is what we refer to as the "violet" and is the edible flower. Later, the showy flower is followed by the low-growing, sometimes subterranean, fertile flower from which most of the seeds arise.

We recommend that the sweet-smelling, blue-flowered plants be used as a foodstuff.

Violet and Dandelion Salad
(a superb source of vitamins A and C, for 2)

2 cups each of young violet greens and dandelion greens

⅓ cup olive oil
¼ cup red wine vinegar
salt and pepper to taste

Wash the freshly collected greens thoroughly, and toss with the oil, vinegar, and condiments. This is probably one of the most healthful salads you could eat.

Boiled Violet Leaves

Take the desired amount of violet leaves and place them in a small quantity of salted boiling water. Lower heat, cover the pan, and cook for 5 minutes. Butter and serve (including the juice).

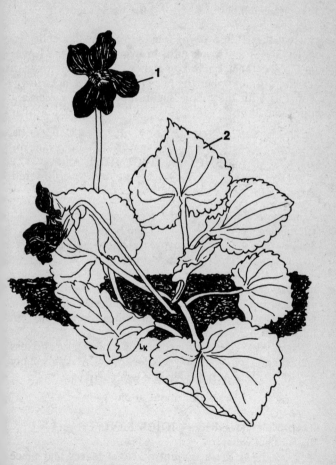

Violet. 1, Showy flower—confection, syrup, soup. 2,
.eaves—confection and raw or cooked vegetable.

Fried Brown Violet Leaves
(an old English recipe, for 2)

3 cups violet leaves
⅓ cup soybean oil

½ orange
3 tsp maple sugar

Heat the oil in a frying pan, add the freshly collected violet leaves and cook until brown. Remove the leaves and place them on brown paper to drain. Place in a serving dish and pour the juice of the orange over them. Top this with the maple sugar. This makes a pleasant luncheon dish.

Violet Flower and Acorn Candy Cakes

4 cups violet flowers
4 large lemons
3 cups water

6 cups maple sugar
1 cup baked acorns
    (coarsely ground)

Steep the violet flowers in the lemon juice and water mixture until a deep red color develops. Add the sugar and boil until it is candied. Remove from heat, add the acorn meats and stir. Pour out into a flat pan and cut into cakes before it is cold.

Violet Flower Syrup
(yield, about 1 pint)

3 cups violet flowerheads
2½ cups hot water

1½ cups raw sugar
⅓ lime

Remove all greens from the flower heads and macerate the flowers. Add water, stir and let steep 12 to 24 hours. Strain out the juice through a cloth. Add the juice of the lime and the sugar; cook over medium heat 10 to 12 minutes. Cool and store in a clean, covered jar.

This syrup tastes like a cross between cranberry and blueberry syrup. Use on ice cream, in milk shakes, and as a sauce for ham.

Violet Soup

For a simple, flavorful, luncheon soup made from blue violets, use the flowers and vegetable bouillon cubes.

For every cup of soup desired, use one cup water, one bouillon cube, and a half cup of violet flowers. Combine together and simmer until tender.

Try this rich new taste and be pleasantly surprised.

Beech Leaves

The American Beech (*Fagus grandifolia*)

Collection and Preparation

The lovely smooth-barked beech is known for its excellence as a shade tree and for its fine nuts (pg. 247). However, it is not commonly known that its newly emerged leaves are a delicious vegetable.

In Vermont, beech leaves emerge from their elongate rust-colored buds around midspring, and for a few weeks these young greens are tender enough to be eaten. Beech leaves wilt rather rapidly and should be used soon after being collected. Wash and drain before cooking.

Beech Leaves
(for 2)

2 cups young beach leaves	1 tbsp butter
¾ cup water	salt and pepper to taste

Salt the water, add butter, and bring to a boil. Stir in the beech leaves, cover and cook over medium heat 5 to 8 minutes. Drain and serve as hot hors d'oeuvres.

Beech leaves must be handled with the fingers. Hold by the leaf stalk (petiole), eat the blade and discard the tough stalk.

Enteromorpha

A Green Alga (*Enteromorpha*—several species)

Introduction

Enteromorpha is a widespread and cosmopolitan green alga which is represented by numerous species in a diversity of marine habitats throughout the world. Anyone who has spent time on our Atlantic coast has probably seen the green matlike or ribbonlike strands of these plants clinging to the undersides of boats or piers.

Marine algae are valuable as a food chiefly because they furnish necessary salts and a number of essential vitamins and trace elements. However, *Enteromorpha*, like its other marine relatives, has not been utilized in this country as a food source, even though it is a tasty cooked vegetable and can be dried to produce a fine sea salt.

Habitat and Range

The various species of *Enteromorpha* occur in all seas of the world and they also grow abundantly in brackish waters and salt marshes.

Description

Enteromorpha consists of bright green, grasslike strands which grow in dense clumps to a length of 2 feet. The strands are actually branched or unbranched hollow tubes which can be filamentous or ribbonlike or inflated. The plant is attached to the substrate by tiny basal holdfasts.

Collection and Preparation

Enteromorpha can be found sprouting in shallow, brackish water in early spring. It attaches to rocks or other suitable substrates and usually grows so close to shore that it can be gathered readily in a few inches of water. It also grows in deeper waters and can be found on wharves, jetties, floats, and boat bottoms, where it grows profusely in the northeast throughout late spring to early autumn; some species are also found year-round.

It can be gathered by ripping or cutting it away from the substrate and should be washed in several changes of fresh water before it is prepared for eating.

Enteromorpha Cooked Greens
(an early spring seaside vegetable, for 2)

2 cups *Enteromorpha* (wet) 3 tbsp butter
½ cup water salt and pepper to taste

Bring the butter and water to a boil, add the *Enteromorpha,* cover the pan and cook over low heat 20 to 25 minutes. Cut the cooked vegetable into small pieces, and serve. Add salt and pepper to taste. The flavor of this vegetable is similar to spinach.

Enteromorpha Salt
(a fine sea salt)

Dry the plants in the sun or in a slow oven (200°F) until the strands are crisp. Crumble the dried plant in your hands and, if desired, pour through a fine sieve. Place in a salt shaker and store the remainder in clean, covered jars. Use as you would table salt.

Enteromorpha Chowder
(an instant chowder)

See the recipe on page 200 for *Ulva* sea chowder and substitute *Enteromorpha* for *Ulva*.

Killifish

(*Fundulus*—several species)

Introduction

The killifish (Cyprinodontidae) are small, minnow-like fish with unforked tail fins that are found in fresh, brackish, and sometimes marine waters. They can be readily caught with a small mesh net or a minnow trap and when gutted, make a good-tasting panfish.

Three of the more common species of *Fundulus* found in eastern waters are the common killifish or mummichog (*F. heteroclitus*), the striped killifish (*F. majalis*), and the freshwater killifish (*F. diaphanus*).

Common Killifish and *Enteromorpha* in Brackish Water. 1. *Enteromorpha* plants with grass-like strands of hollow leaves—cooked vegetable, condiment, chowder. 2. Common killifish (× 1) to show characteristic body size and shape. 3, Rather dorsally located mouth with protruding lower jaw. 4, Single dorsal fin. 5, Fairly convex tail fin—sauté whole fish.

The first two species are often found together in the shallow water of salt marshes during the warmer months of the year, while the last species is most commonly found in freshwater lakes and streams.

Description

The various species of *Fundulus* can be recognized by their small size (2–8 inches in length), elongate body, squared off or slightly convex tail fin, single dorsal fin, large scales, and the rather dorsally located mouth with a projecting lower jaw.

Collection and Preparation

Beginning in spring and continuing throughout the warmer months of the year, quantities of killifish can be found in the shallow waters of salt marshes, bays, and inlets; another convenient place to catch these fish is in the narrow part of a stream. Either a minnow trap is set in the water or a net is used to scoop up these fish which feed along the surface. A suitable net can be fashioned from a mesh bag (such as that commonly used for packaging onions), a metal coat hanger, some

TABLE 3

**Habitat, Range, and Description of
Three Species of Killifish**

Species	Habitat	Range
Common killifish (*Fondulus heteroclitus*)	Usually brackish waters of salt marshes and inlets. Sometimes freshwaters	Gulf of St. Lawrence to Gulf of Mexico
Striped killifish (*F. majalis*)	Same as above	Cape Cod to Florida
Freshwater killifish (*F. diaphanus*)	Usually freshwater of streams, lakes and ponds. Sometimes brackish water	Quebec west to Iowa and North Dakota. South to South Carolina

fish line and an old mop or broom handle. Numerous fish can be caught in a short time but, remember, take only what you will use.

To clean the fish use a razor-sharp knife and make a longitudinal slit along the ventral surface. Remove the viscera and wash out the fish with fresh water.

Sautéed Killifish
(for 2)

1 doz killifish (cleaned)	3 tbsp butter
¾ cup unbleached white flour	4 lemon wedges
	salt and pepper to taste

Wash the fish, pat dry with a towel, and roll in flour. Place in a hot, greased skillet and sauté over medium-high heat until they are golden brown on both sides. While the fish are cooking, brown the butter in another skillet.

Place the cooked fish on a platter, pour butter over them, and serve with lemon wedges and condiments.

In our opinion killifish are finer tasting than smelts.

Description

Length: to about 5–6". Dark green dorsally and yellow below. Males develop bright orange-and-blue color during the breeding season (spring and summer)

Length: to about 6". Dark green dorsally and light below. Males have short, dark, vertical bars on sides and develop bright yellow on fins and ventral surface during the breeding season (spring and summer). Females have 2–4" longitudinal bars

Length: to about 4". Olive dorsally and silver sides. Has about 20 slender, dark, vertical bands on sides

---

Alewife

(*Pomolobus pseudoharengus*)

Introduction

Each spring along our Atlantic coast, alewife linger at the mouths of coastal streams prior to their annual spawning migration from the sea to fresh water. Some local newspapers keep their readers informed of the activity of these fish, and the beginning of the run is a much anticipated day.

Areas where alewife migrate used to be spots of great Indian activity, and in spring these streams were crowded with masses of foot-long fish intent on their ancestral goal of reproducing in fresh water. The silvery alewife were easily taken from the water by the many Indians who had gathered there to pack them into baskets to bring them to the villages. These fish were eaten or used to nourish the soil around the hills of Indian corn.

The early Massachusetts settlers noted this prudent Indian husbandry and soon began to emulate the natives. Alewife were smoked and salted for winter use or added to their gardens for fertilizer. Since these early days, the alewife has become less favored for human fare and is mainly used for bait or cat food. However, the roe is prized by some people of seacoast towns who continue the vernal tradition of gathering alewife in spring for food and fertilizer.

Habitat and Range

The alewife is found in coastal waters from Nova Scotia to Florida. The adult fish spawn in fresh water

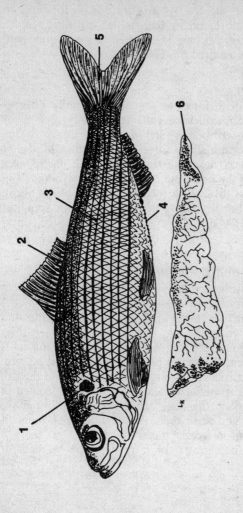

Alewife. 1, Adult fish to show the prominent dark spot posterior to the dorsal surface of the gill cover. 2, Single dorsal fin. 3, Large, silvery scales. 4, Sharp ridge on abdomen. 5, Deeply forked tail. The whole fish can be smoked, salted or used for fertilizer. 6, Roe —a delicacy sautéed.

during the spring and then return to the sea while most of the young remain in fresh water until autumn when they return to the sea, where they remain for three or four years before making their initial spawning run.

Alewife have become landlocked in many areas and recently have entered the Great Lakes.

Description

The alewife belongs to the herring family (Clupeidae), whose members are characterized by their laterally compressed bodies and deciduous scales which commonly form a sharp ridge along the middle part of the underside. There is a single dorsal fin placed near the center of the body and the tail is deeply forked. The alewife grows to about a foot in length, is bluish above and silvery below, and is marked by a dark spot just posterior to the dorsal surface of the gill cover (operculum).

Collection and Preparation

Alewife are generally caught by hand or with a dip net when they are on their spawning run. Check local regulations before taking any. Take a few at a time and sex them as you go along. The females exude a reddish substance from near the anus when the abdomen is gently pressed; the males produce a whitish substance.

To extract roe, cut through ventral surface of the fish and the pink granular-appearing roe will be located in two bands along the sides of the body. Gently remove the bundles and wash them thoroughly. Cook immediately or wrap in freezer paper and freeze. Use the rest of the fish for chowder or bury it in your garden for fertilizer.

Herring Roe
(for 2)

roe from 4 or 6 fish   2 lemon wedges
½ cup unbleached white   salt and pepper to taste
    flour

Roll the roe in flour and place in a hot, greased skillet over low heat. Brown on both sides and cook until firm. Garnish with lemon and serve with salt and pepper.

Wild Grape Leaves

(*Vitis*—several species)

Introduction

The abundance of wild grape plants* growing throughout the eastern United States can be readily located along roadsides, in thickets, and in woods. While they are best known for their fruits, they should also be utilized for their leaves, which can be eaten fresh or cooked and can be preserved for winter use.

Upon hearing about our book on wild foods, a Lebanese-American friend related to us her association with grape leaves. "When I was a child, my mother used to send me to gather young grape leaves whenever she needed them, from spring until they stopped being produced in autumn. She would chop them fresh into salads, sometimes used them as an eating implement

* See pages 277–80 for description of grape plants and additional information.

instead of a fork, and, of course, used them in one of our traditional dishes: stuffed grape leaves."

Collection and Preparation

Search for vines that produce leaves that tend to be smooth, not hairy. If the leaves are going to be eaten fresh, gather only the smallest, most tender young ones. Those used for cooking can be a little larger. They should be used on the same day they are collected, or preserved for later use. Grape leaves that are to be preserved are gathered on a dry day and spread in the sun for an hour. After which, take a clean quart jar, put in a thin layer of salt, then a grape leaf, and cover with olive oil. Repeat this process until the jar is full. Cover and store in a dry room. Before use, wash the salt off with a gentle spray of water or soak in a bowl of water for about an hour. If you have a freezer, wrap individual freshly picked grape leaves in freezer paper and store in your freezer until ready to use.

Sautéed Grape Leaves
(a tasty appetizer)

small grape leaves   salt
butter

Melt butter in a frying pan over medium heat. Add the grape leaves and sauté until brown and crisp, turning once. Salt and serve.

Stuffed Grape Leaves
(a good way to use leftovers)

6 medium-size grape   1 tsp dried wild carrot
  leaves   leaves (optional)
1 cup brown rice (cooked)   3 tbsp tomato paste
½ cup cooked fish

Combine rice, fish, carrot leaves, and tomato paste. Place a tablespoonful or so of this mixture in the center of each leaf and roll from the tip of the blade towards the petiole, taking care to tuck in the sides. Place in a covered baking dish or pan and bake for 30 minutes in an oven set at 300°F. (You might prefer to dip each leaf in boiling water before adding the filling.)

Water Cress

(*Nasturtium officinale*)

History

Water cress is an Eurasian native that was introduced to this country and is now naturalized in streams and clear, cool pools throughout most of the United States. Both the wild and cultivated forms are prized for their crisp, pungent stem tips and leaves, which are used fresh in salads or are served between slices of gluten toast in serenely elegant restaurants that also feature such gourmet dishes as water cress soup.

Habitat and Range

This native of Eurasia grows in springheads, brooks, streams and cool, clear water throughout the United States and southern Canada.

Description

Watercress is a succulent aquatic perennial with creeping or floating stems about a quarter inch to one half inch in width, from which emerge sundry fibrous white roots. The compound leaves have three to eleven small leaflets, which are sometimes toothed; the lateral

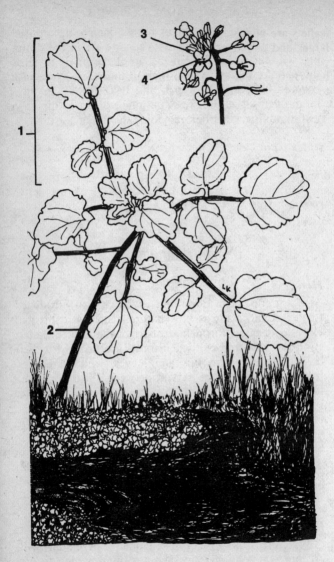

Water Cress. 1, Compound leaf showing 3 leaflets. 2, Stem. Leaves and small stems—soup or a vegetable (raw or cooked). 3, Developing seed pod. 4, Flower with 4 white petals.

leaflets are globose or oblong, while the terminal one is larger and usually globose. The tiny flowers have four white petals and are located towards the tips of the branches. The fruits are linear seed pods which grow to about an inch in length.

Collection and Preparation

This plant can be gathered year-round in most areas, for it will live as long as the water in which it grows does not freeze solid. However, it is more abundant and accessible once ice out has occurred. Pick the stem tips and leaves; do not pull the plant up by the roots. Above all, pick carefully and avoid gathering the leaves and stems of other aquatic and possibly poisonous plants.

Water cress does not store well and like all greens should be eaten as soon after being gathered as possible. Wash the greens thoroughly and rinse in a disinfectant bath if the plants come from water of questionable purity. Disinfectant tablets can be purchased in any pharmacy.

Water Cress Salad
(for 2)

2 cups water cress
(packed tightly)
1 onion (sliced)

oil and vinegar to taste
salt and pepper to taste

Toss the water cress, onion, and dressing together. Add condiments and toss again. Serve immediately.

This simple salad is a highly nutritious dish, for watercress is exceptionally rich in vitamin A and is a fine source of minerals and vitamin C.

Water Cress Sandwiches
(for 2)

½ cup water cress (chopped)   4 slices pumpernickel bread
cream cheese

Spread cheese on the bread to desired thickness, add watercress, and serve with a cup of mint tea.

Chilled Water Cress Soup
(for 2)

1 cup water cress (finely   ½ cup water
   chopped)   1 cup ice cubes
1 vegetable bouillon cube   1 cup milk

Dissolve the bouillon cube in water over medium heat. Remove from stove, add ice cubes, and stir. When the broth has cooled, stir in the milk and water cress.

This nutritious soup takes a short time to prepare and can serve as that "different" luncheon dish.

Sweet Fern

(*Myrica asplenifolia*)

History

Among the favorite beverages of the eastern Indians were the sap of trees, such as the birches and maples; berry drinks, which were prepared by crushing fruit and adding water; and hot teas, made by steeping plants in boiling water. Many of these teas were used for medicinal purposes rather than to please the palate, but aromatic plants were favored and the sweet fern was among them. The colonists learned to use a variety of native plants for teas, and by the time of the American Revolution, over four dozen species were employed as substitutes for the scarce Chinese tea.

Habitat and Range

Sweet fern is distributed from Nova Scotia to Saskatchewan and Minnesota, south to northern Georgia. It thrives on dry, sandy soil and is found in sterile, open woodlands, pastures, dunes, and waste areas.

Description

Sweet fern is a woody shrub 1 to 3 feet tall with elongate, deeply toothed, dark-green leaves which resemble fern leaflets. These slender leaves grow 2 to 4 inches in length and when crushed are pleasantly aromatic. The male flowers are borne in elongate catkins; the female flowers are in globose catkins. The fruit is a round, burr-like structure. The leaves and flowers appear in late spring; the fruit matures in summer.

Collection and Preparation

This is the only woody shrub in our area with fragrant, fern-like leaves. The fruits appear in early summer and can serve as a nibble; the leaves are collected from late spring until autumn and used fresh or dried. Sweet fern leaves should be dried slowly, without artificial heat or sunlight. Take several sprays, tie them together and hang in a dry room until the leaves are crisp. Leaves can be stored in clean, covered jars.

Sweet Fern. 1, Plant silhouette. 2, Close-up of a branch showing fern-like leaves—condiment, tea, or air freshener. 3, Male flowers in elongate catkin. 4, Female flowers in globose catkin. 5, Woody stem.

Sweet Fern Spice
(a source of flavoring for campers)

Sweet fern leaves can serve as a fine wild spice. Add a spray of sweet fern to flavor your seaside or mountain stew. After the soup is cooked, dip the spray into it for 2 to 3 minutes (the soup should be hot, but not boiling). Remove the sweet fern before serving.

Sweet Fern Tea
(for 2)

1 handful fresh sweet fern leaves	2¼ cups water raw sugar (optional)

Bring the water to a boil, add the leaves, remove from heat, and steep for 10 minutes. Serve hot or cold.

Sweet Fern Air Freshener

Before the advent of the aerosol can, a variety of natural air fresheners were made at home by placing the dried leaves of aromatic plants into cloth bags that were suspended from bed posts and chair backs. Sweet fern leaves were commonly used in this way, and the air of many colonial cabins and houses was scented by the fragrance of this plant.

Witch Hazel

(*Hamamelis virginiana*)

History

Decoctions made from the leaves, bark, and root of the witch hazel were used by eastern tribes as astringent healing agents for strains, bruises, hemorrhoids, and ophthalmias. This Indian medicine was soon adopted by the colonists, who used witch hazel extract in a number of remedies, some of which are on the market today. Dried witch hazel leaves are the source of the well-known astringent witch hazel extract called hamamelis. However, the whole plant can be used for this purpose if necessary.

Habitat and Range

The genus *Hamamelis* is represented by trees and shrubs in eastern North America and in eastern Asia. The common witch hazel is a native of North America and is found in moist woods from Nova Scotia and Ontario to eastern Minnesota, south to Texas, and east to Florida.

Description

Witch hazel is a shrub with toothed, broad, ovate leaves that are uneven at the base. The elongate, claw-shaped buds have only two small scales and are hairy. The flowers, which appear in autumn have conspicuously long, ribbon-like, yellow petals. The fruits mature a year after the appearance of the flowers. They are brown, cone-shaped capsules about ½ inch in length.

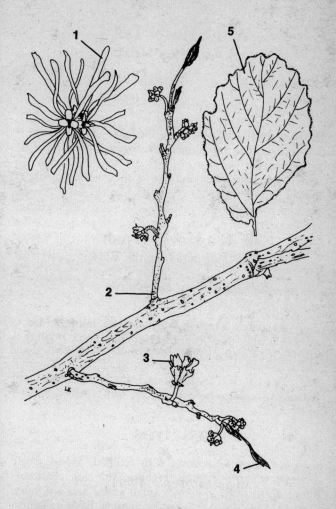

Witch Hazel. 1, Flower with long, ribbon-like yellow petals. 2, Twig—with bark from trunk, used as a cooling wash. 3, Old fruit capsule. 4, Brown, hairy, claw-shaped bud. 5, Leaf—tea.

The shiny, black, wingless seeds are ejected from the mature capsules for distances of up to 20 feet.

Witch Hazel Tea
(from the Cayuga Indians)

1½ tsp dried witch-hazel
    leaves or
5 fresh leaves

1¼ cups water
maple sugar to taste

Bring the water to a boil, add the leaves, cover, lower heat, and simmer for 5 minutes. Sweeten with maple sugar and serve.

This is a fine woodland tea with a rich nut-like flavor.

Witch Hazel Wash
(a soothing fluid from the wild)

1 handful witch hazel twigs
    or bark

2 cups water

Boil the witch hazel in water for 10 minutes. Let cool a bit and then rub this aromatic and cooling decoction on the face and body.

Sassafras

(Sassafras albidum)

History

Sassafras is native to the eastern United States and was widely utilized by the Indians for a variety of purposes. Its roots were employed to make brilliantly colored scarlet, yellow, orange, and green dyes; the leaves were used in teas and to thicken soups. However, it was most famed for its various medicinal uses. Tonics made from the root bark were consumed by those suffering from rheumatism and were regularly used by Indian women following childbirth. A mucilagenous eye wash was made by steeping the pith of sassafras shoots in water for a while and then applying the viscous liquid to the eyes. The dried, powdered leaves were applied to open wounds as healing agents and were carried into battle by Seneca warriors for this purpose. When venereal diseases became rampant among the eastern tribes after the advent of the white man, the "savages" turned to warm infusions of sassafras as a treatment for these maladies which accompanied colonization.

The white man was impressed and excited by the possible medicinal applications of sassafras, and towards the end of the sixteenth century, sassafras plants were brought to Spain from Florida, where French Huguenot refugees learned of their application as a tonic for fevers by the Indians. Its use spread throughout Europe and for several decades, ships laden with sassafras plied the seas between the New World and Old. However, sassafras never proved to be the medicinal or economic miracle it had promised to be. Nevertheless, its use as a medicinal plant and food plant became established in the colonies. Colonial cooks used sassafras leaves and root bark for teas and as a spring tonic, and the leaves and pith from the young stems were added to soup as thickeners or were dried and used as condiments. Today, sassafras is of some economic importance as a flavoring for tobacco, patent medicine, gums, and root beer and other beverages. It is also an ingredient in some soaps and perfumes. Sassafras bark and pith are still employed in medicines. Most of the commercial sassafras comes from trees in the south.

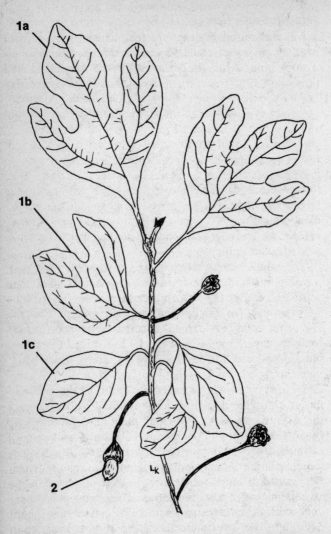

Sassafras. 1 (a-c), Twig showing the 3 basic leaf types. Twigs, leaves, and root—tea. Leaves and pith of twigs —thickener for soup. 2, Blue berry on a red fruit-stalk —fruit.

Habitat and Range

There are three known species of sassafras, two from eastern Asia and our own native species, *Sassafras albidum,* found throughout most of the eastern United States. Sassafras grows in old fields, roadsides and dry or rich woods from southwestern Maine to southern Ontario and Michigan, and south to east Texas and Florida.

Description

Sassafras is commonly shrub-like, but it can develop into a tree up to 90 feet in height. The mature bark is deeply furrowed and red-brown in color, while the twigs are smoother and greenish-yellow. The bark, twigs, roots, and leaves are aromatic. The leaves are variable in shape and are the morphological characteristic by which sassafras can be most easily identified. A single tree can have three main types of leaves: one is unlobed and egg-shaped; another has a single lobe so situated that the leaf looks like a mitten, and the third type has three lobes. The greenish-yellow flowers appear with the new leaves. The fruit is a shiny, blue, bead-like structure suspended at the tip of a red stalk.

Collection and Preparation

Traditionally, sassafras root bark has been employed in making sassafras tea. However, gathering suitable material for this tea requires that trees be uprooted, and the bark peeled away from the root. Then the bark is washed and preferably dried before being used. If you do not wish to go to all this trouble, try steeping the leaves or twigs for tea. The twigs are accessible year round and the leaves can be obtained from spring until autumn; both can be used fresh or they can be dried in an attic room for winter use.

Sassafras Leaf Tea
(a soothing aromatic drink, for 1)

8 fresh sassafras leaves or   1¼ cups water
  2 tsp dried leaves   maple sugar to taste

Bring the water to a boil, remove from heat, and add leaves. Cover pan and allow the leaves to steep for 10 minutes. Sweeten and serve hot or cold.

Sassafras tea is an old-fashioned remedy for colds and bronchitis, being especially favored for its mucilaginous quality.

Sassafras "Gumbo"

Collect young sassafras leaves and twigs in spring and dry in the sun or in an attic room. Crush the leaves and pith to a powder and put through a sieve. Store in clean, covered jars.

This powder is used as a thickener for soups. Add during the last 15 minutes of cooking, using about 1 tablespoonful of powder per pint of soup.

Elder—Flowers

The Common Elder (*Sambucus canadensis*)

Introduction

In late spring the elder plant* puts forth its flattened

---

* See pages 175–177 for additional information concerning this plant.

clusters of small, round flower buds and by early summer its white blossoms have emerged. Both the buds and blossoms can be used as a foodstuff.

Pickled Elder Flower Buds

2 cups young elder flower
   heads
½ cup maple sugar
1 cup white wine vinegar

1 cup water
1 cinnamon stick
1 tsp cloves (whole)

Collect the flower heads when the green flower buds are swelled but before the blossoms appear. Wash the flower heads and set aside to drain. Combine remaining ingredients in a saucepan (do not use aluminum, copper, or galvanized pans) and bring to a boil. Add the flower heads and simmer gently for 5 minutes. Pack into hot, sterilized jars, cover the flower heads with the liquid, and seal immediately. Store in a cool place.

Elder Flower Fritters

2 handfuls elder flower
   heads
1 cup brandy (optional)
1 egg
1 cup milk
½ cup raw sugar
1 tsp nutmeg

1½ cup unbleached white
   flour or
¾ cup cattail pollen and
¾ cup unbleached white
   flour
1 tsp baking powder
fresh berry sauce (optional)

Collect the flower heads when the blossoms begin full bloom. Wash thoroughly and break the heads into three or four smaller pieces. Use immediately or soak in brandy for an hour before using. Meanwhile, combine remaining ingredients and mix well. Dip flowers in the batter and cook in hot fat until they are golden brown. Drain on brown paper and serve as is or top with a fresh berry sauce (pg. 162).

Elder Flour

Pick or shake the buds and petals from the broad flower clusters and use half and half by volume with flour for rolls, hot cakes, and muffins. For winter use, place the flower clusters on sheet pans and dry in a slow oven. Shake the petals free and store in covered tins.

Pigweed

Pigweed, Goosefoot, Lamb's Quarters
(*Chenopodium album*)

History

Chenopodium is a nearly cosmopolitan genus of primarily weedy annuals which are represented in the United States by several native and introduced species. Many of these species are edible. Some Indians of the east and several western tribes utilized the leaves, stem tips, flowers, and seeds for food. One of our more common edible species is the ubiquitous pigweed (*C. album*), which annually plagues gardeners by its uninvited presence. This is another of the weed plants that were introduced* by the settlers and rapidly became

---

* Gleason (1968) disagrees that *Chenopodium album* is solely an introduced species and he states that our *C. album* consists of both introduced and native types. Whatever the case may be, pigweed flourished in the newly cleared lands of what was to be the United States.

naturalized here. However, long before it gained its reputation as a persistent weed, it was prized in Europe for its superior-tasting greens. As early as 1748 pigweed was recorded as being abundant on the streets, dunghills, and grain fields around Philadelphia. Today it is a rare waste area or roadside that does not host a few pigweed plants. The Mohawk Indians were so struck by this prolific species that they named it "skanadanuum'we" ("loves the village") to signify its habit of growing along the paths and roads of settlements.

Habitat and Range

Pigweed grows in waste areas, gardens, roadsides, and dry woods throughout the United States and southern Canada. It is also found in Eurasia and has been introduced into other parts of the world.

Description

The annual, *C. album,* usually grows to about 3 feet in height but can be as tall as 7 feet. It bears alternate, long-stemmed, diamond- to lance-shaped leaves that can grow to a length of 4 inches; the larger leaves are usually toothed. At the apical end of the older plants are borne elongate clusters of tiny, green flowers followed by fruits with black seeds shaped like biconcave discs. The seeds are up to ⅛ inch in diameter.

The young plants are lime-green in color but take on a reddish hue as they mature. Pigweeds are usually described as being covered with a white, mealy substance, particularly on the underside of the leaves. Actually "mealy" is a misnomer but it is a convenient term to describe the appearance of cells located on the surface of the plant, which are distended and full with water.

Collection and Preparation

Search for pigweed along roadsides and in waste areas. If you have a garden, you should have a ready

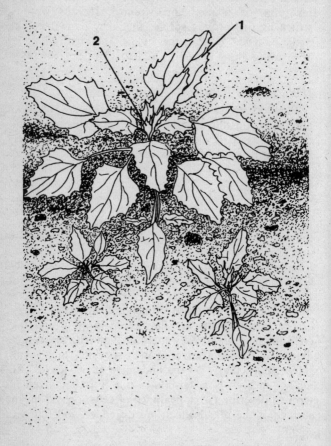

Pigweed. 1, Sprouting plant with somewhat diamond shaped leaves—raw or cooked vegetable and soup. 2, Region from which the tiny, green flowers will emerge.

supply of this weed plant. It requires no care and can provide delicious greens from midspring until the frosts of autumn take it. The leaves and tops of the younger plants can be used as greens, but as the plants mature, only the leaves are tender enough to be eaten. The seeds can be taken from late summer until early winter and ground to be used in bread or gruel.

Pigweed Greens
(an exceptionally delicious vegetable and
a fine source of vitamin A, for 2)

4 cups pigweed greens   1 tbsp butter
½ cup water   salt and pepper to taste

Wash and drain the greens. Place the water in a saucepan, add the salt and butter and bring to a boil. Add the pigweed, cover pan, and simmer over low heat 3 to 5 minutes or until the greens are tender. Stir once or twice while cooking. Serve immediately.

Pigweed Dumplings
(for 2)

¼ cup pigweed greens   1 egg
  (chopped)   salt and pepper to taste
2 slices whole wheat bread

Mix the egg and bread together until a paste is formed. Add the greens and form into balls. Drop balls into boiling water for 3 minutes and use as dumplings in soup.

If dumplings are not to your taste, flatten the egg, bread, and pigweed mixture, and sauté in a little butter until lightly crisp. This can be served as a vegetable pancake or main dish.

Pigweed Soup
(for 2)

2 potatoes (peeled and
　　diced)
water
6 green olives (pitted and
　　mashed)

1 clove garlic (optional)
1 onion (sliced)
¼ cup sesame oil
2 cups pigweed greens

Place potatoes in a saucepan, cover with water, and cook over medium heat until tender. Heat the oil in a skillet, add olives, garlic, and onion. Sauté over medium heat for 3 or 4 minutes. Stir in the pigweed and sauté for an additional 3 minutes. Add the sautéed vegetables to the potatoes and water, simmer for a few minutes, and serve in large bowls.

Campers might wish to substitute bacon or salt pork for the olives.

Pigweed Italian
(for 2)

spaghetti
1 or 2 cloves garlic
pinch of pepper flakes
½ cup olive oil

2 cups pigweed greens
grated cheese
salt and pepper to taste

Cook desired amount of spaghetti according to the directions on the label. In a separate skillet, sauté the garlic in oil for 3 or 4 minutes, add the pigweed and pepper flakes, and cook for 3 more minutes. Stir these vegetables in with the drained spaghetti and serve hot with grated cheese and condiments.

Oxeye Daisy

Oxeye Daisy, White Daisy, Marguerite
(*Chrysanthemum leucanthemum*)

History

It is not widely known that the common oxeye daisy is edible, but in parts of Europe its celery-flavored young leaves have been used for salad greens, and in China several related species are also used in salads. This native of Eurasia was early introduced into this country and is now naturalized throughout most of temperate North America.

Habitat and Range

The genus *Chrysanthemum* is represented by about 100 species, which are mainly native to the northern parts of the Old World. The oxeye daisy was introduced from Europe and is now very abundant in the northeast. It is common in waste areas, fields, and roadsides and is considered a pernicious weed in some areas.

Description

This perennial grows to a height of 2 or 3 feet and has a square, wiry stem which is only slightly branched. At the stem tips are borne the individual flower heads which have a yellow disc and white petals. The diameter across these heads is about 1¼ inches. The lower leaves have a long petiole and are shaped somewhat like a deeply and irregularly toothed skin-diver's fin, while the leaves farther up on the stems have a much attenuated petiole and are slender and elongate.

Oxeye Daisy. 1, Flower head with white petals and yellow center disc. 2, Elongate upper leaf without leaf stalk (petiole). 3, Square stem. 4, Basal leaves with leaf stalks—these leaves (when young) are used as a raw or cooked vegetable.

Collection and Preparation

Daisy plants are most easily located once they have flowered, but the leaves are at their best before flowering occurs. Use the young, basal leaves.

Iceberg Lettuce and
Oxeye Daisy Salad

iceberg lettuce	oil and red wine vinegar
daisy leaves	to taste
radishes	salt and pepper to taste

Mix the lettuce and daisy leaves about 2 to 1, add radishes, oil, and vinegar. Toss. Serve immediately with salt and pepper.

Creamed Daisy Leaves
(for 2)

2 cups daisy leaves	2 tbsp unbleached white
½ cup water	flour
2 tbsp butter	1 cup milk
	salt and pepper to taste

Add daisy leaves to the salted boiling water, cover, and cook over medium heat for 10 minutes. Melt the butter in a separate skillet, and stir in the flour until a paste is formed. Slowly stir in the milk over low heat and flavor with salt and pepper. Stir the cooked leaves into the cream sauce and serve hot.

Day Lily

Orange Day Lily (*Hemerocallis fulva*)
Yellow Day Lily (*Hemerocallus flava*)

History

The familiar day lilies are Asian horticultural species that were early introduced into this country and cultivated in flower gardens for their lovely fragrant blossoms. Their generic name, *Hemerocallis,* comes from the Greek, *hemera,* a day, and *kallos,* beauty, in reference to the short-lived flowers which expand for only a single day.

The sturdy and prolific orange day lily escaped from cultivation and is now naturalized here, while the yellow species is a more occasional escapee. These plants are tasty edibles, which is a fact long familiar to many Asians who use various species of *Hemerocallis* for their crisp, delicious roots and their flavorful flowers.

Habitat and Range

These day lilies are found in gardens throughout the northeast and have spread to roadsides and thickets near old houses.

Description

Day lilies are perennials with tuberous roots, basal, sword-like leaves and a leafless flower stalk from which emerge the upward facing, unspotted blossoms. The flower stalk of the orange day lily grows to about 3½ feet in height and the flower averages about 5 inches in the width. The leaves are a little shorter than the flower

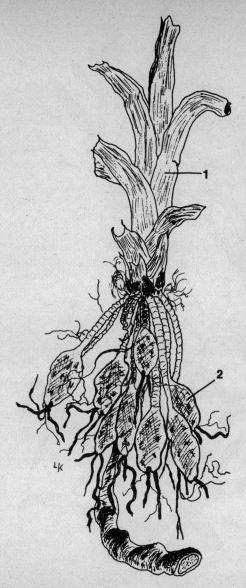

Sprouting Day Lily. 1, Sprouting leaves. 2, Tuberous root—cooked vegetable.

Orange Day Lily. 1, Close-up of orange flower—raw or cooked vegetable, dessert, soup. 2, Flower stalk with buds—cooked vegetable.

stalk and grow to almost an inch in width. The yellow day lily plant is a bit smaller than the orange species and flowers a little earlier than its large relative.

Collection and Preparation

Early in spring, the green patches of day lily plants are quite noticeable as they sprout along roadsides, while later in the season they are apparent due to their tall, cylindrical flower stalks which bear at their apical ends, numerous elongate buds and yellow or orange flowers. The tip of the flower stalk and the young buds can be used for cooked greens. The flowers can be served as an hors d'oeuvre, a cooked vegetable, or a dessert, and the numerous tuberous roots can be used as a boiled vegetable. For those of you who do not want to tamper with the young flower buds or the lovely blossoms, wait until the flower has completed blooming and droops. You can then easily remove the petals, leaving the expanding ovary with its contained seeds intact on the plant. These spent blooms can be sautéed, used in fritters, or dried and added to soups as a thickener. To dry day lilies, put a layer of blossoms on a sheet pan and place in a warm, dry room until crisp. Store in covered jar.

Sautéed Day Lily Blossoms
(a delicious hot hors d'oeuvre, for 2)

6 blossoms	salt to taste
2 tbs butter	

Melt the butter in a skillet over medium heat, add the blossoms, and sauté until they are crisp. Serve hot with salt.

Boiled Day Lily Blossoms
(for 2)

2 cups blossoms (packed)   butter, salt and pepper
½ cup water   to taste

Bring the water to a boil, add the blossoms, cover and cook over low heat for 3 minutes. Serve as a hot vegetable with butter, salt and pepper.

This vegetable tastes similar to summer squash.

Day Lily Desserts

1.

Top fully expanded day lily blossoms with a tablespoonful or two of whipped cream. This is a light, aromatic dessert.

2.

Prepare day lily flower fritters according to the procedure given for elder flower fritters on page 101. Serve day lily fritters hot or cold with a berry sauce or whipped cream.

Boiled Day Lily Roots
(a vegetable dish, for 2)

12 roots   butter, salt and pepper
1 cup water   to taste

Wash the roots and slice in half. Bring the water to a boil, add the roots, cover, lower heat, and cook until tender. Peel and serve hot with butter and condiments.

Summer

Roses

(*Rosa*—several species)

History

Bleak would this world be without the rose family
(Rosaceae) whose members have provided us with a
wonderful variety of sweet-scented rose blossoms and
have given us such aesthetically pleasing and useful
plants as the apple, peach, pear, plum, apricot, cherry,
raspberry, blackberry, and strawberry. These fruits have
nourished us since the days when foraging and hunting
were a way of life. But of all these plants, the rose
stands apart. It is the rose whose beauty has drawn
generations of men to carefully nurture it in gardens,
both great and small, and it is the rose whose allure
has stimulated the imaginations of poets since the days
of Homer.

In addition to their decorative qualities, roses have
long been cultivated commercially in parts of Europe
and Asia for use in perfumes and soaps, for medicinal
purposes, and as a foodstuff. The production of roses
for perfume continues to be a busy industry today, particularly in Bulgaria and France, where thousands of
acres of the damask rose (*Rosa damascena*) and cabbage rose (*R. centifolia*) are cultivated for their blossoms which are distilled to extract the aromatic volatile
oil. It takes about 20,000 pounds of flowers to produce
one pound of this rose oil, which has been a favored
perfume since the beginning of the seventeenth century.
A by-product of this industry is rose water, which consists largely of the water left behind after distillation
along with a little rose oil. Rose water is used as a

vehicle for medicines, is employed to make a fragrant rosewater ointment and has a variety of culinary uses. In France, rose blossoms are also used commercially to make crystallized rose flowers, which are sold as a confection, or the petals are employed to make rose syrup, which is used to flavor ices and beverages.

Rose hips, commonly known as the fruit of the rose, have long been used in parts of Europe for jellies, jams, teas, and soups. They are also recorded to have been a popular food with some American Indians, particularly those of the northwestern states. Recently, modern Americans have become aware of the culinary possibilities of these fruits, mainly due to the widely publicized findings that rose hips are an extraordinarily good source of vitamin C. It is of interest to note that rose hips were used as antiscorbutics by Alaskan Indians long before the word "vitamin" was coined.

Habitat and Range

The genus *Rosa* is represented by about 100 species, all of which are natives of the north temperate zone. In the United States there are several native and introduced roses which in many cases have freely hybridized and are found growing cultivated or wild in a variety of habitats throughout the country.

Description

Roses are shrubs or woody vines which are usually thorny or bristly and commonly bear aromatic glands on the flowering stalk and foliage. The compound leaves consist of 3 to 11 toothed leaflets, and the flowers have five (sometimes more) petals that can range from white, to yellow, pink, and red. Following the blooms, are the fleshy rose hips, which are called "false fruits" by plant taxonomists. Actually the true fruits are found within the hip and consist of little hairy structures which surround an individual seed. Taxonomic considerations aside, the whole ripe hips can be used for

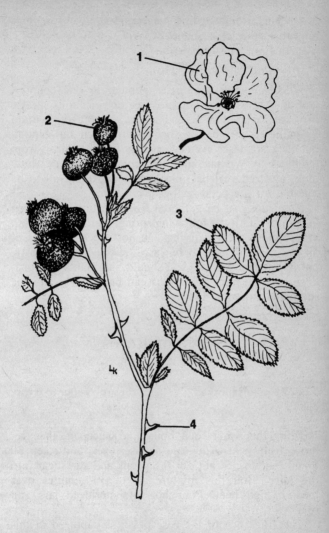

Virginia Rose. Illustrating the general characteristics of wild roses: 1, aromatic flower with 5 pink petals—syrup, confection, jelly, conserve, perfume, rose-water; 2, red rose hip—tea, soup, preserve; 3, compound leaf; 4, thorny stem.

food. The urn-shaped, sometimes rounded, rose hips are small, colored orange.

Collection and Preparation

Wild and cultivated roses abound in this country, and as long as the plants are free of poisonous sprays, they can be used as a food source. Rose petals should be gathered just before the flowers reach full bloom, but they are tasty even when they begin to drop from the blossom. We have used the aromatic petals of white, pink, and red varieties and have found them all to be suitable for the petal recipes given here.

Rose hips can be gathered from the time they ripen in summer until the following spring, and are used fresh or are preserved by drying. Do not expect the hips of all varieties of rose to be large, succulent, and tasty, but if you search a bit, you should find plants that produce suitable hips. Rose hips can be dried in an attic room and stored in tins.

Syrup of Roses
(about 1 pint)

1 qt rose petals (packed)   1½ cups raw sugar to a cup
3 cups water   of juice

Bring the water to a boil in a saucepan, then remove from heat. Add rose petals, cover, and steep 30 to 60 minutes. Strain out the petals and stir sugar into the juice. Boil this mixture 20 to 30 minutes over medium-high heat. Pour hot into sterilized jars and seal.

The fragrance of the rose petals is captured in this syrup, which is an exquisite topping for baked apples, ice cream, and pancakes.

Rose Petal Candy
(about 5 dozen pieces)

3 cups raw sugar   ½ lemon
2 cups water   waxed paper
2 cups rose petals (packed)

Place sugar and water in a saucepan, stir until the sugar is dissolved, and boil over medium-high heat. Meanwhile, macerate the rose petals in a bowl and mix in the juice of the lemon. When the sugar in the saucepan begins to crystallize, stir in the rose mixture. Boil for 1 or 2 minutes or until the sugar begins to crystallize again. Drop this fragrant mixture by teaspoonfuls onto waxed paper and allow to cool.

These candies are a delicious, delicate confection.

Candied Rose Petals

rose petals   raw sugar
egg white

Not all rose petals taste alike, and for this recipe it is important to search for petals that are exceptionally sweet and aromatic. If necessary, snip off the white basal end of the petals, which is sometimes very bitter.

Spread brown paper on sheet pans and place the individual petals on the paper. Spoon the whipped egg white over the petals and allow to drain for 5 minutes, then sprinkle sugar on the petals. Dry in the sun or in a very slow oven. Pack in covered tins.

Rose Petal Jelly
(about 5 medium glasses)

3 cups rose petals (packed)   1⅓ cups raw sugar to a cup
3 cups water   of juice
1 box powdered pectin

Bring water to a boil, remove from heat, add rose
petals, cover and steep 30 to 60 minutes. Pour through
a sieve and add pectin to the juice. Stir until the pectin
is dissolved, then bring to a hard boil. Add the sugar,
stir and bring to a hard boil again 1 to 2 minutes.
Skim and pour into sterilized jelly glasses. Seal with a
thin layer of paraffin.

Rose Petal Conserve
(about 5 medium glasses)

3 cups rose petals (packed)   1⅓ cups sugar to a cup of
3 cups water   juice
1 box powdered pectin to   1 lemon (juice and grated
   2 cups juice   rind)

Bring the water to a boil, then remove from heat.
Add rose petals, cover, and steep 30 to 60 minutes.
Pour through a sieve and set petals aside to be used
later. Measure juice and add pectin. Stir and bring to
a hard boil, then stir in the sugar and lemon. Boil hard
for 1 to 2 minutes, add the rose petals, and pour into
sterilized jelly glasses. Seal immediately with a thin
layer of paraffin.

This fragrant conserve is a delicious topping for
muffins and crackers.

Rose Hip Tea
(a fragrant, pink beverage)

Dried and ground rose hips are most commonly used for this tea, which is a popular beverage in Germany. For every 2 cups of boiling water, steep 1 level teaspoonful of dried, ground hips for 10 minutes. Serve hot or cold with a sweetener.

Rose Hip Soup
(for 2)

1 cup fresh rose hips
  (quartered) or
¾ cup whole dried hips

1 pt of water
raw sugar and sour cream
  to taste

Bring the water to a boil, add rose hips, cover and cook over medium heat 10 to 15 minutes. Mash hips and pour the mixture through a sieve. Add water to the puree to bring it back to its original volume. Sweeten to taste and serve chilled with sour cream.

Old-Fashioned Rose Hip Jam
(about 4 medium glasses)

4 cups fresh rose hips
  (quartered)
1 qt water

1⅓ cups sugar to a cup
  of juice

Bring the water to a boil, add hips, cover, and cook over medium heat 10 to 15 minutes or until the hips are tender. Mash and pour through a strainer. Stir in the sugar with the puree and bring to a boil. Cook until the mixture sheets from a spoon. Skim and pour into sterilized jelly glasses and seal with a thin layer of paraffin.

If you prefer to use a commercial source of pectin, reduce the sugar to 1¼ cups per cup of juice and use 1 box of powdered pectin.

Once you have your puree, stir in the pectin and bring to a rolling boil, then stir in the sugar and bring to a rolling boil again. Cook 1 more minute. Skim and pour into sterilized jelly glasses and seal with paraffin.

Clover

White Clover (*Trifolium repens*)

History

In this country there are several native and introduced clovers, but among the sweetest is the common white clover (*Trifolium repens,* whose fragrant flowers bloom throughout the summer. Bees are drawn to these aromatic blossoms whose flavor is captured in the delicious honey made from their nectar. Man is also attracted to these plants and has learned to make both food and drink from its sweet blooms. White clover blossom tea is a wholesome beverage that used to be popular in the eastern United States; dried white clover flowers and seeds can be used as a bread-food, as was the case in Scotland during times of famine. Even today, some country people continue to make their annual keg of white clover wine or boil down a quart or two of their own homemade white clover honey.

Habitat and Range

White clover is a native of Eurasia and possibly northern North America, where it has been widely

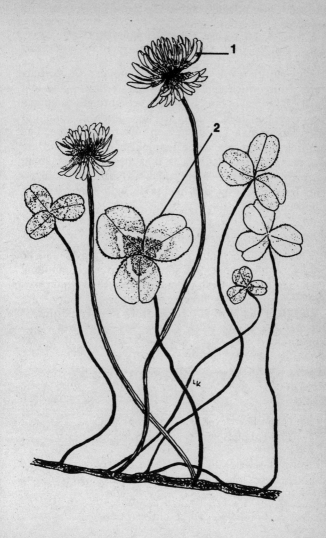

White Clover. 1, Head of white to pinkish flowers—tea, honey. 2, Trifoliate leaf with each leaflet exhibiting a pale chevron towards its base.

planted. It is cultivated and is also found growing wild on lawns, roadsides, and fields.

Description

This clover is a low-growing perennial with creeping stems from which emerge the separate flower and leaf stalks. The leaves are trifoliate with broadly elliptical to egg-shaped leaflets that are lime-green in color but often have a pale-green chevron toward their base. The pea-like flowers are white to pinkish in color and are grouped into rounded heads that measure from about ½ inch to a little larger than an inch in diameter. The fruits are tiny pea-like pods with three to four globose seeds.

Collection and Preparation

The sweet blossoms of this common clover can be collected throughout the summer into early autumn. They can be used fresh or may be dried for winter use. To dry, spread the flowers on paper in a dry, airy room, until the clover is crisp. Store in covered tins.

Clover Blossom Tea
(for 1)

⅓ cup fresh white clover or   1¼ cups water
   1½ tsp dried blossoms   honey to taste

Bring the water to a boil, add blossoms, cover and simmer over low heat for 5 minutes. Sweeten and serve.

Clover Blossom and Rose Petal Honey
(an old New England recipe)
about 1 pint

2 cups fresh white clover
  blossoms (packed)
4 cups water

6 cups raw sugar
1 cup fresh rose petals
  (packed)

Place all ingredients except the rose petals into a saucepan, stir, and bring to a boil. Lower heat, cover, and simmer slowly for 30 minutes. Remove from heat, stir in the rose petals, cover and let stand overnight. Strain off the flowers and reboil the juice over medium heat until it is of the desired consistency. Pour into hot sterilized jars and seal.

Use this dark, rich sweet in the same ways as ordinary honey.

Wild Mints

(*Mentha*—several species)

History

The mints are perennial plants of the genus *Mentha,* the majority of which are native to Eurasia and Australia. These herbs have been commonly used since pre-biblical times and have been popular for their culinary uses and for their medicinal value, which is probably due in part to their high amount of vitamins A and C.

We have one native mint, *Mentha arvensis,* whose leaves were used by some tribes of American Indians for tea and as a relish. However, the settlers and subsequent generations of Americans favored the imported mints, which had been crossed and recrossed in Europe for generations. Many of the progeny of these crosses have been introduced into the United States, where they have thrived both as domesticated and wild plants. Our two most popular mints, peppermint (*M. piperita*) and spearmint (*M. spicata*), have been with us since colonial times and have spread across the country growing in waste places and damp grounds. Spearmint and peppermint are also extensively cultivated in the midwest and in the northwestern United States. Their volatile oils are used for a variety of purposes, such as flavorings for ice cream, candy, chewing gum, and tooth paste.

Habitat and Range

Because most mints like moisture, you can expect to find them along brooksides, in moist meadows, and along marshes. You will probably first notice them as you walk through moist areas and become aware of their pungent minty odor. They can be found throughout the northeast from late spring until frost, but are most abundant in summer.

Description

Mints are aromatic perennials with the well-known minty odor; they have erect, square stems; opposite, toothed leaves, and tiny blue to lavender flowers that are either borne in the leaf axils or in terminal spikes. (For more information on the speciation of mints, see Gleason 1968.)

All mints are edible but if you favor spearmint and peppermint they usually can be identified by their characteristic odor. In addition, peppermint tends to produce a pronounced cooling sensation when you inhale after chewing a leaf.

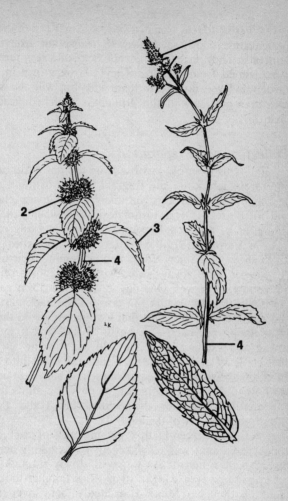

Wild Mint (left) and **Spearmint** (right). 1, Tiny flowers on a spike. 2, Flowers in leaf axil. 3, Opposite, toothed leaves—chew, flavoring, confection, jelly, tea. 4, Erect square stem.

Cultivating Mint

Mints are hardy and easy to transplant from the rootstalk. They do best on level black soil areas recently reclaimed from swamps. They can be grown in the garden and will do best in loam soils but will also survive in sandy soils if the ground is mulched around them.

Collection and Preparation

Mint! This is an old favorite from the past. Although our forefathers knew the fragrant beauty of mint, few people today really care or know about these plants and their uses. I* was fortunate in that when I was a youngster of fourteen I spent a summer working on a farm in Vermont. My boss, a farmer in his sixties, enjoyed showing me new things and explaining their uses. His stories were always laced with the richness of his boyhood experiences. One day he took me down along the bank of a brook that ran through the back pasture and showed me some mint that was growing wild there. "Rub it in your hand and smell!" I did, and it was a strong and exciting odor. He told me how he always chewed leaves as a boy. That summer I got into the habit of chewing mint leaves myself. Later he taught me how to distinguish some of the common mints from one another. But soon the summer faded and along with it, the memory of the mint.

It was only recently that my memory of that first exposure to mint was reawakened. I was hiking across the edge of a marsh. As I moved slowly through the sawgrass, my eyes caught sight of a familiar-looking plant. I thought, Mint! I excitedly bent over and plucked off a sprig, and was rewarded by that same heady fragrance that so excited me as a boy. I eagerly looked around at the patch of mint and after much comparing of plant structure and odor, I concluded that

* L.K.

I had both peppermint and spearmint. I picked from each type of plant and put them in my car. I eagerly drove home, for I was a man with a plan. I had always wanted to have a real mint julep and decided that this was a fitting occasion.

Mint Julep
(for 2)

⅓ cup fresh mint leaves   8 oz bourbon
6 tsp raw sugar   2 cups shaved ice

Wash freshly picked mint in cold water and set it on an absorbent towel to drain. Pinch off the leaves and place ⅓ cup of them with the sugar in a blender. Run the blender at a slow speed until the ingredients are well mixed. Add 8 ounces of your favorite bourbon and 2 cups of shaved ice. Blend again at high speed until the mixture is close to freezing. Pour into two glasses. Need I say more?

We have included some other recipes using mint to demonstrate what a great variety of foods you can prepare with these plants.

Candied Mint Leaves
(for 4)

2 cups fresh mint leaves   1 cup maple sugar
6 whipped egg whites

Wash and sun-dry large mint leaves. Hold each leaf by the petiole (the elongate stem-like part attached to the leaf blade), dip the blade into the egg white and then into the sugar. Lay the leaves carefully on brown paper. Allow to dry in a slow oven. Pack in covered tins.

They will keep for a year and are delicious with a cup of tea.

Mint Butter

½ cup fresh mint leaves   1 pt water
½ cup parsley leaves   ½ lb butter

Pour boiling water over the mint and parsley leaves and steep for 10 minutes. Drain and rub the pulp through a sieve. Take ½ pound of butter and work in the leaf preparation.

Mint and Currant Pastry Filling

Take equal quantities of fresh chopped mint leaves, currants and maple sugar. Use as fillings for pies or turnovers.

Mint Jelly

2 cups crushed fresh mint   6 cups raw sugar
   leaves   1½ boxes pectin
3¼ cups boiling water   1 cup water
2 tbsp lemon juice

Crush the fresh mint in a blender and pour into a saucepan. Add the boiling water, quickly cover the pan, and steep 10 to 15 minutes. Strain and measure 3 cups of the infusion. To this add the lemon juice and sugar. Stir until the sugar is dissolved. Take the powdered pectin and boil hard for 1 minute in 1 cup of water. Stir the pectin mixture into the mint infusion. Pour into glasses and seal. Store in freezer.

Peppermint Tea

1 pt boiling water   lemon and raw sugar
½ cup mint leaves   (optional)

Pour the boiling water over the leaves and steep for 10 minutes. If desired, serve with lemon.

This is not only delicious, it is also an old remedy for indigestion, colic, and colds.

Wild Carrot

Wild Carrot, Queen Anne's Lace
(*Daucus carota*)

History

Daucus carota originated in Eurasia, where it was first taken from the wild state over 2,000 years ago and brought under cultivation in Central Asia and around the Mediterranean area. Slowly its range extended beyond its native lands partly due to its being purposely distributed and cultivated by peripatetic man who prized the fleshy roots of the domesticated varieties, and partially due to its own tough nature and ability to thrive as a wild plant. By the sixteenth century, the carrot was cultivated in England, both as a food and medicinal plant. In the early part of the seventeenth century it was introduced into the New World. True to its wild spirit, the carrot escaped from domestication and spread throughout what was to be the United States. Today, the wild carrot is known by most people here as the common, yet beautiful weed, Queen Anne's Lace,

whose graceful foliage and elegant flowers brighten
many a bleak waste area, parking lot, and roadside.

Habitat and Range

This native of Eurasia has become established in
fields, waste areas, and roadsides throughout the United
States, southern Canada, and many other parts of the
world.

Description

The wild carrot is a biennial that produces a rosette
of feathery leaves and a slender white taproot in its
first year. During its second season, it puts forth erect,
branching, hairy stems that usually grow to a height of
2 to 3 feet. The leaves are hairy, finely divided and
much longer at the base of the plant than on the stem.
At the apex of the stems are numerous small umbels
of white (sometimes pinkish) flowers which together
form a large compound umbel that usually has a purple
flower in its center. These compound flower clusters
generally range from 3 to 6 inches in diameter and may
be flattened or convex. However, as the fruit begins to
mature, the umbels curl upward, thus forming a beautiful structure that somewhat resembles an oval bird
cage. All parts of this bristly plant have an aromatic
carrot-like odor when bruised.

NOTE

Be careful when collecting wild carrot as it
resembles poison hemlock (*Conium maculatum*),
which is extremely toxic when eaten. To illustrate
the gravity of mistaken identification here, we remind you that the hemlock which Socrates imbibed
was an extraction of *C. maculatum*.

To distinguish between these two species, note
that the wild carrot has hairy stems and leaves
while those of poison hemlock are smooth. In addition, poison hemlock has an ill-smelling "mousy"

Wild Carrot. 1, Compound umbel with tiny white flowers. 2, Erect, branching, *hairy* stem. 3, *Hairy,* finely divided leaves—flavoring. 4, White tap root—cooked vegetable, soup.

Wild Carrot Close-up. 1, Hairy flower stalk with compound umbel—the peeled young stalks are a peppery chew. 2, Brown fruit—flavoring.

odor when bruised as compared to the aromatic odor of the wild carrot.

Collection and Preparation

Wild carrots begin to bloom in early summer and continue to put forth blossoms until autumn. They can be easily recognized once they have begun to flower in early summer. At that time, the flavorful roots, leaves, and flower stalks should be gathered. The roots can be dug up with a shovel. The roots can be used in the same ways as the domestic varieties of carrot, although the core of the wild carrot is usually too tough to eat; the fresh or dried leaves can be used to flavor soups, and the freshly peeled, young flower stalks are a crisp and peppery nibble when eaten raw. Soon after the carrot blooms, its small brown fruits can be gathered and dried for use as a flavoring in soups, chowders, breads, and salads. Toward the end of summer, the roots of the new young plants can be gathered. Dry the carrot leaves and seeds in an attic room or in a slow oven and store in covered jars.

Boiled Wild Carrots
(for 1)

8 medium-size wild carrot roots (about 4" long and ½" in width)	½ cup water 1 tsp butter salt and pepper to taste

Wash and dice carrots into inch-long pieces (if desired, peel before dicing). Place water, butter and a little salt in a saucepan and bring to a boil. Add the carrots, cover and cook over medium heat for 20 minutes or until the carrots are tender. Serve with condiments taking care to remove the inner core if it is tough.

Wild Carrot and Pigweed Soup
(for 2)

10 medium-size wild carrot roots

4 large carrot leaves (about 8" long)

1 cup pigweed tops (packed)

3 cups water

1 tbsp butter

salt and pepper to taste

Wash vegetables and dice carrot roots. Place water, butter, and some salt in a saucepan and bring to a boil. Add the carrot leaves and roots, cover and cook over medium heat for 20 minutes. Remove the carrot leaves, add pigweed, lower heat, and simmer 3 to 4 minutes. Serve in bowls with condiments.

Wild Cherry

(*Prunus*—several species)

History

The genus *Prunus* is mainly concentrated in the north temperate zone and is represented by many economically important plants, such as the peach, apricot, cherry, and plum. In North America there are several species of native wild cherry and plum, but the peach and apricot were introduced by the settlers.

Indians of the east ate the fresh or dried fruit of the pin cherry (*Prunus pensylvanica*), the black cherry (*P. serotina*) and the choke cherry (*P. virginiana*). They also made a tea from the twigs of the black cherry and choke cherry, and the dried and leached fruits of the choke cherry were used in pemmican. The

Choke Cherry (1), with small white flowers in a long cluster, egg-shaped leaves with bristly teeth, and round, wine-red fruit—jelly. **Black Cherry** (2), with flowers in an elongate cluster, leaves that have blunt teeth, and round blackish fruit—wine, jelly. **Pin Cherry** (3), with flowers borne in an umbrellalike cluster, leaves with rather blunt teeth and red fruit—raw, soup, wine, jelly.

colonists made a medicinal tonic of black cherry bark and utilized the fruits of the various wild cherries for jams, cordials, and wines.

Collection and Preparation

The bark of cherry trees has many horizontal streaks (the lenticels) which remind one of birch bark. Sometimes cherry trees are mistaken for black birch. When you think you have a wild cherry, break a twig and

TABLE 4

Habitat, Range, and Description of
the Wild Cherry

Characteristics	Pin Cherry (*Prunus pensylvanica*)
Habitat	Burned-over areas, woodlands, and clearings
Range	Newfoundland to Indiana, South Dakota, Colorado, and south to Virginia. Throughout a large part of Canada
Height	Thin, reddish brown, often shiny
Bark	Lenticels lens-shaped
Buds	Crowded at twig tip
Leaves	Simple, alternate; lance-shaped; blunt teeth; yellow-green
Flowers	5 white petals. Borne in umbrella-like clusters
Fruit	Globose, red. Sour, but can be eaten raw
Available	Early summer

smell. If it has a strong wintergreen smell, you have a black birch; if it has a rather bitter odor, you probably have a cherry.

Note. The leaves, twigs and pits of peach, apricot, bitter almond, and wild cherries discussed here concentrate dangerous levels of a cyanogenic glycoside. We suggest you employ only the pitted fruit as a food.

Black Cherry (*P. serotina*)	Choke Cherry (*P. virginiana*)
Forests, roadsides and waste areas. Does best in deep moist soil	Found in a great variety of habitats, such as waste areas, roadsides, swamp borders, and dunes
Nova Scotia to Minnesota, south to east Texas, and east to Florida Tree up to 90′	Throughout the northeast and most of the rest of the country. Southern Canada Usually a shrub but can be a small tree up to 30′
Young stems reddish brown. Old trunks black with plate-like scales. Inner bark aromatic. Lenticels elongate	Smooth gray brown with small lenticels
Solitary at twig tip	Same as black cherry
Same as pin cherry. Oblong to lance-shaped. Blunt teeth. Lustrous dark green above and "hairy" along midrib below	Same as pin cherry. Egg-shaped. Bristle-like teeth. Yellow-green
Same as pin cherry. In elongate clusters	Same as pin cherry. Same as black cherry
Globose, almost black. Wine-flavored	Globose, reddish purple. Use only for cooking
Autumn	Late summer

Chilled Pin Cherry Soup
(2 to 3 cups)

4 cups pin cherries
5 cups boiling water
raw sugar to taste

6 to 8 tbsp sour cream or
yogurt

Mash the berries through a coarse sieve. Add the pulp to a saucepan containing the boiling water. Cover and simmer slowly for 20 to 30 minutes. Remove from heat. Slightly sweeten with sugar; if the juice seems too strong, dilute it a bit with water. If desired thicken the juice with one tablespoonful of cornstarch that is first dissolved in a little water and then stirred into the hot liquid. Chill the soup and serve topped with some sour cream or yogurt.

Wild Black Cherry Wine

6 qt dried cherries
3 lemons (sliced)
6 oranges (sliced)
2 lb raisins (white)

5 to 7 lb raw sugar
3 yeast cakes
3 gal water

Place cherries, lemons, oranges, raisins, and sugar into a 5 gallon crock, cover with the boiling water, and set aside to cool. Dissolve the yeast in a little warm water and stir in with the rest of the ingredients. Cover the crock with a clean towel and let work in a cool room for 2 weeks or until it stops bubbling. Stir daily. Siphon the liquid into wine bottles as is described for dandelion wine (page 9), and store in a cool dark room for 6 months or more before serving. This is such a ripe, rich wine that we suggest it be sipped as an after-dinner drink.

Wild Cherry Jelly

All of these cherries can be used for jelly as long as the fruits are fully ripe. The pamphlet which comes with Certo has a jelly recipe for these pectin-poor fruits.

Sweet Goldenrod

(*Solidago odora*)

History
Some eastern Indian tribes used the flowers and leaves of this anise-flavored native goldenrod to make a fine tea. Presumably the settlers learned the use of this plant from the Indians, and by the time of the Revolutionary War sweet goldenrod tea was a common substitute for oriental teas. Indeed, for a while after the Revolution, the flowers of sweet goldenrod were dried and exported to China and used there as a tea.

Habitat and Range
The goldenrods are mainly North American herbs that are represented in the eastern United States by an impressive array of species which towards summer's end, begin to paint our countryside with their brilliant golden-yellow hues. Sweet goldenrod prefers dry open sandy soil or thin woods, and grows from east Texas to Florida, north to New Hampshire and southern Vermont.

Description
Sweet goldenrod is a perennial herb that grows to 3

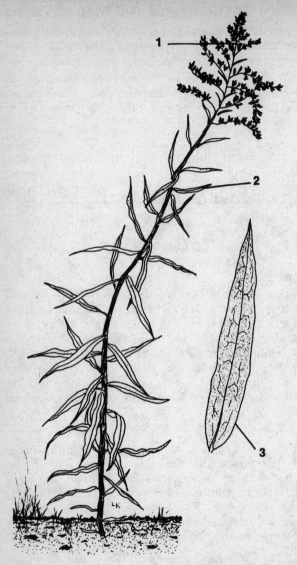

Sweet Goldenrod. 1, Flower head with golden blooms
—tea. 2, Lance-shaped alternate, untoothed leaf—tea.
3, Close-up, leaf held to light illustrates the tiny translucent dots.

or more feet in height and produces its golden blooms from midsummer to late summer. The lance-shaped leaves grow to 4 inches in length and are hairless, alternate, and untoothed. When a leaf is held up to the light, many translucent dots can be seen along its length. Both the leaves and inflorescences give off a strong anise-like odor when crushed.

Collection and Preparation

Sweet goldenrod begins to flower around midsummer and can be recognized by its smooth, untoothed leaves which smell of anise. Collect the leaves or flowers on a dry, bright day, and dry in an attic room. Store in clean, covered jars.

Sweet Goldenrod Tea
(for 2)

2 tsp sweet goldenrod
   flowers or leaves (dried)
2⅓ cups water

1 tsp fresh lime juice
maple sugar to taste

Bring the water to a boil, add the goldenrod, cover and simmer over low heat for 15 minutes. Pour through a sieve, add the lime juice, and serve with maple sugar.

This is a light, smooth flavored tea that should have wider use.

Wild Rice

Wild Rice, Water Oats (*Zizania aquatica*)

History

Wild rice is not a true rice, but its grains have long served as a vital food for some eastern Indians, particularly those located near the Great Lakes. In years gone by, fierce battles were waged among various tribes over the rights to some of the great northern rice-filled waters, which today, continue to serve as a source of food and income for some Indians. The Indian method of gathering wild rice is legend and was described in detail by the early explorers who noted that the natives went two or three to a canoe among these aquatic plants and with a stick, beat the seeds out into the canoe bottoms.

An account (Dale 1906) of a harvest among the Mississauga Indians in 1906 relates that late in August, the tribe gathered in canvas houses around the stands of wild rice, awaiting the week of harvest when the plants would be bent with the heavy, black grain. Their competitors for this nutritious and highly marketable food was a neighboring band of Indians who claimed collecting rights to parts of this particular stand, myriads of wild ducks, which feed upon it with relish, and the ominous September winds which could whisk a whole harvest from the laden plants, depositing it in the water. Until harvest time, the women wove baskets and the men went out in their canoes to fish the waters or hunt the abundant waterfowl. But when the appointed day arrived, the canoes were manned by a male and female; while the man worked the boat through

146

the dense stands of rice, his squaw in the stern, beat the stalks with a cedar stick to remove the rice which dropped into the boat. Four hours of working in this way could yield three bushels. Back at camp, the women would gather together and sing while cleansing the rice—it was parched in great pots and stirred hard to remove the husks and then was cast into the air and the chaff blown off by the wind. Some of the rice was kept for winter use and the surplus was sold for $2.00 a bushel.

Habitat and Range

Zizania is represented by one species in North America (*Z. aquatic*) and another in Asia. Our species is an aquatic annual that grows in stream borders, shallow waters, fresh or even brackish marshes, and tidal flats. It ranges from Nova Scotia and eastern Quebec to Manitoba, south to Louisiana and Florida. However, it reaches its greatest abundance around the Great Lakes and upper Mississippi River valley region and has been widely planted both in and out of its range as food for waterfowl.

Description

This striking annual of the grass family is noted for its aquatic habit, large size, prominent flower stalk, and beautiful color which is a yellow-green in late spring and early summer, often ripening to a dramatic straw-yellow at harvest. Wild rice has flat grass-like leaves and can grow to about 10 feet in height although some varieties are small, particularly the variety, *brevis,* which only reaches a height of about 2 feet. The cluster of flowers is erect and the lower portions contain the widely spreading male branches, while the terminally located female branches are at first erect and then ascending. The almost cylindrical-shaped fruits are about ½ inch long and have a loosely rolled husk about the hard, slender seed which ranges in color from olive green to brown or black.

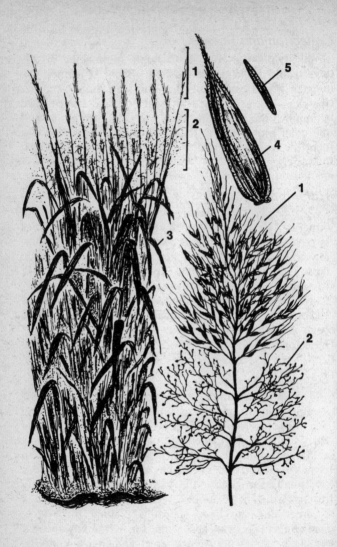

Wild Rice. 1, Female flower cluster. 2, Male flower cluster. 3, Long, grasslike leaves. 4, Fruit inside of which is 5, the green-to-black seed. The seed is the edible wild rice.

Collection and Preparation

Wild rice can be recognized by its aquatic habit and the large flower stalks that appear around early summer in the northeast. The Indian's method of gathering and cleaning wild rice has not been substantially improved upon, but before you harvest the grains check to determine whether your collecting area has been set aside for Indian use, as is the case in some areas near the Great Lakes. Also, to remove some of the smoky taste, you might want to wash the wild rice and drain it before storing in dry, covered containers.

Before cooking wild rice, pour it into a sieve and rinse with cold water.

Fried Wild Rice
(a garnish or snack)

Place wild rice into a fine mesh frying basket. Lower basket into hot fat and fry until the grain pops open (about 3 minutes). Lightly salt and serve as an appetizer or use it hot or cold as a garnish for salads, vegetables, poultry, and game.

Boiled Wild Rice
(for 4)

1 cup wild rice	butter to taste
4 to 5 cups water	salt and pepper to taste
1 tsp salt	

Bring the salted water to a boil, add wild rice, cover, and cook over medium heat, stirring occasionally, until the rice is tender and fluffed (about an hour). Serve as a vegetable with butter and condiments. If desired, during the last 5 minutes of cooking add ½ cup each of blueberries and chopped butternuts.

Wild rice is the plant from which the Menomini tribe derived its name. Their customary way of boiling this grain was to cook it with venison broth and season with maple sugar. If you happen to have these ingredients, why not try cooking wild rice in this traditional way.

Wild Rice Stuffing

Use boiled wild rice in lieu of bread in your favorite stuffing recipe.

BERRIES

Introduction

Wild fruits and berries have always been important items in the diets of aboriginal peoples. The American Indians utilized almost 300 species of berries and berry-like fruits which were eaten fresh, used in cooking, mashed for fresh berry drinks, or dried for winter use when they would be added to soups, breads, and puddings.

Some of the most highly prized and abundant berries gathered by the eastern Indians were the strawberry, mulberry, juneberry, raspberry, blackberry, dewberry, blueberry, huckleberry, elderberry, and cranberry.

Waugh, in his book *Iroquois Foods and Food Preparation,* tells of the important role berries played in the life of the Iroquois: "Amongst the earliest berries to ripen is the strawberry followed closely by the raspberry and others. These welcome events are celebrated by longhouse ceremonies in which thanks are given, while quantities of the fruit are eaten in the feasts which follow" (Canadian Government Printing Bureau 1916, p. 25).

The chief nutritional value of berries is that they provide carbohydrates, minerals, and vitamins A and C. To retain the vitamin content, berries should be eaten raw or used fresh in cereals, short cakes, and other dishes.

We have assumed here that people will use berries fresh or cook them in pies and tarts for which there are many recipes available in most cook books. Rather than repeating ways of preparation already familiar to many, we have attempted in several of our recipes to include lesser known ways of serving berries. For example, we have an English recipe for fresh berry syrup that is far superior to any fruit syrup on the market today. Also, we have included some ways the Indians used berries and berry plants along with some traditional berry medicines.

Wild Strawberries

(*Fragaria*—several species)

History

Strawberries are one of the most popular small fruits of the temperate zone, acclaimed both for their fragrant taste as well as for their rich supply of vitamin C. Like many of the more favored wild food plants, the wild strawberry has been taken from the woods and fields and put under cultivation. Written records indicate that it was planted in English herb gardens at least as far back as the fifteenth century. Both medieval and modern herbals recommend the strawberry for food and medicine: strawberries and cream and strawberries and wine are perennial household favorites; strawberry juice can be used as a complexion wash; strawberry leaves make fragrant, vitamin-C-rich teas and decoctions of the root or leaves can be used as astringents.

When the colonists came to the New World, they found that its Indians collected and consumed quantities of these sweet fruits. Soon the gardening-prone settlers began cultivating the rich-tasting American species, *Fragaria virginiana,* and sent plants to England, where this species has been cultivated since the seventeenth century.

Modern commercial strawberry production is centered around the growing of vigorous hybrid plants that originated from crosses between wild North American species and a Chilean species. Although mass production of strawberries has been achieved, the domesticated fruits cannot compare in flavor and taste with the succulent fruit of our common wild strawberry, *F. virginiana.*

Habitat and Range

Fragaria is represented by about 35 species and many varieties which grow throughout the north temperate zone and in the Andean region of South America. The most common wild strawberry in the eastern United States is *F. virginiana,* which can be found in and around woods, on open slopes, and in undisturbed areas.

Description

Wild strawberries are low-growing perennials which usually spread by runners. They can be readily recognized year-round by the leaves which are basal and consist of three toothed leaflets which in some varieties are hairy. These leaflets are soft when young but become more firm as they mature; the younger leaflets are recommended for food and medicine. The flowers have five white petals and the fruit is the familiar tiny, soft, sweet red strawberry.

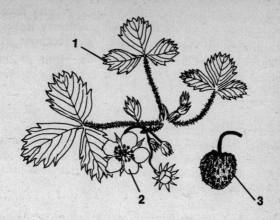

Wild Strawberry (top). 1, Compound leaf with three-toothed leaflets—tea, astringent. 2, five white petals of flower. 3, Red strawberry—numerous uses as a fresh, dried or cooked fruit.

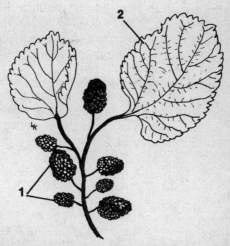

White Mulberry (bottom). 1, Mulberry fruits which resemble blackberries—fruit drink, syrup, candied apples. 2, Leaf which is rather globose in shape, alternate and toothed.

Some species of cinquefoils (*Potentilla*) resemble the wild strawberry plant in their leaf and flower structure and could confuse those uninitiated to the finer points of plant identification. Fortunately, the fruit of the cinquefoil cannot be confused with that of the strawberry.

Collection and Preparation

Because wild strawberries are soft and fragile fruits, they should be either eaten or preserved within a few days of being collected. Wash strawberries thoroughly and hull before using.

Strawberry Leather
(a simple and inexpensive way to preserve fruit)

Mash berries and mold into pancake-size cakes, place on large basswood leaves or platters, and dry in the sun (remember to screen from insects) or in a slow oven (200°F). When dry, store in covered containers.

The Indians used these berry cakes as is or added them to pottages. The Europeans employed them for pies, short cakes, sauces, and tarts.

Most all of the berries discussed in this section can be substituted for strawberries in this recipe, but those with large seeds or a stemmy pith, such as blackberries, dewberries, and mulberries must first be mashed through a sieve before being molded into cakes.

Strawberry Syrup
(a superior natural fruit flavoring)

strawberries
white wine vinegar

equal parts raw sugar and juice

Clean the berries, place in a crock and cover with the vinegar. Place a clean towel over the crock and let stand for 3 days. Strain the liquid through a sieve. Measure out the liquid, stir in the appropriate amount of sugar, and boil gently for 5 minutes. Remove scum from the top and pour into sterilized bottles. Cover and store in a cool place.

Use as a topping for hotcakes or desserts. Add a teaspoonful to a glass of water to make a pleasant fruit-flavored drink, or use as a topping for ice cream.

Blackberries and raspberries can be substituted for strawberries in this recipe.

Fresh Wild Strawberry Soup
(for 2)

1 pt berries   raw sugar to taste
1 cup sour cream

Place berries and sugar in a blender and mix well. Chill. Serve in bowls and top with sour cream.

Wild Strawberries and Wine
(a pleasant, cool summer drink)

1 cup strawberries (crushed)   1 orange (sliced)
peel from 1 cucumber   1 qt soda water
ice cubes   Rhine wine (one fifth)
1 lemon (sliced)

Place the fruits and ice cubes in a glass pitcher or punch bowl. Add the wine and soda water. Stir and serve cold.

Mulberries

The Red Mulberry (*Morus rubra*)
The White Mulberry (*Morus alba*)

History

Among the first of our native fruits to ripen is the prolific red mulberry which reaches maturity soon after the wild strawberry. The red mulberry was a popular fruit with both northern and southern Indians, and some southern tribes cultivated tracts of land with the red mulberry tree. The settlers reportedly used the red mulberry instead of raisins and currants, and employed it in drinks and syrups which were mildly purgative. It has never been widely used as a table fruit, perhaps this is due to the chewy axis running through the center of the fruit. The bark has been used for cordage, thread, and rope. The inner bark of the root can be powdered and used as a purgative. A teaspoonful of the powdered root to a cup of hot water is the dose that has been used.

Before the American Revolution and during the early part of the nineteenth century, the Asian white mulberry tree was imported and extensively cultivated in the east for its leaves and fruit, which are the preferred food of the silkworm larvae. While the production of silk was not a successful business endeavor in this country, the effects of this industry remain with us today in the presence of the white mulberry trees, which persisted and spread. Because the fruit is not as fine as that of the red mulberry, it has been used as fodder for poultry and swine, and was employed in the Civil War by the Confederacy to make mulberry wine and to color confections.

Habitat and Range

The mulberries are represented by about a dozen species found in temperate regions of the northern hemisphere. Our native red mulberry is a forest tree found in rich woods from southern Vermont to Minnesota and South Dakota, south to Texas, and east to Florida. The introduced white mulberry has become naturalized and is well established in the east, being especially abundant west and southwest of New York State. Both these mulberries have been planted as ornamentals.

Description

These mulberries are small to medium-size trees with milky sap, flowers that are borne in catkins and abundant fruits that resemble blackberries. The leaves are alternate, egg-shaped to roundish, and simple with entire, toothed or lobed margins.

To distinguish between the red mulberry and white mulberry tree, note that the red mulberry has red-brown bark, leaves that tend to be coarse above and are hairy beneath, and its succulent, tasty fruits are dark purple in color, while the white mulberry has yellow-brown bark, shiny soft leaves that are only hairy along the veins on the underside, and its rather bland-tasting fruit ranges from white to almost black.

Collection and Preparation

Mulberry trees are easily recognized in summer, when they are producing their numerous fruit which attract many birds and squirrels. Pick the ripe fruit directly from the tree or spread old, clean sheets or spreads beneath it to catch the fruit and gently shake the branches. Check through the fruit and remove debris or overripe berries. Mulberries will keep well a week or two under refrigeration. Wash and drain before using.

Mulberry Drink
(a refreshing summer beverage)

2 qt mulberries   raw sugar to taste
1 qt water   juice of 1 lemon

Mash berries and squeeze the juice through a straining bag. Stir in remaining ingredients, cool, and serve.

Mulberry Candied Apples
(a natural fruit treat)

1 qt mulberries   ½ tsp cinnamon
2 cups water   12 medium-size apples
1½ cups raw sugar waxed paper
8 whole cloves

Wash apples thoroughly, allow to drain, then insert a stick in the stem end. Set aside.

Crush berries, add water, and bring to a boil over medium heat. Cook for 15 minutes. Pour through a jelly cloth and squeeze to obtain all the juice. Stir in the sugar and spices and boil 15 minutes. Remove from heat and strain out the cloves. This will yield about a quart of juice (which can be stored in sterilized jars), or you can continue to boil it until it forms threads when dropped from a spoon. Immediately dip apples into the syrup until they are covered. Set on waxed papers to drain.

This recipe is particularly suited for mulberries. We recommend that some juice be stored for candying apples year-round.

Blueberries

(*Vaccinium*—several species)

History

Blueberries are one of America's favorite small fruits. While most of our commercial supply still comes from wild plants, vast tracts of clayey or sandy acidic soils in the east are now planted with cultivated hybrid varieties.

Blueberries were popular with the eastern Indians and quantities were eaten as fresh fruit or crushed and added to water for a cooling fruit drink. Large stores of the easy-to-keep berries were dried or smoked and used with cornmeal to make a variety of breads and pudding or added to vegetable or meat soups. Blueberries were also popular with the colonists who used them much as we do today in pastries, cakes, and preserves.

Habitat and Range

The genus *Vaccinium* is represented by sundry berry-producing shrubs that grow throughout much of the north temperate zone and in parts of the tropics. However, the true wild blueberries are confined to eastern North America, where there are several species that can be found in diverse habitats from bogs and swamps to dry woods and old fields.

Description

Blueberry plants can be recognized by their speckled, slender, reddish or green twigs, their small, smooth egg-shaped leaves; the white, bell-shaped flowers, and the

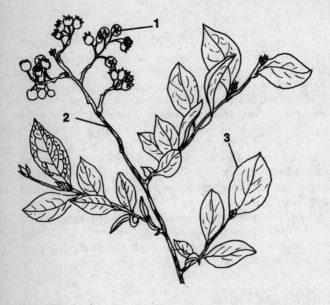

Blueberry. 1, Blue fruit—numerous uses as raw, dried, or cooked berry. 2, Slender twig. 3, Egg-shaped leaf.

round, blue to black berries which contain many seeds. There are low-bush and high-bush varieties. The latter predominate in the south.

Blueberries share their range with several related, edible berry plants, such as those of the huckleberry (*Gaylussacia*), bilberry (*Vaccinium*), and whortleberry (*Vaccinium*). Generally, these fruits are picked interchangeably with blueberries, but for those who want to distinguish these plants from true blueberries, note the following characteristics: a huckleberry contains only 10 seeds while a blueberry has more; bilberries and whortleberries bear their fruits in stalks that emerge from the leaf-axil, while blueberry fruit is borne on stalks separate from the leaves.

Collection and Preparation

As mentioned above, blueberries grow in a variety of habitats but if you live in the northeast and want to locate quantities of plants, try searching in cleared and burned-over lands, where the low, sweet blueberry, *V. angustifolium,* tends to invade and propagate itself quite readily.

Once the fruits are gathered they should be checked over for debris and inferior berries, then the suitable berries can be washed, drained, and loosely packed in jars. Blueberries will keep well one to two weeks in the refrigerator or they can be frozen as is. Use the thawed berries as you would fresh berries. Dried blueberries are also a useful food item especially for those who spend a lot of time in the woods. Some techniques for drying berries are given below.

Drying Blueberries

The Iroquois Indians used to spread their berries upon wood or shallow baskets and dry them in the sun or by a fire. The fruits were then packed away in covered baskets.

Berries can be dried at home by spreading them on clean towels or paper in a warm attic room or they can be placed on sheet pans and dried in a slow oven (200°F) for several hours.

Dried berries may be added to soups, used instead of currants and raisins in bread and cake recipes, and soaked in warm water and cooked as a sauce.

Pumpkin, Corn, and Berry Bread
(an Iroquois recipe)

1 small pumpkin	2 tbsp butter
cornmeal	1 cup dried blueberries

Slice off the top of the pumpkin, remove the seeds and set aside to bake as described on page 267. Peel off the rind and then cut the pumpkin into small cubes. Take equal quantities of pumpkin and water and boil until you have a thin mush. Stir in the berries and then add sufficient cornmeal to form a paste. Mold the batter into patties about one inch thick and sauté in butter.

This is a delicious breakfast bread that goes well with fried eggs. The mixture keeps well when refrigerated and can be made a night or two before it is to be used.

Blueberry Sauce
(a wild-fruit topping for meat and breads)

blueberries	raw sugar

Place equal amounts of berries and sugar in a skillet. Add enough water to just cover berries, and stir. Bring to a boil then lower heat and simmer to desired thickness.

Serve hot over ham or pancakes. Store leftover sauce in sterilized, covered jars.

Old-Fashioned Wild Blueberry Jam

raw sugar   blueberries

Weigh fruit and an equal amount of sugar. Place fruit in a large kettle, crush, and cook for 15 minutes. Stir in the sugar and cook until the mixture thickens to a jelly-like consistency.

Ladle into sterilized jars and seal with a thin layer of paraffin.

Shadbush, Juneberries, Serviceberries

(*Amelanchier*—several species)

History

The shadbush received this appellation from the settlers along the East Coast who associated the appearance of the showy blossoms of this plant with the annual spring spawning run of the shad. One of its other names, the Juneberry, was in reference to the fruit that ripens as early as June in some areas.

Shadbush berries are insipid to tasty when fresh but they improve in flavor with drying. This fact was not lost on the Indians. These berries were among the more popular of the 50 or so types that were dried for winter use by the various American tribes. The whole berries were dried in the sun or over a fire or they were reduced to a paste and pressed into cakes which were then dried. The dried berries were considered a delicacy when added to the broths of meat or fat. They were regularly mixed with cornmeal for breads and puddings, and they were added to pemmican* as a flavoring. Lewis, of the Lewis and Clark Expedition, described the dried berry cakes which were sometimes pressed into loaves 10 to 15 pounds in weight. Bits of these were broken off and eaten raw or were added to hot soups.

The use of shadbush berries was much more common among the explorers and settlers than among modern Americans. We are the poorer for this as the fruits of some of the species have a delicious almond flavor when cooked and are especially good as a muffin berry or when used in cakes and pies.

Habitat and Range

Amelanchier is represented by about 20 species and many varieties that grow in the north temperate zone. Eighteen of these species are in North America, where they occupy a variety of habitats from the banks of tidal streams, to rocky slopes, barrens, and open woods. Like some of the blueberries, certain varieties of shadbush quickly invade burned-over or cleared areas and spread rapidly.

Description

These plants are small shrubs or trees with simple, toothed, alternate leaves that are elliptical to egg-shaped. The striking five-petaled flowers are white or pink and appear with or just before the leaves. The mature fruit resembles a huckleberry and is red to black in color. A characteristic by which the shadbush can be conclusively identified is its slender buds, which are pink to red, and bud scales, which are dark at the tip.

---

* Pemmican: Dried lean meat pounded into a paste with fat, formed into cakes and allowed to become solid. The Indians often added dried berries and maple sugar to their pemmican.

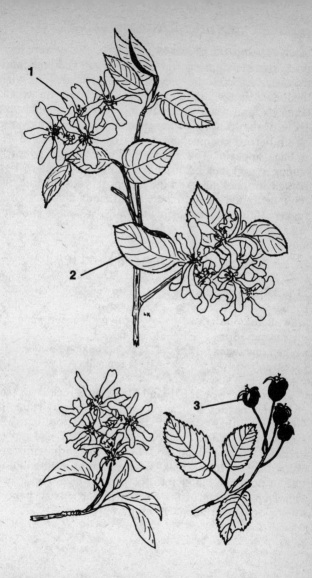

Shadbush. 1, Striking flower with five elongate white to pink petals. 2, Simple, toothed, egg-shaped leaf. 3, Red-to-black fruit—baking.

Collection and Preparation

Early each spring, the white to pinkish shadbush blooms brighten the newly foliating land with their brilliant display along stream banks, edges of woods, thickets, and waste areas. At this time one should take note of the location of the shadbush plants as they and their berries become much less conspicuous once the foliage appears. The berries are usually ripe by early summer and can be used fresh or dried but are best suited for cooking. Add the berries to your favorite biscuit or muffin recipe or try one of our favorites, gold cake with a shadbush berry topping.

Gold Cake and Berries

1 to 1½ cups shadbush berries
raw sugar, to taste
¼ cup margarine
½ cup raw sugar
¼ tsp salt
½ tsp vanilla
2 egg yolks
1 cup unbleached white flour
1¼ tsp baking powder
⅜ cup milk

Set the oven at 350°F and grease an 8-inch layer pan. Mix the berries and sugar and set aside. Cream the margarine, the ½ cup of sugar, and salt together. Mix in the vanilla and egg yolks. Sift the flour and baking powder together and add to the margarine mixture, alternately with the milk. Beat well after each addition. Then pour the batter into the greased pan. Top it with an even covering of the sweetened berries and bake in a slow oven for about 30 minutes.

Blackberries and Dewberries

(*Rubus*—several species)

History

Blackberries are common wild-fruit plants of the north temperate zone, with a long history of use as medicinal and food plants. The ancient Greeks used blackberries as a remedy for gout, and the English peasantry used decoctions of blackberry root and leaves as a treatment for diarrhea. Chemical analysis of blackberry plants reveals that the roots and leaves of this plant concentrate a large amount of tannin, which accounts for their astringent properties.

The English developed sundry recipes for blackberry cordials, syrups, and wines that were taken as foods or as pleasant tonics for intestinal afflictions. These blackberry recipes traveled to the New World with the colonists, who found the prickly fruit plants growing profusely here. They observed that during summer, the juicy black fruits were gathered by the Indians of the region and eaten in huge quantities or dried and stored in covered baskets for winter use.

The cultivation of blackberries commenced here sometime after the colonists arrived, but this endeavor has never proved to be of great commercial importance. However, wild blackberries were used throughout the colonies for jams and for their various salubrious liqueurs. Perhaps the blackberry plant reached its apogee in this country during the Civil War when it was widely used in diverse field remedies for the perennial bowel

disorders that plague armies. A great advocate of blackberries and of spirits was the Confederate army sur-
geon, Dr. Porcher, who said of blackberry wine, "It is
not easy to overvalue the great utility of so mild an
alcoholic a drink, combining slightly astringent vegetable properties, and which may be placed within the
reach of almost anyone. Cheap good wines are certainly
the greatest boon that could be conferred on any country" (Porcher 1970, p. 143).

Habitat and Range

Rubus is an almost cosmopolitan genus that is best
represented by innumerable species in the north temperate zone. Blackberry and dewberry plants are common in the United States and are found in a variety of
habitats, except where winters are very severe or where
there are droughts or extremes of heat.

Description

Blackberry plants usually grow erect and then arch
back toward the ground; dewberry plants tend to creep
along the ground. The stems of both are green or red
and are usually armed with thorns and prickles. The
leaves of both typically consist of three or five leaflets
and the white, five-petaled flowers resemble wild roses.
The mature fruits grow to about ½ inch in length and
consist of many juicy black kernels.

One thorny plant that might be confused with blackberry is the greenbrier (*Smilax*). To readily distinguish
between these, note that unlike the stout blackberry
stems which form arching clumps, the greenbrier is a
climbing vine that adheres to the foliage of other plants
by means of its tendrils.

Collection and Preparation

Blackberry and dewberry plants can be readily recognized in summer by their copious black fruit; after leaf
fall, they can be identified by their spiny stems, which

tend to be erect and angular in shape in the former and low-growing and rounded in the latter.

It is advisable to use gloves when gathering these berries. Use only the firm fruit because the overripe berries tend to be indigestible when eaten fresh. Wash berries and remove stems before using.

Blackberry Root Decoction
(an old field method of treating diarrhea)

1 oz blackberry root   1½ pt water

Boil down the root and water until you have 1 pint of fluid. The dose is 2 to 3 teaspoonfuls for a child per day and a wineglassful several times a day for an adult.

Blackberry Leaf Tea
(a delicious camp tea, for 2)

1 handful fresh blackberry   2¼ cups water
  leaves   honey (optional)

Add freshly picked leaves to boiling water, cover and remove from heat. Let steep for 10 minutes. Serve hot or cold. Wild raspberry or strawberry leaves can also be used in this manner.

Blackberry Ice
(a cooling summer treat)

1 cup blackberries   4 paper cups (4 oz)
1 cup water   shaved ice
1 cup raw sugar

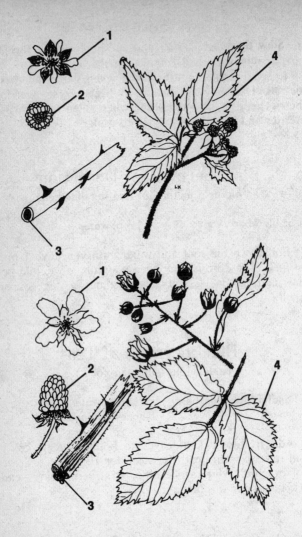

Red Raspberry (top) and **Blackberry** (bottom). 1, Flowers with five white petals. 2, Fruits have a wide variety of culinary uses raw, dried, or cooked. 3, Spiny or bristly stems, rounded in raspberry, angular in blackberry—raw vegetable (when newly emerged). 4, compound leaf—tea. Also, decoctions of root, leaves, or fruit of blackberry used as a remedy for diarrhea.

Stew the blackberries, water, and sugar together 15 to 20 minutes. Gently mash through a fine sieve. Set the syrup aside to cool. Save the pulp and serve as a dessert with cream.

Shave ice with an ice scraper or in a blender. Pack the paper cups with the shaved ice. Pour syrup over the ice. Serve with small spoons.

An interesting variety of ices can be made by using different berry syrups. Store extra syrup in sterilized, covered jars.

Blackberry Cordial
(an English recipe)

1 gal blackberries to each qt of water

2 lb raw sugar to each gal of juice

Pour boiling water into the crushed berries and stir. Let stand for 24 hours, stirring occasionally. Strain off the liquid into a cask and mix in the sugar. Cover tightly and let stand for 2 or 3 months in a cool room. Siphon the rich, ripe liquid into sterilized bottles, stopper, and store in a cool, dark room.

We usually serve this as an after dinner cordial.

Red and Black Raspberries

(*Rubus*—several species)

History
Raspberries are hardy fruits which are widely distributed throughout the north temperate zone and range

well into Alaska and Canada. These tender fruits were enjoyed by the ancient Greeks and Romans and were cultivated in Europe, perhaps as long as 2,000 years ago, and eaten fresh or prepared into a variety of tasty preserves, syrups, cordials, and wines. In addition to their use as a food, raspberry fruits were employed as a source of dye and the leaves were steeped in water to make a slightly astringent tea.

In the New World, raspberries were utilized by eastern and western tribes wherever the plants were available. The fruit was eaten fresh or dried or pressed into cakes, and dried. Some tribes ate the peeled fresh young shoots; others used the twigs and leaves for tea.

Today, most of the raspberries produced commercially in this country are either sold fresh or preserved by canning and freezing. The black raspberry of commerce is mainly derived from our native eastern wild black raspberry plant, *Rubus occidentalis,* while most of the commercial red raspberries come from a European plant, *R. idaesus.*

Habitat and Range

The habitat and range of the raspberries are about the same as those of the blackberries except that the range of the raspberries extends farther north.

Description

In general, the leaves, flowers, and stems of the raspberries resemble those of the blackberries (see p. 168). However, the raspberry stem tends to be rounded and often has a white "powder" on it; blackberry stems tend to be angular and lack the white substance. The fruits of both are similar in that each "berry" actually consists of several fruits aggregated together. These fruits can be readily distinguished from one another in that the ripened raspberry separates from its supporting central stalk, thus producing a hollow, bowl-shaped aggregate, but the ripened blackberries remain attached to their stalk and form a more solid aggregate.

Preparation

Fresh Raspberry Shoots
(from the Onondaga Indians)

Gather the fresh shoots, wash, peel and eat raw. Salt can be added if desired. Blackberry shoots can be used in the same way.

Raspberry Tea
(from the Seneca Indians)

1 handful of young raspberry twigs	2 cups boiling water maple syrup to taste

Pour the boiling water over the twigs, cover, and steep for 15 minutes. Sweeten with maple syrup and serve.

Steamed Berry Pudding
(for 8)

Steamed puddings are one of the oldest and most delicious of desserts. The pudding is cooked in a well-greased mold, such as a coffee can that is covered with waxed paper and secured with twine. The mold is placed on a rack in a large kettle. Boiling water is poured into the kettle until it reaches halfway up the sides of the mold. The kettle is then covered and boiling is continued over moderate heat for the appropriate length of time.

The steamed berry pudding recipe given here was kindly offered to us by Mrs. Josephine Petelle of Derby Line, Vermont. She and her husband raised eight children on their farm in northeastern Vermont. Wild berries were an important item in the diet of their sturdy family, whose members gathered hundreds of quarts each summer.

Berries

1 qt fresh wild raspberries
or blueberries (stewed
berries can be used)

raw sugar to taste

Wash berries and combine with sugar. Set aside.

Batter

1 cup raw sugar
1 egg
1 cup milk
2 cups unbleached white
flour

2 tsp baking powder
¼ tsp salt

Make a batter of the above ingredients, then put a thin layer in a well-greased 2-pound coffee tin or other suitable mold. Add a generous layer of berries. Continue layering and cover the top with batter. Do not fill any more than two-thirds full because the pudding expands. Cover with waxed paper and secure. Place in the steam kettle and steam as described above for 3 hours. Serve with cream.

Raspberry Relish
(for 4)

1 cup raspberries
1 pt sour cream

grated rind from ½ an
orange

Blend together all ingredients. Use as a topping for sliced cucumbers or fruit salads.

Raspberry Ice Cream
(for 5)

1 cup fresh raspberries
1 tsp lime juice
⅓ cup water
½ cup raw sugar

2 egg whites (whipped)
⅔ cup heavy cream
(whipped)

Crush raspberries, add lime juice, and set aside. Bring the water and sugar to a boil and cook until a thread is formed when the mixture is dropped from a spoon. Add the sugar mixture to the egg whites, beat together until thoroughly mixed, and chill in the refrigerator. Fold the raspberry and egg-white mixtures into the whipped cream. Pour into a chilled, freezing tray, and freeze 2 to 4 hours.

Strawberries, mulberries, blueberries, and blackberries can be substituted for raspberries in this recipe. For a smoother ice cream mash the crushed berries through a sieve before using.

Elderberries

The Common Elder (*Sambucus canadensis*)

History

The European black elder (*Sambucus nigra*) has a colorful history of use as a medicinal and food plant from the days of Hippocrates right up until modern times. It has been called "the medicine chest of the country people" and all parts of the plant can be utilized for one purpose or another, some of which follow. The inner bark can be used to produce a strongly purgative drink, and a black dye can be extracted from the bark of the older branches and roots. Elder flowers can be prepared into a delicate skin wash or gentle lotion, the fresh flowers can be cooked as fritters or added to pancake batter to produce aromatic pancakes; the dried flowers can be used as a tea. The fruit makes a powerful purgative drink. It can be used for wine and a variety of preserves and can be mixed with alum to produce a blue dye. The leaves can be prepared into an ointment for wounds; they can be used to produce a tea with strongly diuretic properties. When mixed with alum the leaves yield a green dye. When the leaves are rubbed on the body or crushed and worn in the hat, they act as an insect repellent, particularly for flies and midges.

When the settlers came to the New World, they found the common elder. *S. canadensis,* growing in damp soils throughout the east and utilized it in many of the same ways they had used its European cousin, the black elder. In the colonies, elderberry wine was a favorite medicinal drink, but perhaps the most exciting use of our native elder was as a natural insect repellent. Boiling water was poured over the leaves, flowers, or berries to make a wash for wounds which was noxious to flies. Elderberry ointment was used for the same purpose and was prepared by boiling lard and elderberry juice together and straining the product through a coarse sieve.

Habitat and Range

Sambucus is represented by about 40 species in the temperate zones and mountainous regions of the tropics. The common elder, (*S. canadensis*) is found in the east from Nova Scotia to Manitoba, south to Texas and Florida; it is also in the West Indies and Mexico. It prefers damp or rich soils and is found in moist fields, woods, and around marshes.

Description

The common elder is a tall shrub that grows to a height of 10 feet or more. The younger stems are slightly woody and have a large white pith. Elder leaves are opposite and compound with 5 to 11 (usually 7) toothed, egg-shaped or lance-shaped leaflets. The white flowers are tiny and are grouped in flattened clusters. Usually the fruits (elderberries) are purple-black in color, but there are varieties with red, green, or yellow fruit. The blossoms appear in late spring and the fruits are ripe some time after midsummer.

Note. Unfortunately, elder has some poisonous look-alikes that share its predilection for moist habitats. One is the poison sumac, or poison elder, *Rhus vernix,* which can cause a painful dermatitis if the foliage, flowers or fruits are touched. The other is the water hemlock, *Cicuta maculata,* whose tuberous bundle of roots has a sweet parsnip-like odor but is deadly poisonous if eaten.

If you think you have an elder, check again to ensure that the plant has opposite, toothed leaves. Both the poison sumac and water hemlock have alternate leaves and in addition, the sumac leaves are entire, not toothed.

Collection and Preparation

Both the young flowers and flower buds can be used for food (see page 101) while the mature fruits are usually converted into jelly or wine. Wash the elderberries thoroughly before using. If they are to be stewed or added to pastries, the dried fruits are preferred over the fresh ones.

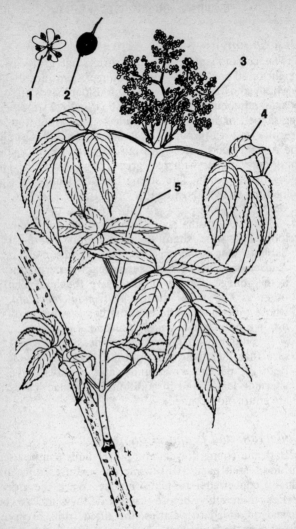

Elder. 1, Close-up of a tiny white flower—fritter, flour substitute. 2, Fruit (usually purple-black)—baking, jelly, wine, syrup. 3, Clusters of flower buds—flour substitute. 4, *Opposite,* toothed, compound leaves. 5, Warty bark. Also, decoctions of elder plant used as a purgative, insecticide, or skin lotion.

Elder and Apple Jelly
(about 12 medium glasses)

2 qt elderberries
2 qt apples (sliced)

raw sugar
1 large lemon

Place the freshly picked fruit in a saucepan and heat slowly. Crush, then add the apples and simmer for 10 minutes or until the fruit is soft. Mash fruit and then strain the juice through a jelly bag. Use 1 to 1½ cups of sugar per cup of juice. Return to heat, add lemon rind and juice. Cook until the mixture sheets when dropped from a spoon. Pour into sterilized jelly glasses and seal with a thin layer of parafin.

Elder Rob
(for colds)

1 qt elderberries
¼ cup water

raw sugar

Place the elderberries and water in a saucepan and bring to a boil. Lower heat and simmer slowly. Crush berries and strain juice through a sieve. Take equal amounts of juice and sugar, mix together, and gently boil for about 20 minutes. Cool then store in sterilized jars.

This decoction has laxative properties and should also bring on perspiration and act as a demulcent. Place a tablespoonful of elder rob in a cup of boiling water and serve hot in the evening.

SEASHORES, SALT MARSHES, INLETS, AND ESTUARIES

Introduction

Whether on the rocky coast of New England or on the sandy southern beaches, the sea and shore are replete with interesting and sometimes exotic-tasting animals and plants. To aid the reader in locating these organisms, we have divided this section into three subsections: shore plants, algae, and shellfish and fish. Where possible, we present the organisms within each of these subsections in the order they can be expected to occur in reference to their location from shore to water. For example, the algae are listed in the following order: sea lettuce, Irish moss, dulse, and *Laminaria* (expect sea lettuce to occur closest to shore and *Laminaria* in deeper water with the other algae somewhere between). The shore plants are a bit more difficult to separate in relation to land and water because many times they can be found rather clustered together. But in general the first named are found closest to shore and the upper levels of the beach; the last named, the glasswort, are common in salt marshes, where they grow in and around the area reached by high tide. The animals discussed can be found in the intertidal zone or adjacent subtidal, with several also located in shallow brackish water.

We have chosen the species included here on the basis of their availability in summer and also because of personal biases. For example, we have not included scallops and oysters because they cannot be taken in many areas during the summer; but for those interested in gathering these succulent mollusks, we advise you to check local laws concerning when and where they can be gathered. *Bon appétit!*

Shore Plants

Beach Pea

(*Lathyrus maritimus*)

History

The beach pea is another of our wild plants that is fairly common but little used here. However for centuries, ripe beach peas have served as a famine food in various northern regions throughout the world. They were never very popular in fatter times, presumably due to their small size. The boiled shoots are reported to have been used in Labrador for salads, and the Iroquois Indians ate the sprouts and leaf tips, fresh or boiled. We recommend the young sprouts and pods because the tiny peas are tedious to shuck.

Habitat and Range

The beach pea is a plant of sea beaches and lake shores in the cooler regions of Eurasia and North America. In the northeast, it ranges on the Atlantic coast from New Jersey north, and is found on the shores of the Great Lakes, Lake Oneida, and Lake Champlain.

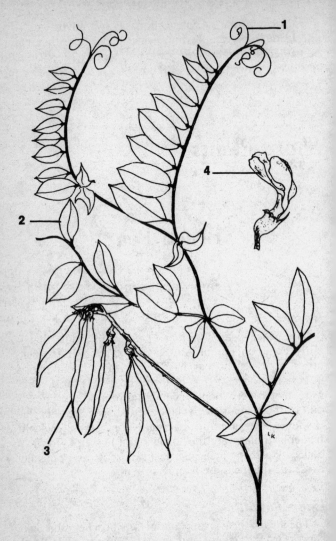

Beach Pea. 1, Tendril. 2, Compound leaf with 4 pairs of leaflets: young stem and leaf shoots—cooked vegetable. 3, Pod with enclosed seeds—young seeds, raw or cooked vegetable; young pods, cooked vegetable. 4, Flower.

Description

This perennial has stout prostrate to erect stems that grow up to 3 or so feet in length; its leaves are compound with 3 to 6 pairs of egg-shaped, untoothed leaflets that grow to 1 to 2 inches in length; each leaf terminates in a tendril. The flowers resemble those of the sweet pea and vary in color from almost white to a deep purple; the seeds are similar to the garden pea and are borne in a pod.

Note. The herbage of several species of *Lathyrus* is poisonous, so be careful in identifying these plants.

Collection and Preparation

At the shore, search for the beach pea on the upper beach, facing the water. It is easy to recognize by its resemblance to domesticated pea plants and is available from late spring until early autumn. From the time the plant first sprouts until frost, both the tender new stem and leaf shoots can be picked and eaten; in early summer a large crop of pods are produced, while in late summer and early autumn a smaller crop can be harvested. We prefer to cook the young pods oriental style, but sometimes we take an hour and shuck enough peas to serve as a cooked vegetable or add a few raw peas to salad.

Sautéed Beach Pea Sprouts
(a tasty appetizer for 2)

1 pt stem or leaf sprouts   salt to taste
2 tbsp butter

Sauté the sprouts in butter for 3 minutes and serve hot with salt.

Beach Pea Pods and Rice

young pods
butter
brown rice (cooked)

soy sauce
salt and pepper to taste

Sauté the pea pods in butter until tender, then stir in with the hot, cooked rice. Serve immediately with the soy sauce and condiments.

Orache

Seabeach-orache (*Atriplex arenaria*)
Spearscale, Orache (*Atriplex patula*)

History

Atriplex is a nearly cosmopolitan genus represented

TABLE 5

**Habitat, Range, and Description of
the Most-common East-coast Oraches**

Characteristics	Seabeach-orache (*Atriplex arenaria*)
Habitat	Sandy seashores and borders of salt marshes
Range	Southern New Hampshire to Florida
Stem	Erect or prostrate. Up to about 1½′ in length. Green to purple in color
Leaves	Alternate, oblong to oval, gray-green, scurfy, short to much attenuated leaf stem, blade up to 1½″ in length
Flowers	Tiny, green. Borne in clusters at stem tips
Fruiting structure	Wedge-shaped to round. Up to about ⅕″ in width. 4–7 teeth along the top

in the United States by several species, some of which are important forage crops in our western states and some which have been used as vegetable plants by Indian tribes of the southwest. In addition, one introduced species of *Atriplex,* the garden orache (*A. hortensis*), has been cultivated in this country for its succulent leaves which are cooked like spinach. The wild oraches of our northeastern states have not had such extensive use as their western cousins, but the two most common species along our coast, *A. arenaria* and *A. patula,* annually produce abundant greens which could be utilized as a foodstuff.

Collection and Preparation

The oraches resemble their close relative the pigweed (*C. album*) in appearance and in taste, but there is no problem because both can be used in the same ways. Gather orache leaves and plant tops from late spring through early autumn. Chop them into salads or cook them in the ways described for pigweed on pages 105–106.

Orache, spearscale (*A. patula*)

Saline and alkaline soils, waste places
Throughout the United States and parts of Eurasia
Erect or prostrate. Up to about 3½′ in length. Same as *A. arenaria*
Alternate, opposite or both, lance shaped to triangular shaped, green, mealy—especially young leaves, long leaf stem, blade up to 3″ in length.
Tiny, green. Borne in clusters at stem tips
Triangular to diamond shape. Up to about ⅟₁₆″ in width. Entire or toothed

---

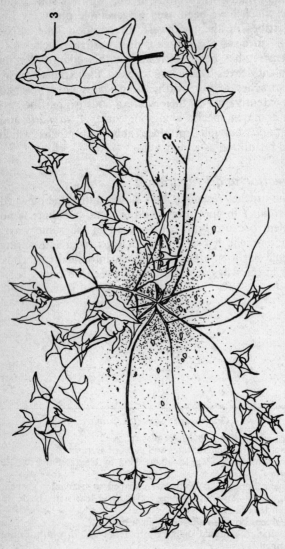

Orache. 1, Erect stem. 2, Elongate prostrate stem. 3, Triangular leaf—raw or cooked vegetable.

Sea Rocket

(*Cakile edentula*)

History

Sea rocket is a member of the mustard family (Cruciferae) and has as its relatives such food crop plants as cabbage, cauliflower, broccoli, rutabaga, kohlrabi, turnips, brussel sprouts, radishes, watercress, mustard, and horseradish. Sea rocket is reportedly used as a cooked green in parts of southern Labrador.

Habitat and Distribution

Cakile edentula is found on sandy and gravelly beaches as well as on inlets and bays from southern Labrador to South Carolina. It is even found around the Great Lakes. It flowers from June through September.

Recently while living on St. Croix, I* found a tropical form of sea rocket growing profusely on a number of beaches. It is also edible.

Description

This is a very easy plant to identify. It can grow up to 2 feet in height and can be distinguished by its leaves, which are large (around 2 inches long), fleshy, dark green, and shaped much like a skin-divers fin. As the summer progresses, the new leaves are more slender and elongate than the earlier leaves. If you think you have a sea rocket plant, pluck a leaf and take a nibble

_____

* A.M.S.

of it. The sharp horseradish taste will convince you that you are correct.

The tiny purple flowers are borne at the tip of the plant. The flowers are about ¼ inch across and the four petals of the flowers are arranged in the shape of a cross. All members of the mustard family have flowers shaped like a cross, hence the family name, the Cruciferae.

The fruit is a rather large two-jointed structure. The basal joint is an elongated, rather wide, cylinder; the upper joint is oval with a beak-like tip. As the summer progresses, the fruits become more numerous and at the end of summer the sea rocket plant consists almost entirely of fruit and is bare of leaves.

Collecting Sea Rocket

On Cape Cod, sea rocket begins to sprout in May and provides large leaves from about the end of June until mid-August. However, if you are fortunate enough to live by the sea for several months, you can extend the sea rocket season until October. I* learned to my delight that sea rocket will continue to produce new leaves after the old ones have been picked. In addition, unpicked sea rocket plants will go to seed much sooner than those which have had their leaves and apical stems plucked by the forager. Once you have found a plot of sea rocket plants, plan to stagger your picking. In other words, pick from one group of plants one day and another group the next day. You will find that it takes about seven days for the plants to regenerate their leaves. In this way you will have a continuous source of sea rocket leaves all summer and early fall. You should allow some plants to seed so that you can ensure a new crop of sea rocket year after year.

* A.M.S.

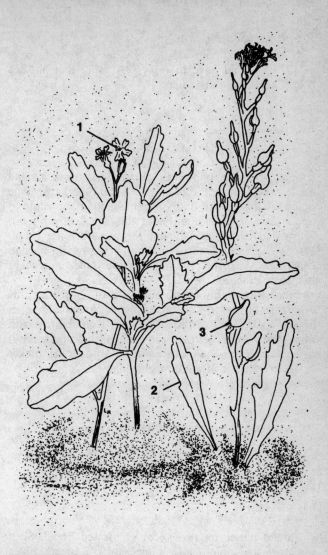

Sea Rocket. 1, Tiny flower with 4 purple petals. 2, Fleshy, dark green leaf—raw vegetable. 3, Fruit—raw vegetable.

Preparing Sea Rocket

If anybody should ask me, "What is your favorite salad?" I would have to reply, "A salad that has sea rocket as its main ingredient."

Sea Rocket Salad

Sea rocket fans who are "purists" will want a salad made solely of sea rocket greens and perhaps some onion. A dash of oil and vinegar is added according to one's taste. I must admit that this salad is a bit too sharp and eye-wateringly hot for most people. I suggest to these less hardy souls that they prepare a salad using half sea rocket and half a milder green as iceberg lettuce or orache.

In addition to the memorable taste of sea rocket, this vegetable has good keeping qualities. A day-old salad of sea rocket still tastes and looks fresh. I often add new greens to my leftover sea rocket salad and serve it again to my family. Another use for leftover sea rocket salad is to use it in a club sandwich.

Sea Rocket Club Sandwich
(for 2)

4 slices toast
2 tbsp butter
leftover meat

leftover sea rocket salad
onion and bacon

Spread butter on two slices of toasted bread. Slice tomatoes and onion onto a piece of the bread. Place leftover meat on the vegetables (steak, ham, bacon, or poultry are all suitable). Top the meat with a generous amount of sea rocket that has marinated in oil and vinegar for a day or two (we use leftover sea rocket salad).

A cup of hot tea made with the leaves of the sweet goldenrod beautifully complements this club sandwich.

Note. I would not recommend sea rocket from the temperate zone as a cooked vegetable—it is extremely bitter. However, the tropical form is delicious.

Sea Blite and Hairy Bassia

Sea Blite (*Suaeda*—several species)
Hairy Bassia (*Bassia hirsuta*)

History

Several species of this nearly cosmopolitan genus (*Suaeda*) were employed as a foodstuff by Indians of California, Arizona, Utah, and Nevada who used the ground seeds for mush and biscuits or boiled the leaves as greens. Although five species are found in the northeast, we found no evidence they were used as a foodstuff by the natives or the colonists.

Habitat and Range

Suaeda is represented by about 50 species which are found in both hemispheres. Of the five species in the northeastern United States, four grow in salt marshes and sometimes in sea strands, and a fifth grows in saline soil and ranges from western Minnesota and Manitoba to California and Texas.

Description

The various species of *Suaeda* range from forms with prostrate stems to those that grow erect, sometimes reaching a height of 2 feet or more. However, they all are characterized by their numerous, slender, fleshy, linear leaves that are arranged alternately on the stems. In the upper part of the stems, the leaves are reduced to bracts and in late summer, the tiny greenish flowers are borne singly, or often in triplets, in the axils of these bracts.

> *Note.* Saltwort (*Salsola kali*) resembles sea blite but it is inedible due to its leaves, which have prickly points. It is a common plant of sandy seashores in the northeast and has also spread to cultivated fields, waste places, and roadsides.

Hairy bassia (*Bassia hirsuta*) is another look-alike of sea blite but it is an edible plant. Although it is not a native species, it has become a common inhabitant of salt marshes and seashores from Massachusetts to New Jersey. It is a densely branched, low-growing plant usually less than one foot in height and bears numerous short, succulent, linear-shaped leaves that are covered with a fine white down. Its flavor is similar to that of sea blite and it can be cooked in the same ways.

Collection and Preparation

Sea blite can be located growing along the shores of inlets and salt marshes from late spring until early autumn, but is at its best from early summer to midsummer. Often it will be found growing in the company of three other edibles: orache, sea rocket, and hairy bassia. Early in the summer, the emerging stems and leaves can be plucked and cooked, but as the season advances, only the stem tips are tender enough to eat. By late summer, only the fleshy leaves can be used.

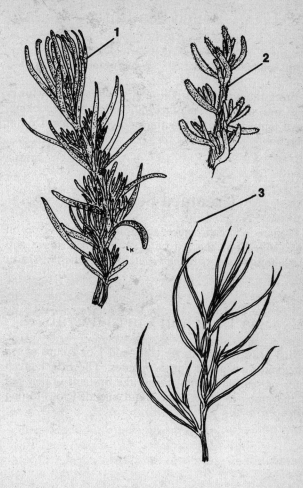

Sea Blite (1). Characteristic numerous, fleshy, linear leaves—cooked vegetable. **Hairy Bassia** (2), with the downy, succulent leaves—cooked vegetable. **Saltwort** (3), with spiny-tipped leaves—not edible due to the spines.

Because sea blite is a succulent plant, pick it just prior to use.

Boiled Sea Blite
(for 2)

2 cups sea blite   ⅓ cup water

Bring the water to a boil, add sea blite, cover, lower heat and simmer 3 minutes. Stir once while cooking. Serve immediately with butter and condiments. Do not overcook!

Creamed Sea Blite

Prepare a cream sauce according to the recipe on page 169. Cook the sea blite as described above and just before serving stir the vegetable into the hot sauce.

Sea Blite and Curried Crab

Just prior to serving the crab, add 1 or 2 cups of sea blite and let simmer for 3 minutes. The bright green color of sea blite complements the brilliant orange-red of the crabs to effect a beautiful and delicious-tasting dish.

Glassworts

Glasswort or Samphire
(*Salicornia*—several species)

History

Colonial housewives pickled a number of foods that are seldom, if ever, eaten by modern Americans. Among the more popular were the glassworts (*Salicornia*), which the early settlers on the Atlantic coast mistakenly believed to be the "samphire" of Europe, a pickle plant long popular there. This error was rather fortuitous as the glassworts proved edible and made a fine pickle. Colonial households also had pickled elder buds, young black and white walnut fruits, barberries, radish pods and nasturtium buds. This year when you are making your pickles, why not emulate our forebears and put up a few jars of these lesser known food plants.

Habitat and Range

Three species of glasswort found in the northeast are inhabitants of salt marshes, while a fourth is found in saline soil from Minnesota west to Saskatchewan, Kansas, and Nevada.

Description

Glassworts are bright green, fleshy herbs that commonly reach a height of 6 inches to a foot. The stems are conspicuously jointed, usually branched and bear reduced, opposite, scale-like leaves with the uppermost scales forming a cylindrical terminal spike. The flowers are inconspicuous and are borne in groups of three on

Glasswort. 1, Region from which the tiny flowers will emerge. 2, Jointed, succulent stem with opposite branches. Upper parts of plant used as a raw or cooked vegetable, pickle.

the upper joints of the stem. In late summer and early autumn, salt marshes are made brilliant with the pink to crimson colors of the fading glassworts.

Collection and Preparation

Glassworts first emerge in spring but are most abundant and conspicuous in summer and early fall. Take only the tender plant tips because the lower parts of the stem tend to be tough and rather bitter. Either fresh or boiled glasswort can be chopped into a salad, but we do not recommend salad consisting solely of this plant. For pickling, use the recipe on page 101 for pickled elder buds. Or cover freshly picked glasswort with boiling vinegar and let stand for 24 hours and serve. If pickles are not to your taste, try sautéed glasswort.

Sautéed Glasswort
(a crisp, salty appetizer)

glasswort	butter
unbleached white flour	salt and pepper

Roll the tender plant tips in flour and sauté in butter until brown and crisp. Serve hot with salt and pepper.

Sea Lettuce

(*Ulva*—several species)

Introduction

Sea lettuce, and the previously mentioned seaweed, *Enteromorpha,* are the most conspicuous and wide-

'spread of the marine green algae. Sea lettuce is found throughout the world in oceans and brackish waters.

Some Americans do utilize this alga as a food plant but its use is not nearly as widespread as that of the brown and red algae which are imported into this country and sold in health food stores. We have seen foot-long pieces of dried Japanese seaweed selling for a dollar or more in health food stores on Cape Cod while quantities of sea lettuce were being washed up on the Cape's shores and ignored. This is a rather absurd situation; sea lettuce is as common in our shallow marine waters as dandelions are on our lawns and fields. Chopped sea lettuce is a fine addition to vegetable soups, and the dried plant is a tasty condiment and can be converted into an extraordinarily delicious instant marine chowder.

Habitat and Range

Many species of this cosmopolitan genus grow along the Atlantic coast in the open ocean as well as in salt marshes and brackish water. They grow in shallow water attached to rocks, wood, shells, or other suitable substrate and are often ripped away and found floating in the water or washed onto shore.

Description

Ulva is the largest of the green algae. Its various species grow in bright green, membranous ribbons or sheets to lengths of 6 feet or more.

Collection and Preparation

Sea lettuce can be gathered from the shore or can be collected by snorkeling along a jetty and plucking it from the rocks where the plant grows in great abundance. Wash the plant thoroughly in fresh water before using it for consumption.

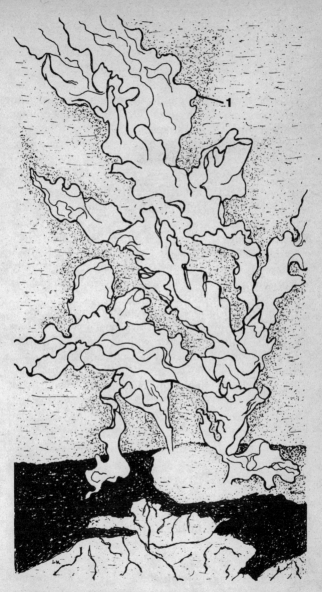

Sea Lettuce. 1, Green sheets of sea lettuce underwater
—condiment, chowder.

Sea Lettuce Condiment
(a mineral-rich seasoning)

Dry the plant according to the method suggested for *Enteromorpha* salt on page 79. Use as a condiment on fish, vegetables, and soups.

Sea Lettuce Chowder
(a dish rich in the flavor of the sea)

1 tbsp sea lettuce (dried and finely chopped)	1 tbsp butter or oleo
	1 small onion (chopped)
	2 cups milk
¾ cup water	salt and pepper, to taste

Place the sea lettuce, butter and onion in the water, cover the pan, and cook over low heat for 15 minutes. Stir in the milk and flavor with the salt and pepper. Heat the chowder until it is hot but not boiling. Serve with crackers.

We highly recommend this instant sea chowder.

Irish Moss

(*Chondrus crispus*)

History

Irish moss, along with dulse, has been a popular food alga in western Europe for centuries. It was primarily used for blancmange, which is a sweet jelly-like dessert made by cooking Irish moss with milk, sweetening it with sugar and adding fruit or vanilla for flavoring. It was also employed as a treatment for diarrhea, urinary disorders, and consumption, and was used to make soothing hand creams and medicinal salves. In Japan, it is even employed in making a gelatinous shampoo which reportedly leaves the hair with a fine sheen. The plant was brought to our East Coast by the early colonists, who imported it until it was discovered growing prolifically on our northeastern coast. This is one alga that is widely utilized today in this country. During the warmer months of the year, rich harvests of Irish moss are gathered commercially along the coast from New England to Nova Scotia. Carrageenan, which gives this plant its jellying qualities, is extracted and used as a food stabilizer for such products as ice cream, whipped cream, eggnog and sherbet; it is utilized to aid emulsification of puddings and frostings and is added instead of starch as a thickener for soups.

Habitat and Range

Irish moss is found from the coast of North Carolina to Newfoundland, but forms its richest stands from Cape Cod, north. It grows in the lower part of the intertidal zone and the adjacent subtidal, where it attaches to rocks, shells, and other suitable substrates, sometimes forming a dense moss-like turf.

Description

Irish moss is a low-growing plant with a short, disk-like holdfast, slender stalk (stipe), and tough, flattened blades that tend to branch dichotomously. It reaches a length of about 6 inches and is variable in branch shape, in width of the blades, and in color (ranging from cream-colored to green, red, purple, and jet black). The darker colored specimens are often strikingly iridescent and are among the most beautiful plants to be found in a tide pool.

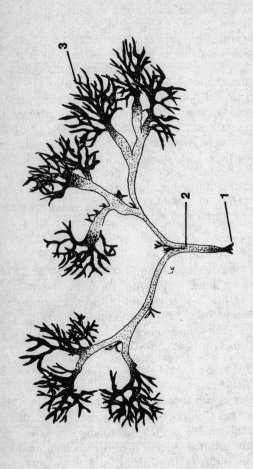

Irish Moss. 1, Holdfast. 2, Stalk. 3, Flattened blades—gelatinous carrageenan extracted from whole plant—pudding, soup, shampoo.

Collection and Preparation

Irish moss is washed onto the beach year-round, where it can be found bleached out and brittle; more pliable and colorful specimens can be plucked from the rocks at low tide. The fresh or dried plant can be used as long as it is washed in several changes of water (do not over-wash, because the gelatinizing properties will be reduced). For winter use, Irish moss can be sun-dried and stored in covered containers.

Jellied Irish Moss Soup
(for 4)

1½ cups Irish moss (packed)	1 medium onion (chopped)
2½ cups water	1 tbsp butter
3 vegetable bouillon cubes	salt and pepper to taste

Bring the water to a boil in a saucepan and add the Irish moss. Cover and cook over low heat for 15 minutes, stirring once or twice to prevent the plant from sticking. Meanwhile, sauté the onion in butter until tender, then set aside. Remove the cooked Irish moss from the heat, allow to cool for a few minutes, then place the plant in a sieve. Catch the gelatinous material in a bowl or pan. You will obtain about 1½ to 2 cupfuls of this rather unappetizing appearing substance (have patience, it makes a delicious soup). Add 2 to 3 cups of water to this as well as to the bouillon cubes and onions. Bring to a boil, stir to help dissolve the bouillon cubes, then simmer for about 5 minutes. Remove from heat, allow to cool, then refrigerate the soup in bowls. Serve chilled with salt and pepper to taste.

Note. Use the spent Irish moss as fertilizer for your garden. Leftover jelly can be stored in the refrigerator for several days.

Blancmange

¾ cup Irish moss
1 cup water
2 cups milk (scalded)
1½ tsp vanilla

2 tbsp sugar
1 cup cooked brown rice
(optional)

Cook the Irish moss and extract the gelatinous material as described in previous recipe. Take ½ cup of jelly per 2 cups of milk and stir together with the vanilla, sugar, and rice. Allow to cool, then refrigerate. It will set in about ½ hour.

Many recipes recommend adding berries as a flavoring for this dessert. We prefer vanilla alone or berries plus vanilla.

Irish Moss Demulcent
(an old New England treatment for coughs)

dried Irish moss
water

honey
lemon or orange juice

Place a small quantity of Irish moss in a saucepan, cover with the water, and heat gently until the liquid is syrupy. Strain off the juice and add to this a little honey and lemon juice. Take as needed to sooth the throat.

Algae

Dulse

Dulse, Dillisk, Sol, Sea Kale
(*Rhodymenia palmata*)

History

In general, algae have not been popular food plants in western countries as compared to their wide utilization in some eastern countries. But *Rhodymenia palmata* is an exception, for it has been used as a source of food for several centuries in Scotland, where it is commonly known as dulse; in Ireland, where it is called dillisk; and in Iceland, where it is known as sol. Some traditional ways of eating this alga is to use it fresh or dry as a salty chew, cook it with butter and fish or boil it in milk with a little rye flour as a thickener. During times of famine in Ireland, dulse and potatoes were a staple of people living along the coast. In Mediterranean countries today, dulse is added to ragouts for color and thickening.

Dulse, along with another edible seaweed, *Alaria esculenta,* has also been utilized as a forage crop. In Scandanavia, Iceland, the British Isles, and along the coast of France, goats, cows, and sheep are driven or wander out to the shore during low tide to graze upon the fronds of these algae. Also, in some sections of Ireland and Scotland cattle and sheep are fed almost exclusively on dulse. Some Americans have emulated this thrifty animal husbandry of the Europeans and now *Macrocystis,* a large and prolific alga of the Pacific coast, is harvested and processed for use as a mineral-rich food supplement that is fed to cattle, poultry, and sheep. However, dulse grows abundantly on our rocky northeastern coast but is generally unrecognized and unused here.

Habitat and Range

The genus *Rhodymenia* is represented by over four dozen species; they are found throughout the world growing in the intertidal and subtidal zones. In this country, dulse is common in the Puget Sound area of Washington; it also grows from North Carolina north, and is especially abundant in New England and around the Bay of Fundy.

Description

This red alga grows to about a foot in length and consists of a small disk-like holdfast, an inconspicuous stalk (stipe), and flat, veinless, broad blades which tend to branch dichotomously or palmately above. These forking branches can grow to about 6 inches in width but are more commonly half that size, and often near the base of the blades there are numerous, small outgrowths. The whole plant somewhat resembles a hand with the branches serving as the "fingers."

Collection and Preparation

Either gather dulse at low tide on a rocky shore or search for specimens that are washed onto the beach year-round. Wash the plants thoroughly and dry the fronds in the sun or in an attic room for several days. When dried, dulse will be rubbery, not brittle. Roll it and store in clean, covered containers.

Dried dulse is a fine source of salts and a wad of it is easily carried in a pocket for hiking and camping trips when it can serve as a salty chew.

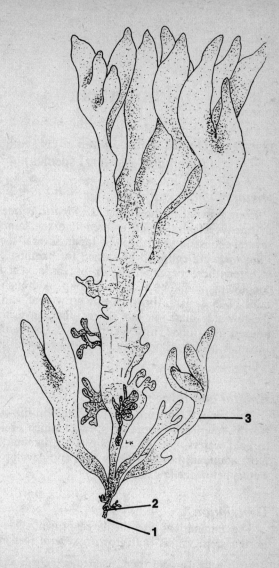

Dulse. 1, Tiny holdfast. 2, Inconspicuous stalk. 3, Dark-red flattened blades which resemble fingers—diced for chewing, cooked vegetable.

Laminaria

Oarweed, Devil's Apron, Sea Tangle, Kelp*
(*Laminaria*—several species)

History

Long popular in the Orient, *Laminaria* is one of the marine vegetables which entered into the human diet several thousand years ago. In Japan several species of *Laminaria* are collected and dried for "kombu", which is eaten there or exported for use as a vegetable, a condiment, and for sauces and soup. Although quantities of these large brown kelps grow near and below the low tide mark on our shores, they have not been utilized as a food. However, imported *Laminaria* from Japan is sold here in health food stores and gourmet shops.

Habitat and Range

The genus *Laminaria* is represented on the coasts of North America by about 20 species, which prefer cool to cold waters. On the Atlantic coast, laminarians are most abundant north of Cape Cod and develop best in waters below the low tide level.

Description

The laminarians are the large brown algae of our northeastern waters that grow to several feet in length

---

* Originally the word "kelp" referred to the soda and potash-rich ash derived from burning *Laminaria* and other brown algae, but today in America, the word is commonly employed as an appelation for any large brown seaweed.

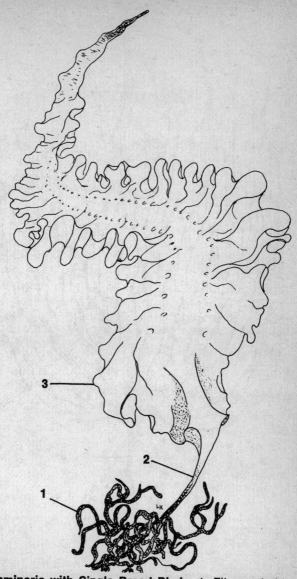

Laminaria with Single Broad Blade. 1, Fibrous hold-fast. 2, Stalk. 3, Large, brown, ribbonlike blade—condiment, chowder, sauces.

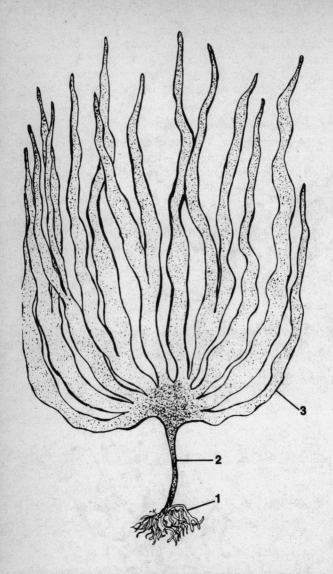

Laminaria with Blade in Several Ribbons. 1, Fibrous holdfast. 2, Stalk. 3, Single brown blade divided into several ribbons—condiment, chowder, sauces.

and consist of a fibrous or disk-like holdfast, a slender, unbranched stalk (stipe), and a blade which is smooth and imperforate, without ribs. In some species the blade is a single elongate ribbon; in others it is broad and divided into several long ribbons.

Collection and Preparation

Most species of *Laminaria* are large, tough plants, which are washed ashore year-round relatively intact and can be gathered on the shore. They can also be obtained at low tide by snorkeling in the area where they grow and cutting them from the substrate. Chop the freshly gathered blades for soup using the recipe on page 28 or grate it into chowders for flavoring. We have dried *Laminaria* for soup but prefer sea lettuce.

Shellfish and Fish

Periwinkles and Rock Purple

Periwinkle and other species (*Littorina litorea*)
Rock Purple, Dog Whelk (*Thais lapillus*)

Introduction

The cosmopolitan genus, *Littorina,* is represented by numerous species that often are abundant on rocks and seaweed in the intertidal zone. The common or edible periwinkle (*L. litorea*) was introduced to our Atlantic coast in the nineteenth century from Europe via Iceland, Greenland, and Labrador. It is now perhaps the best known snail on our northeastern coast; it is found as far south as Delaware Bay and often accumulates in areas that are only briefly submerged at high tide. Scores of these small snails can be observed at low tide as they move about the intertidal area grazing on minute plant material they scrape from the substrate with their rasping organ, the radula.

In Europe, *L. litorea* is roasted and sold on city streets from pushcarts, being especially popular in England. They are the tastiest of the numerous marine snails we have eaten from cold northen waters to the tropics.

Habitat and Range

This European species is found along our Atlantic coast from Delaware Bay north, being particularly abundant on our rocky northeastern coast, where it accumulates in the intertidal zone.

Description

The common periwinkle has a rather thick, squat, conical shell that varies from brownish olive to black or yellowish in color and is often banded with brown or dark red. The interior of the shell is brown or whitish with a dark blue outer rim. The species can grow to an inch in length and about half that size in width and height. On exposed shores it grows larger and has a thicker shell than in more protected regions.

Note. The common periwinkle is frequently found with a few other edible periwinkles: The rough periwinkle (*L. saxatilis*), which often lives high on the rocks in regions only periodically splashed by the highest tides and can be distinguished by its smaller size, rough shell, and drab color; the small, colorful and shiny smooth peri-

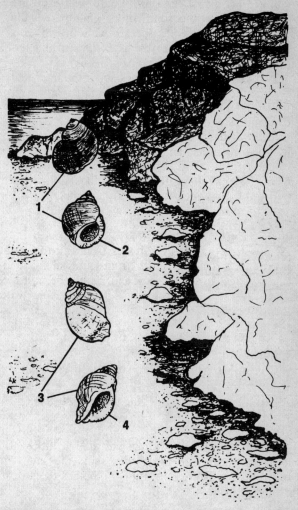

Common Periwinkle (1), with squat, conical, dark-colored shell; interior of shell is whitish or brown with 2, a dark-blue rim. **Rock Purple** (3), with a more elongate, white to yellow, orange, or purple shell. 4, Large aperture. These snails are served as an appetizer.

winkle (*L. obtusata*), which remains in the wet seaweed because it can survive only brief exposure to the air; and the southern or Gulf periwinkle (*L. irrorata*), a white species with brown dots that is about the same size as *L. litorea* and has extended its range north to Massachusetts.

A common snail that moves about the intertidal zone is the predatory dog whelk (*Thais lapillus*), which is highly carnivorous, feeding on barnacles, mussels, oysters, clams, and sometimes periwinkles. It has a thick shell with a large aperture; it grows to about an inch in height, and ranges in color from white to yellow, orange, or purplebrown. It can be gathered and cooked like the periwinkle, although it is not as flavorful.

Collection and Preparation

At low tide, gather periwinkles from the rocks and seaweeds of a rocky beach or from jetties along sandy beaches. They are a delicacy and should be collected on the day they are to be eaten. Rinse in cold water and cook briefly.

Sauteed Periwinkles

periwinkles
butter

garlic salt or dried leek
leaves

Melt the butter in a frying pan, add a little garlic salt or leek leaves to taste, then sauté the snails for 3 to 5 minutes. Serve hot, using toothpicks to extricate the animals from their shell.

Periwinkles in Tomato Sauce

Take your favorite tomato sauce and add 1 cup of periwinkles per 2 cups of sauce: Simmer together over low heat in a saucepan for 30 minutes. Serve with bread, a soup spoon, and toothpicks.

Mussels

The Blue Mussel (*Mytilus edulis*)

History

Mytilus edulis is a very tasty food and a good source of protein, but it has never become very popular in the United States. Perhaps this is due to the abundance of larger bivalves here, such as the oyster. It could also be due to the fact that Pacific coast mussels can be safely eaten only in the winter. Whatever the case may be, the blue mussel from the Atlantic coast is a safe and delicious food all year round.*

In France and in other parts of Europe, the blue mussel has been widely used as a food for years. Over there, it is cultivated in shallow coastal water "farms", much as we grow oysters in this country. Tree branches or other substances are driven into the sand. These materials provide a surface on which the mussels can attach themselves and feed. Cultivated mussels usually grow larger than wild mussels, and shells two inches or over are considered marketable.

Mytilus is a sessile organism that attaches itself to the substrate by several strong secreted threads called

---

* Provided there is no outbreak of Red Tide or other such pollutant.

byssal threads. Like its relatives the clams and oysters, the blue mussel is a filter feeder. It has incurrent and excurrent siphons through which sea water enters and leaves its body. The incurrent siphon brings in oxygen and microscopic planktonic food and the excurrent flow removes carbon dioxide and solid waste material.

Habitat and Range

The blue mussel is found along the eastern seaboard from North Carolina to the Artic, but is most abundant in the colder waters. It also is found all along the European shore.

During low tide, acres of blue mussels are sometimes exposed where they are attached to stones and pebbles or other stationary or floating objects. They also hang in masses from wharf timbers and are abundant on jetties and rocky shores.

Description

Mytilus edulis can grow up to 3 inches in length and has a fairly smooth blue-violet to blue-black shell. The shape of the shell is roughly an elongated triangle. On the outer surface of the shell are many fine concentric lines. The interior of the shell is white with violet margins.

The beginner often confuses the blue mussel with another East Coast species, the ribbed mussel (*Modiclus demissus*). The ribbed mussel is not recommended for eating because it is very bland in taste and because of its ability to thrive in polluted waters.

To distinguish between these two mussels, look for the following:

1. Although both mussels are shaped like elongated triangles, the ribbed mussel is much more slender and elongate than the blue mussel.
2. The shell of the ribbed mussel has numerous radiating ribs, it is finely scalloped at the edges,

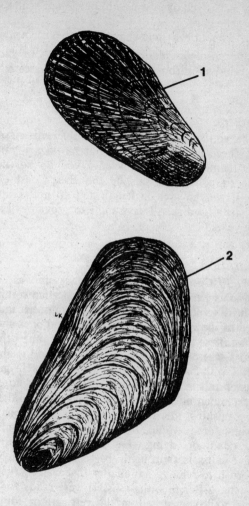

Ribbed Mussel (1), Elongate, with prominent radiating ribs—not recommended for eating. **Blue Mussel** (2), Less brittle, without ribs—main course or appetizer.

and is very brittle while that of the blue mussel is relatively smooth and is not scalloped at the edge.

3. The ribbed mussel prefers brackish water and tidal flats and is often embedded in the peat-like earth. The blue mussel prefers clear ocean water and is not usually embedded in the earth.

Collection

Once you have found a bed of blue mussels at the shore, there is nothing to do but to take a pail and gather them. (To our knowledge you do not need a license to collect mussels on the East Coast). Take mussels over an inch in length and do not scrape the area bare of mussels. Leave some to provide spawn for future years.

Preparation

*My first encounter with blue mussels was several years ago when I was working in an Italian restaurant. The boss took me to a sink full of mussels and proceeded to show me how to check for dead ones and how to clean those suitable for eating. At that time I thought the boss was crazy for the mussels looked inedible, all covered with barnacles, algae, and debris. He grasped a mussel and held it between his thumb and forefinger and explained how he was putting pressure on the mussel by pushing the shell in opposite directions. This shearing force would force open any mussels that were dead or dying. He then told me to wash the live mussels thoroughly by scrubbing them with a stiff brush to remove any matter that was encrusted on the shells. After this, the mussels were ready for cooking or could be stored in the refrigerator for a few days.

---

* L.K.

Steamed Mussels
(A simple way of preparing mussels, for 4)

2 qt mussels
1 qt water

½ lb butter
lemon wedges optional

Place mussels in a pot and add enough boiling water to cover ⅓ of them. Add a cover and steam until the mussels are fully opened. This should take about 10 minutes. Overcooking will make the mussels dry up and lose their flavor. Serve with drawn butter and eat as you would steamed clams.

Baked Mussels
(for 4)

4 doz mussels
1 pt mussel broth
1 cup seasoned bread
   crumbs

1 clove chopped garlic
¼ cup chopped parsley or
   sea lettuce
½ cup olive oil

You can use either fresh mussels or leftovers from the previous day. Take the steamed mussels on the half shell and put on a cooking sheet or flat pan. Pour broth on the mussels and then sprinkle them with the garlic and bread crumbs. Top them with the parsley or sea lettuce. Pour the olive oil over the preparation. Place in a broiler or a hot oven and brown.

Many Italian Americans still appreciate the gourmet possibilities of blue mussels. Here are two recipes gleaned from my* experience of working in Italian kitchens. These easy-to-prepare dishes should delight the most sophisticated gourmet.

Mussels in Red Sauce
(for 6)

6 cloves of garlic
1½ cups olive oil
5 to 6 doz mussels

1 #10 can of tomatoes
¼ cup fresh basil

Crush the garlic bulbs to release the cloves, peel and place in a large frying pan. Partially cover the garlic with olive oil and add the fresh basil leaves. Sauté until the cloves are golden brown. Drop this preparation into a large pot and add the mussels. Stir in the tomatoes and mix all ingredients thoroughly. Cover and steam over medium heat for 10 minutes.

Note. If you want a hot sauce, add some crushed pepper flakes before serving.

Keep the cloves of garlic whole so that the person who does not care for garlic can remove it from his plate.

If you do not have fresh basil, use dried basil, but stir it in at the end of the cooking or else the basil will impart a bitter taste to the food.

Mussels in Wine Sauce
(for 6)

1 large onion
6 cloves of garlic
5 to 6 doz mussels

½ bottle white wine
¼ cup fresh basil

This procedure is similar to the previous one, with a few exceptions.

Sauté the onion, the cloves of garlic, and the basil leaves. When the cloves are brown, add the preparation to a large pot. Place the mussels in the pot and pour the white wine over the whole mixture. Stir, cover, and steam over medium heat for 10 minutes.

Note. See note on garlic and basil leaves above.

Blue Crabs

Blue Crab, Edible Crab (*Callinectes sapidus*)

Introduction

Although there are several species of edible crab in the waters of our northeastern coast, the blue crab is the one most economically important as a source of food. It prefers brackish waters and is caught commercially by fishermen who use trawl lines and by sportsmen and amateurs who employ a variety of devices, such as traps, baited lines, and nets. While crabbing is a popular summer and early autumn activity all along our eastern coast, 75 percent of the annual catch is yielded by the waters of Chesapeake Bay and Louisiana.

Habitat and Range

Blue crabs range from Cape Cod to Louisiana, where they occur offshore and are common in the bottom of coves, bays, and in the shallow, brackish waters of estuaries; during winter they move into deeper water. They are strong swimmers and are often seen as they advance and retreat with the tides. The young, particularly, prefer to hide in the tangle of grass and seaweed near the shore line.

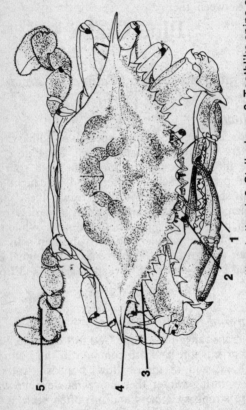

Blue Crab. 1, Large, pincerlike cheliped. 2, Stalked eye. 3, Toothlike spine of carapace. 4, Lateral spine of carapace. 5, Flattened legs used for swimming. Blue crab can be boiled or sautéed.

Description

The dorsal part of this crab is an olive green in color and the legs are suffused with blue. Its construction is unusual due to the shape of its carapace (the shell covering the dorsal part of the thorax), which is twice as long as it is wide and terminates on each side with a spine. Between these lateral spines and the eyes are eight strong "teeth". The first pair of thoracic legs (the chelipeds) are elongate, strong offensive and defensive weapons, while the last pair are specialized at the tips into flat oar-like appendages that facilitate swimming.

The soft-shelled crabs of the market are blue crabs that are moulting. These are delicious when sautéed.

Collection and Preparation

Before taking blue crabs, check local regulations; they are usually very lenient concerning this species. These crabs can be spotted from low bridges and by walking, snorkeling, or boating in the shallow water of inlets and estuaries. One can drop a line baited with old fish and then net the attached crab or just scoop them up with a net as they are located in the water. If you are walking along the water or snorkeling, you will need a container to hold your catch. We float a basket in the center of an old inner tube and tie a line from the tube to the body. Take only the number of crabs you will use within a few days because they must be alive when cooked. About 8 crabs measuring 5 to 6 inches across should make a sufficient meal for a family of four.

Boiled Crabs

Place live crabs in a pot of salted boiling water and cook over medium heat for 30 minutes. Serve hot with drawn butter. Leftover crabs should be shelled and used for salads or crabmeat cocktail.

Curried Crab
(for 2)

4 crabs	1 clove garlic
4 tbsp oil	1 vegetable bouillon cube
1 medium-size onion	1 tbsp curry powder
(coarsely chopped)	1 cup water

Heat oil in a deep saucepan, add the onion and garlic and sauté for 3 or 4 minutes. Quarter the live crabs and add to the mixture. Stir and cook over medium heat for 5 minutes. Add the remaining ingredients, cover, lower heat, and simmer for 10 minutes. Stir occasionally. If desired, add 1 or 2 cups of sea blite or hairy bassia to the pot during the last few minutes of cooking.

Clams

Quahog, Little Neck Clam, Hard-shelled Clam, Cherrystone, Round Clam
(*Mercenaria mercenaria*)
Long-necked Clam, Soft-shelled Clam, Steamer
(*Mya arenaria*)
Surf Clam, Hen Clam (*Spisula solidissima*)

Introduction

All of these clams as well as their close relatives, the mussels, oysters, and scallops are a fine source of nutriment, particularly proteins and minerals. Being filter feeders, they operate far down in the food chain and can produce more food in a shorter time than any other

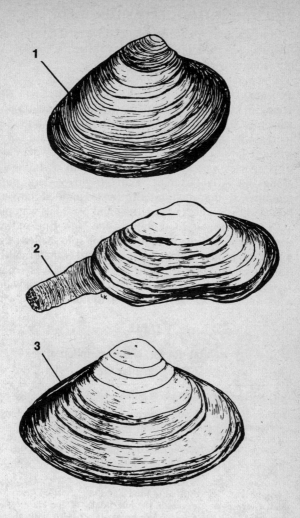

Clams. 1, Quahog with characteristic, rather oval, thick shell which has a gray-white exterior—raw (when young), steamed, baked, chowder. 2, Long-necked clam with a fairly oblong, thin shell that gapes at both ends—steamed, fried, chowder. 3, Surf clam with a thick, rather triangular shaped shell that is white with a yellow-brown covering—chowder, steamed, baked.

kind of animal. As fishing and culture methods improve, they will play a more important role in the diets of our burgeoning world population.

The quahog (*Mercenaria mercenaria*) is the highly esteemed commercial clam of the East Coast and when young is known as the little neck clam, or cherrystone, which is served raw on the half shell. As the clams increase in size, they are used for steaming and baking, with the largest specimens being popular chowder clams. This species was an oft used food clam of Indians all along the Atlantic coast, and the glossy dark purple sections of the shell interior were molded into tiny pierced beads which were strung and prized as wampum.

A very popular food clam of the New England area and elsewhere is the long-necked (or soft-shelled) clam (*Mya arenaria*), which grows wild and is under cultivation in many areas on both the East and West coasts. It is also often served as fried clams or in chowders. This species is a favorite food of the walrus, which

TABLE 6

Habitat, Range, and Description of Three Popular Clams

Species	Habitat	Range
Quahog (*Mercenaria mercenaria*)	Shallow ocean water and, particularly, tidal streams, inlets and estuaries. Common in mud to mud-and-sand bottoms	Gulf of St. Lawrence to Texas, particularly south of Cape Cod
Long-necked clam (*Mya arenaria*)	Buried in mud, sand or gravel in the intertidal area, and in brackish water	Arctic Ocean to Cape Hatteras. Also naturalized on the West coast
Surf clam (*Spisula solidissima*)	In the sand of rather shallow ocean water at and below the low-tide level	Labrador to Cape Hatteras

employs its long tusks as a clam rake to extricate these mollusks from the bottom.

The large and abundant surf clam (*Spisula solidissima*) is the biggest bivalve on the Atlantic shores. It is dredged in large quantities and used primarily for chowders; smaller specimens are utilized for steaming and baking. Hundreds of these clams are sometimes washed ashore after a storm.

Collection and Preparation

These three species of clam should be gathered at low tide; a rake or pitchfork can be helpful tools. Where to search for them is perhaps most easily determined by contacting the shellfish warden in the town you desire to collect. He will tell you where, when, and if you can gather in his area.

A sandy beach at the low tide level and beyond should yield some surf clams located just a few inches

---

Description

Shell length: to 5–6". Shell shape and texture: rather oval, thick, and heavy shell.
Color: gray-white exterior; white interior with violet stainings along the margins and about the muscle scars.

Shell length: to 6", usually smaller. Shape and texture: rather oblong, thin and brittle. Somewhat wrinkled by growth lines, and gapes at both ends.

Color: white to gray or blue-white exterior; whitish interior.
Shell length: to 7", but usually about 5". Shape and texture: rather triangular-shaped, thick shell.
Color: white with yellow-brown covering on exterior; dull-white interior.

below the surface. Tidal flats and brackish waters hold
stores of long-necked clams, which must be dug. Muddy
areas and brackish waters are the choice repository of
quahogs which, because they are so close to the surface,
can often be located by prying with your feet.

Refrigerate the clams and rinse in cold water before
using.

Steamed Clams

Add the clams to salted boiling water and cook over
medium heat 20 to 30 minutes. Serve with drawn
butter.

Baked Clams

clams   parsley (chopped)
seasoned breadcrumbs   olive oil

Clams on the half shell are placed onto a sheet pan
or pie pan. They are then sprinkled with the bread
crumbs, parsley, and olive oil. Bake in the oven 20 to
30 minutes or until brown. Serve as an appetizer.

Clam Chowder
(4 large bowls)

1 lg white onion (chopped)   2 cups clam broth
2 lg cloves garlic (crushed)   2 lg potatoes (diced)
¼ lb butter   ¼ lb salt pork (diced)
2 doz chowder clams   2 cups light cream or milk
   (steamed and diced)

In a pot, lightly sauté the onion and garlic in butter
for 10 minutes. Add the clams, clam broth, and diced

potatoes. Simmer slowly until the potatoes are tender. In the meantime, sauté the pork until it is crisp and golden brown. Drain on brown paper. When the potatoes are ready, stir in the cream and salt pork over low heat. Serve hot and if desired garnish with some dried sea lettuce (see page 200) or chopped chives.

Conch

Knobbed Pear Conch (*Busycon caricam*)
Channeled Pear Conch
(*Busycon canaliculatum*)

Introduction

Busycon caricum is the largest snail in the waters north of Cape Hatteras and is found in shallow bottoms where it and another species, *B. Canaliculatum,* wander about in search of their prey, clams and oysters. When they come upon a clam, they grasp it with their large muscular foot and crack it open by delivering a series of hard blows with their large shell. The conch, in turn, is preyed upon by the crushing claws of the stone crab, and by the sea gulls which grasp the exposed mollusk with their bills, carry it aloft and then drop it on a hard surface, such as a jetty or paved road. We use this bit of natural history to help us locate conch by observing where the gulls are hunting.

Habitat and Range

These two species of conch are shallow water animals found on sandy to stony ocean bottoms from Cape Cod to the Gulf of Mexico.

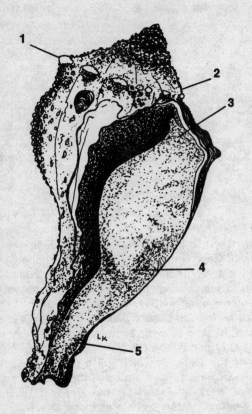

Knobbed Pear Conch. 1, Pear-shaped shell with prominent knobs on the shoulder. 2, Gray-white exterior. 3, Orange-red interior. 4, Aperture. 5, Canal. The muscular foot—appetizer and in salad.

Description

The shell of *Busycon caricam* is knobbed at the shoulder, pear-shaped and is from 4 to 9 inches in height and sometimes reaches a length of one foot. On the exterior it is grayish-white and the interior is a bright orange-red. It has an oval aperture and a long, narrow canal. The body is large and fleshy with a broad edible foot on which it crawls, supporting the shell with the canal projecting forward and upward.

B. canaliculatum is almost as large as *B. caricam* but can be distinguished from it by the heavy, gray, felt-like covering (periostracum) on the exterior of the shell, the lack of knobs and the yellow color of the shell interior.

Collection and Preparation

Search for conch at low tide along sandy and stony beaches. They can be spotted by wading or snorkeling in shallow water and they often are in and around where the gulls are hunting. Just pluck them from the bottom and place in a collecting bag.

To extricate the animal from its shell, place it in boiling water for 20 to 30 minutes, then pull it out and slice off the long muscular foot, which can be used immediately or refrigerated. The remainder of the body can be added to a compost heap or discarded. When ready for use, cut the foot crosswise into paper thin slices.

Conch in Tomato Sauce

Slice cooked conch into your favorite tomato sauce and simmer together over low heat for an hour or two.

Conch Salad
(for 4)

2 large conch feet (cooked and sliced)
1 stalk celery (diced)
1 lb mixed greens or your favorite lettuce
1 lg tomato (quartered)
1 clove garlic (chopped)
sprinkle of red pepper flakes
1 tsp capers
a pinch of oregano and basil
juice of 2 lemons
¾ cup olive oil
salt and pepper to taste

Combine all ingredients and mix well.

Seaside Conch Chef Salad

Same as above except add 4 cooked and peeled shrimp, ¼ cup of crab meat, ¼ cup poached scallops, and 4 slices of shredded Swiss cheese. Toss and serve.

Tautog

Tautog, Blackfish (*Tautoga onitis*)

Introduction

The tautog is common in waters of the north temperate zone and is a popular sport fish along the Atlantic coast, where it summers around jetties, piers, and bridges. This fish belongs to the wrasse family (Labridae), whose members are primarily found in tropical waters and are characterized by their small mouths and large teeth. Tautog feed on mussels and crustaceans which they crush with their teeth.

This large, common fish can be taken by spear fishing in many areas. For those of you who enjoy snorkeling or scuba diving and who like to hunt for their own fish dinners, the tautog can provide a fine meal. However, before doing any spear fishing, check into the laws dealing with this sport in the area you plan to fish.

Habitat and Range

Tautog are found along the Atlantic coast from New Brunswick to South Carolina. In winter they remain in deep waters; during the summer they congregate in rocky inshore areas.

Description

Tautog are husky, blunt-nosed fish that can grow to 3 feet in length and to 20 or more pounds in weight. The back and sides are black and blue-black while the ventral surface is gray. Like most wrasses, the mouth is diminutive but the teeth are large and powerful and the dorsal fin is contiguous with a long spinous portion.

Fishing for Tautog

Tautog are most abundant from Cape Cod to the Delaware Capes; in these areas most any jetty in summer will harbor an abundance of them. When the tide is high, snorkel off the end of a jetty and chances are you will encounter many tautog. They can be readily taken with a spear gun. Remember, only spear as many fish as you will use.

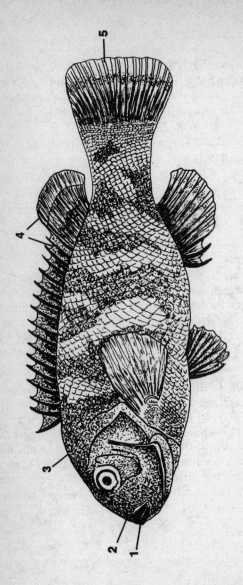

Tautog. 1, Small mouth. 2, Blunt nose. 3, Chunky blackish body. 4, Spinous and soft portion of dorsal fin contiguous. 5, Square to convex tail fin. A delicious fish, broiled or baked.

Broiled Tautog
(for 4)

1 tautog (2 to 3 lb)   ½ tsp paprika
2 lemons   salt and pepper to taste
½ lb butter

Scale, clean, decapitate, and wash fish. Cut into steaks by making crosscuts along the length of the body at 2 inch intervals.

Squeeze a lemon over steaks, brush on butter, add paprika, and salt and pepper. Place over glowing coals and cook approximately 4 minutes on each side or until the fish is golden brown.

Place steaks on platter and serve with lemon wedges and a little drawn butter.

Baked Stuffed Tautog
(for 4)

1 tautog (2 to 3 lb)   ¼ lb butter (melted)
unbleached white flour

Scale, clean, and wash fish. Place in a large baking pan and fill the cavity with stuffing. Dust the fish with flour and bake in a preheated oven at 400°F for approximately 45 minutes.

Before serving, pour melted butter over the fish.

Stuffing

4 slices bacon
1 medium-size onion
  (chopped)
2 tbsp butter
1 vegetable bouillon cube
1 cup water
16 slices whole wheat bread

1 egg
juice of 1 lemon
1 tbsp parsley (chopped)
1 tbsp oregano
1 tbsp thyme
½ tsp paprika

Fry the bacon until crisp and brown. In a separate skillet sauté the onion in butter until tender. Crumble the bacon into a large bowl and add the onions. Boil the bouillon cube in water and pour in with the bacon and onions. Add the remaining ingredients and mix well. Stuff the fish.

Autumn

NUTS

Introduction

The use of nuts as a foodstuff is very limited in the United States today. At best, they are sometimes employed as a garnish, a confection, or as a salted snack. There is a commonly accepted but erroneous belief that nuts are indigestible. It might surprise many Americans to discover that nuts are an important part of the diet in tropical countries where meat is in short supply and to know that nuts can supplement the daily need for proteins and provide an abundance of minerals and fat as well as carbohydrates. For example, our native wild beech nuts and black walnut are a particularly good source of proteins, and acorns contain a rich supply of carbohydrates.

Nuts were used extensively by many American Indian tribes who taught the early colonists how to gather and prepare them for flour, pastes, oil, butter, pottages, and dyes. Part of the Indians' annual cycle of activities included the autumn harvest of the abundant black walnuts, acorns, hickory nuts, and chestnuts. Nuts were an important item in the Indians' diet and as winter progressed and the food supply became low, they depended more and more upon them for nourishment. They deemed nuts so important that several tribes named their moons or times of the year after them. For example, the Natchez Indians called their twelfth moon (around the latter part of January) that of the Chestnut and the thirteenth moon (February) that of the Nuts.

Even today in America some country people are drawn out into the chill October weather to forage for our rich supply of wild nuts. Their path, generations old, tells a simple story. When the season of fall encroaches upon winter, they, like the chipmunks and squirrels, set out to find, nibble upon, and gather the wild nuts which will be a source of winter nourishment and pleasure. Cracking and eating nuts adds to the warm enjoyment of a long farm winter afternoon when men gather to talk, to plan the spring projects, and to sample last summer's homemade wines.

Unfortunately, this lovely fall tradition of collecting wild nuts has been superseded in our culture by such phenomena as the new fall television shows, the new

TABLE 7
Habitat and Range of
Common Nut-bearing Trees

Species	Habitat
Beech (American) (*Fagus grandifolia*)	Rich uplands
Filbert (American) (*Corylus americana*)	Thickets
Filbert (Beaked) (*C. cornuta*)	Rich thickets, clearings, and borders of woods
Hickory (Pignut) (*Carya glabra*)	Dry woods and slopes
Hickory (Shagbark) (*C. ovata*)	Rich woods, bottoms and slopes
Oak (Black) (*Quercus velutina*)	Dry soils
Oak (Red) (*Q. rubra*)	Dry or upland woods
Oak (White) (*Q. alba*)	Dry woods
Walnut (American Black) (*Juglans nigra*)	Rich woods
Walnut (White, Butternut) (*J. cinerea*)	Rich woods and river terraces

models of cars and, of course, football. Now each autumn as the crisp world becomes orange and crimson, an abundant harvest of nuts ripens and falls to the ground ignored and unseen by most of us.

Collecting, Drying, and Storing Nuts

It is difficult to compete with the squirrels and chipmunks for the filbert nuts. We give ourselves an edge in the race by collecting early and usually start picking filberts on Labor Day. We gather hickory nuts and

---

Range

New Brunswick west to Wisconsin, south to east Texas, and east to northern Florida

Central Maine to Saskatchewan, south to Oklahoma, and east to Georgia

Newfoundland to British Columbia, south to east Kansas and Colorado, and east to Georgia

Southern Maine, New Hampshire, Vermont, and New York, west to Michigan, and south to Missouri and Mississippi, east to northern South Carolina

Southern Maine west to southeastern Minnesota, south to east Texas, east to central Georgia

Southern Maine west to southeastern Minnesota, south to east Texas, and east to Georgia

New Brunswick west to Minnesota, south to Oklahoma, and east to Georgia. Not on South Atlantic or Gulf coastal plains

Maine to southern Minnesota, south to Texas, and east to northern Florida

Southern New Hampshire and Vermont west to Nebraska, south to Central Texas, east to western Georgia and South Carolina. Not on the southern coastal plain

New Brunswick west to Minnesota south to northern Arkansas east to western Georgia. Not on the south Atlantic and Gulf coastal plain

---

acorns when the leaves fall, which is around October in southern Vermont. Beech nuts and walnuts are gathered last. Wait until there is a hard frost due in October and then place old blankets or sheets under a beech tree laden with nuts and catch them as they fall. Black walnuts and butternuts are so large that many can be gathered as they lie on the ground.

Husk the freshly gathered nuts and store in a cool, dry place. High temperatures and dampness will only increase the chance of their becoming rancid. Put off husking the walnuts and butternuts because the thick, firm husks are very difficult to remove and will deeply stain your hands and clothes as you wrestle with them. Just pile them in a corner of your yard or outbuilding and let the husks ferment for a month or so until they are soft and can be more readily removed. Unshelled nuts keep better than shelled nuts, but if you want to remove the shells from a batch to put away for future use, store the meats in tightly closed containers in the refrigerator. They should keep for a few months.

We had trouble storing beechnuts and acorns, which tended to spoil after a few months, so we decided to dry them before storing. We had more success with these dried nuts and we suggest that you dry them if you are going to store them over winter. This can be accomplished by placing them in a slow oven (200°F) for two or three hours or, if you wish to emulate the Indians' technique of drying nuts, construct a hurdle of reeds, place the nuts upon it, and dry over a low fire for several hours.

We tried cooking the ten types of nuts (see accompanying table) in a variety of ways and have selected those we thought best suited for particular recipes. It should be pointed out that not all nuts are alike. Each type has its own unique flavor, consistency and nutritional value. Certain nuts are tastier than others when prepared a certain way. Most of the nuts could be used interchangeably in the recipes but in many cases the product will taste different with each kind of nut.

TABLE 8

Uses of the Nut

(* indicates particularly good)

Nut	Fresh	Dried	Butter	Flour	Oil	Salad garnish	Coffee	Pottage	Sautéed	Livestock feed
Beech	*	+	+	+	*		+			*
American Filbert	*	+	+	+	+	+	+	+		
Beaked Filbert	*	+	+	+	+	+		+		
Hickory (Pignut)	*	+	*	+	+	*		*		
Hickory (Shagbark)	*	+	*	+	+	*		*		
Black Oak		+	+	+	+	+		+		
Red Oak		+	+	+	+	+		+	*	*
White Oak	+	+	+	*	+	+	+	+	*	*
American Black Walnut	*	+	*	+	+	+		+	*	*
Butternut (White Walnut)	*	+	*	+	*	+		+		

TABLE 9

Miscellaneous Uses of the Nut-bearing Trees
(* indicates particularly good)

Tree	Leaves as vegetables	Young fruit for pickling	Sap for sugar and syrup	Husk of fruit dye	Bark for dye and tanning
Beech	+				
American Filbert					
Beaked Filbert					
Hickory (Pignut)					+
Hickory (Shagbark)			+		+
Black Oak					+
Red Oak					+
White Oak					+
American Black Walnut		*	+	+	
Butternut (White Walnut)		*	+	+	

The American Beech

(*Fagus grandifolia*)

Habitat and Range

There are ten species of beech all of which are found in the north temperate zone. *Fagus grandifolia* is the only species of beech native to North America. It is a common tree of the eastern hardwood forest and is planted as an ornamental in parks and in yards. The beech prefers rich well-drained soils and is seldom seen growing under swampy conditions.

Description

Beech trees average 80 feet in height and 4 feet in diameter and can be readily recognized by their smooth, clean, blue-gray bark. If grown in close proximity to other trees, the beech develops a straight trunk and a small crown, but if grown in the open, the trunk is squat and has a wide spreading crown. Once you can identify the beech trees, you will recognize the difference in the growth form of the slender forest-grown beech as contrasted with the stouter park-grown type.

The buds are rust-colored, slender, and elongate; the egg-shaped leaves are simple and toothed. The male flowers are drooping yellow-green structures; the female flowers are shorter spikes. Flowers appear when the leaves are about half grown (approximately 3 inches long). The fruit is a three-cornered shiny brown edible nut about ½ inch long and usually borne in twos or threes in a prickly brown husk. Heavy frosts cause the husks to open, thus releasing the beech nuts.

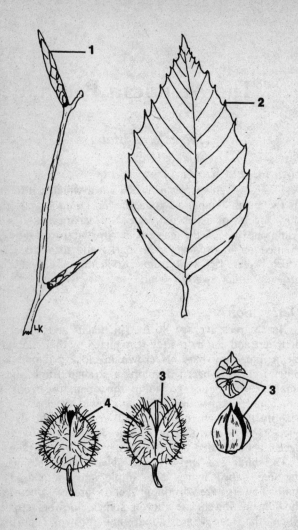

American Beech. 1, Elongate, rust-colored, scaled bud. 2, Egg-shaped, toothed leaf—appetizer (when newly emerged). 3, Brown nut—particularly good as garnish, butter, oil, and coffee substitute. 4, Brown, prickly husk.

Collection and Preparation

When beech trees are about 40 years old they begin to produce nuts. However, heavy crops are produced by an individual tree only every few years. The wise forager will locate several large beech trees to increase his chance of happening upon one that is having its bumper-crop year. As mentioned above, wait for a heavy frost to collect your beech nuts.

Beech nuts are sweet and delicious when eaten fresh, as attested to by their great popularity with wild birds, mammals, and domesticated livestock. They are rich in proteins, carbohydrates and fat and could provide a nutritious supplement to the diet. Their main drawback is their small size. The European beech, *F. sylvatica*, produces a slightly larger nut that is eaten fresh, used for oil, and added to chestnuts and acorns to form a food called "mast", which is a feed for hogs.

Creamed Beech Nut Sauce
(for 2)

4 tbsp butter
4 tbsp unbleached white
   flour
2 cups milk

2 vegetable bouillon cubes
½ cup chopped beech nuts
salt and pepper to taste

Melt butter and blend in flour until smooth. Gradually stir in milk, bouillon cubes, and salt and pepper. Simmer, stirring until mixture thickens. Add nuts and simmer for 2 minutes. Pour over fowl, fish, or vegetables. Serve and enjoy.

Beech Nut Coffee

To Prepare the Nuts: Take the husked and dried beech nuts and place in a moderate oven (300°F) 15 to 30 minutes to crack the shell. Shell the nuts and then dry them in a moderate oven until they are brittle. Grind them fine with a rolling pin and place the "coffee" in clean, covered, screw-capped jars.

To prepare the Coffee: Ground beech nuts can be used alone by allowing a teaspoonful of the nuts per cup of coffee and steeping in boiling water for 15 minutes, or mix 1 part beech nut "coffee" with 2 parts instant coffee, steep for 15 minutes, and serve.

Beech Nut Oil*
(a long process)

Husk and dry the nuts and store until ready to use.

Heat the dried nuts in a moderate oven to crack the thin brown shells. Remove the shells by rubbing in the hands and winnowing.

Grind the nuts to a paste between stones, with a mortar and pestle or in a blender. To prevent the paste from drying, add sufficient water to keep it the consistency of fresh frosting.

When oil can be extracted from the paste due to the pressure of your hand, it is placed in clean bags of wool or linen for pressing. Slowly extract the oil from the bags by putting them under pressure for several hours. Catch the oil in large earthen vessels. When all of the oil is removed from the first press, remove the paste and put it into a pot. Add enough water to keep the paste sticky. Mix and warm under gentle heat for 15 minutes. Place the paste back into the bags and press again.

Store the oil in covered casks in a cool corner of the cellar. After 2 or 3 months draw off the oil into fresh vessels leaving the residue behind. Repeat this last process 2 or 3 times during the first year.

Finally, place the oil in clean, stoppered flasks and store upright in the cellar (preferably in sand). The oil will keep at least 10 years.

---

* After Fernald *et al.* (1958).

Filbert (Hazelnut)

Filbert, American Hazelnut
(*Corylus americana*)
Filbert, Beaked Hazelnut (*Corylus cornuta*)

Habitat and Range

The hazelnuts are shrubs or small trees found in the cool temperate zone of the northern hemisphere. There are two American species and they are both found in the eastern United States. *Corylus americana,* the American hazelnut, grows in thickets and *C. cornuta,* the beaked hazelnut, is found in rich thickets, clearings and borders of woods.

Description

Both the beaked and American hazelnuts are shrubs with alternate, egg-shaped, doubly toothed more or less downy leaves. The male flowers are borne in elongate conspicuous catkins; the female flowers are less conspicuous. The fruit is a brown shelled nut borne in a leafy husk. The husk of the American hazelnut is open and flares somewhat at the summit; the beaked hazelnut has a very bristly husk that forms a tube-like beak at the apex of the nut. The shell of the beaked hazelnut is soft compared to that of the thick-shelled American hazelnut.

Collection and Preparation

Cultivated hazelnuts or filberts are sold on the American market and the wild varieties are still gathered in county areas to be used fresh or in a variety of

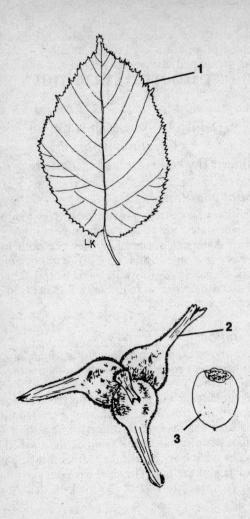

Beaked Filbert (Hazelnut). 1, Egg-shaped, doubly-toothed leaf. 2, Beaked, bristly husk. 3, Brown shell surrounding nut—kernel particularly good eaten fresh or used in baking.

recipes. Filberts are a good source of protein, carbo-hydrate, and the vitamin thiamine (B_1). They are high in fat and are an excellent source of the minerals calcium, phosphorus, and potassium.

As mentioned above, you should gather your filberts early in September as they are very popular with wild mammals. Use gloves when you gather, and husk the beaked hazelnut or the bristles will penetrate your hands.

Hazelnut Fritters

1 egg	½ cup unbleached white
1 tbsp water	flour
1 tbsp lemon juice	a pinch of salt
	⅓ cup chopped hazelnuts

Whip the egg with the water and lemon juice. Fold in the flour, nuts and salt. Mix thoroughly. Spoon out the mixture into hot fat (use a skillet) and cook for 2 minutes, turning the fritters once or twice. Remove fritters from skillet and drain on brown paper.

Serve with sour cream or use like dumplings and place in hot soup or stew.

Hazelnut Orange Squares
(one 7 x 11 inch baking pan)

1¼ cups whole wheat flour	⅔ cup raw sugar
1 tsp baking powder	1 tsp vanilla
⅛ tsp salt	2 tbsp grated orange peel
1 cup hazelnuts	1 egg
¼ cup butter	2 tbsp milk

Blend flour, baking powder, salt, and the nuts to-gether. Cream butter and sugar; add vanilla, orange peel, milk, and egg; whip well. Combine the flour mixture with other ingredients and mix thoroughly. Spread the mixture in baking pan and bake for 20 minutes at 350°F. Cut in squares and serve.

Hickory

Shagbark Hickory (*Carya ovata*)
Pignut Hickory (*Carya glabra*)

Habitat and Range

There are about a dozen species of hickories plus a number of varieties and hybrids found throughout eastern North America and eastern Asia. While the hickories are particularly noted for their lumber, some are commercially important for their nuts. Perhaps the most popular of the food hickories is the pecan (*Cary illinoensis*), which thrives in bottomlands throughout the Mississippi River valley and is widely planted in the South. Two hickories of the northeast with edible nuts are the shagbark (*C. ovata*) and the pignut hickory (*C. glabra*). Shagbark hickory nuts are of such fine quality that they are often found in the commercial market. This hickory prefers rich woods, bottomlands, and slopes; the pignut hickory is found in dry woods and slopes.

Description

Both the shagbark and pignut hickory have alternate compound leaves usually with five egg-shaped, finely toothed leaflets. The scaly buds at the tips of the twigs are much larger than the lateral buds. In the spring the elongate male catkins are below the leaves; the stouter

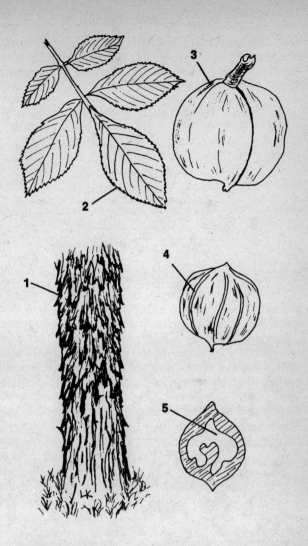

Shagbark Hickory. 1, Gray bark broken into shaggy plates. 2, Compound leaf with five, toothed leaflets. 3, Large husk which tends to separate readily from the nut. 4, Nut with prominent ribs. 5, Kernel—raw, soup, butter, garnish, oil, baking.

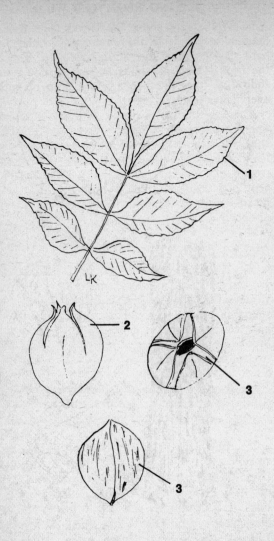

Pignut Hickory. 1, Compound leaf with seven, toothed leaflets (often there are five leaflets). 2, Husk which tends to cling to the nut. 3, Unribbed shell of nut. Kernel —raw, soup, butter, garnish, oil, baking.

female spikes are above the leaves. The fruit, which matures and falls in the autumn, is rounded with a hard shell covering the oily, edible seed. The husk of the fruit is hard and splits lengthwise into four parts. Individual trees produce a heavy crop of nuts about every other year.

These two hickories can be easily distinguished from one another by the bark and the fruit. The bark of the shagbark hickory is broken into long shaggy plates; the bark of the pignut hickory is rough and deeply furrowed. The shagbark hickory fruit has a readily dehiscent husk and the nut is ribbed, while the pignut hickory tends to fall with the husk still attached to the unribbed nut.

Preparation

Hickory nuts are our favorite wild nut because they are abundant, easy to keep, tasty, and can be used in a variety of deliciously different dishes. They are a good source of protein, carbohydrate, fat, and iron and are an excellent source of phosphorus. The tastiest of the hickory nuts are those produced by the shagbark hickory whose nuts are reputed to be among the finest wild nuts in the United States.

Historians who chronicled the early days of our American colonies frequently made reference to the Indians' use of hickory nuts. An excerpt from one of the more colorfully written works is given below.

"Hiccory Nuts have very hard Shells, but excellent, sweet Kernels, with which, in a plentiful Year, the old Hogs, that can crack them, fatten themselves, and make excellent Pork. These Nuts are gotten in great Quantities, by the Savages, and lail up for Stores, of which they make several Dishes and Banquets. One of these I cannot forbear mentioning; it is this: They take these Nuts, and break them very small betwix two Stones, till the Shells and Kernels are indifferent small; And this Powder you are presented withal in their Cabins, in little wooden Dishes; the Kernel dissolves in your

Mouth, and the Shell is spit out. This tastes as well as any Almond. Another Dish is the Soup which they make of these Nuts, beaten, and put into Venison-Broth, which dissolves the Nut and thickens, whilst the Shell precipitates, and remains at the bottom. This Broth tastes very rich" (Lawson 1937, pp. 100–01).

Hickory Oil and Broth
(An old Indian method of preparation)

Crush washed, husked hickory nuts and add to an equal quantity of boiling water and boil slowly 2 to 3 hours. The shells sink to the bottom, the nutmeats float in the water and gradually the nut oil rises to the surface. As water evaporates, keep adding more to keep the water level above the nutmeats. Skim off the nut oil, place in a container and refrigerate. Do not worry if you get some nutmeats mixed with your oil, they add flavor and nutritional value. This oil can be used like butter on your homemade breads or it can be served with vegetables as described below.

Two cups of nuts will yield only about 2 tablespoonfuls of oil, but as long as you use the broth as described below, the process is worth it.

Once you have extracted most of the oil from your mixture, you can now concentrate on making broth from the nutmeats. Add boiling water to your nutmeat shell mixture, stir and cook for about 20 minutes or until the broth is brown and has a nut-like flavor. Pour all the liquid into a storage container. Repeat this process several times and then finally skim off the nutmeats and add to your now copious broth. Hot nut broth can be eaten as is or can be used to make a delicious soup.

Hickory Nut Soup

hickory nut broth and
   nutmeats
leftover venison, pork or
   beef

leftover vegetables
dried herbs (we like
   bayberry leaves)
salt and pepper to taste

Combine all ingredients and let simmer for 10 minutes. Serve hot with homemade bread. This is one of the finest dishes one can prepare with wild foods. We highly recommend it.

Hickory Nut Green Beans
(for 1)

1 cup fresh garden beans
1 tbsp hickory nut oil
1 tbsp nutmeats per serving

6 tbsp water per serving
salt and pepper to taste

Mix half the hickory nut oil and nutmeats into the water and boil. Add the beans, cover, and cook over moderate heat for 10 minutes. Place the vegetable and liquid in a serving dish. Top the beans with the remaining hickory nut mixture. Season to taste and serve.

Hickory Nut Salad Dressing
(for 2)

⅓ cup hickory nut oil plus
   nutmeats to taste

2 cups greens (we suggest
   dandelion or escarole)

Bring the hickory nut oil and nutmeats to room temperature and then add to the greens. Mix thoroughly. This is a tasty blend of bitter and sweet.

Hickory Nut Hot Cakes
(for 2)

1 cup hickory nuts   ½ tsp salt
1 cup boiling water   2 tbsp butter
1 cup cornmeal   1 egg
½ cup milk

Take a cup of husked hickory nuts and crush. Add this to a cup of boiling water and cook over moderate heat for 10 minutes. Skim off the nutmeats and a few drops of the liquid from the top of the mixture and add to the cornmeal. Blend the egg, butter, salt, and milk to mixture. Form into patties. Sauté on medium heat until lightly brown and serve with butter.

Use the remaining nut broth in your homemade soups and stews.

Oak

(*Quercus*—several species)

Habitat and Range

The oaks are a common and widely distributed group of trees. They are found in temperate regions of the northern hemisphere and at high altitudes in the tropics. They are represented by several species in the United States and are the most important timber trees here.

Description

Oaks are a common member of our forest population and they are often planted as shade trees in our cities and towns. They will probably be the easiest of the nut trees for you to locate and identify.

The oaks are tall trees with simple alternate leaves that are either toothed or lobed. An unusual feature of the oaks is that the buds are clustered at the end of the twigs. The bark is deep and furrowed and the male flowers are elongate catkins; the female flowers are inconspicuous. The fruit is an acorn which is a shelled nut covered at the base by a cup consisting of overlapping scales.

Taxonomists divide the oaks into two major groups, the White Oak Group and the Black or Red Oak Group. This taxonomic subdivision is of interest to the forager mainly because the members of the White Oak Group have the sweetest acorns. But keep in mind that the acorns of all the oaks are edible and nutritious. The chief characteristics of these two groups of oaks are listed below.

TABLE 10

Major Groups of the Oaks

Features	Group I White Oaks	Group II Black or Red Oaks
Bark	Scaly	Furrowed and dark
Leaves	Smooth leaf tips	Leaf or lobe tips with bristles
Acorn		
Time to Mature	1 year	2 years
Texture inside the Shell	Smooth	Downy
Taste	Usually sweet	Bitter

Because of their abundance, the white oak (*Quercus alba*) from Group I and the black oak (*Q. velutina*) as well as the red oak (*Q. rubra*) from Group II have been selected as representative types. For additional information concerning the oaks, consult a good tree guide.

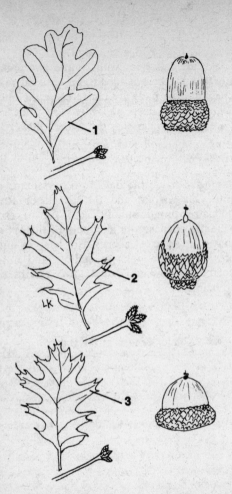

Oaks. 1, White oak with hairless, lobed leaf, hairless twig and buds, and typical acorn. 2, Black oak with lobed, bristle-tipped leaf that is somewhat hairy below; hairless twig, hairy end buds, and typical acorn. 3, Red-oak leaf similar to black-oak but is hairless below; hairless twig and buds, and typical acorn. White-oak acorns are usually sweet but those of the red and black oaks are bitter and must be leached before eating. White oak, fresh or cooked, red and black usually cooked, often ground for flour.

Collection and Preparation

Acorns probably will not be your favorite wild nut but they are an excellent source of carbohydrate and in a few dishes are superior to most of the wild nuts discussed in this section.

One advantage of acorns as a food source is that the oaks are so common and widespread. Acorns can be found easily and many can be gathered in a short time on any pleasant autumn day. However, if you gather acorns from the same trees year after year, you will notice that individual trees have "bumper" crops only every three or four years.

Unfortunately, the acorns of Group II, and even sometimes of Group I, must be leached to release the bitter-tasting tannic acid. Leaching is time-consuming and during the process, some sugar is lost from the acorn kernels. The acorns are still nutritious, but if you want to save time and trouble, try to locate a large white oak tree that produces sweet-tasting acorns that do not have to be leached.

If you must leach your acorns, here are a few suggestions. The most common technique is to dry the nuts as described earlier in this section; then put them aside until there is time to leach them. It was the custom in many Indian tribes to pound the shelled dried kernels, place them in a basket and let running water trickle through for several days until the bitterness was dispelled. The dried kernels can also be boiled in several changes of water for three or four hours. Another variant on the technique is to boil the kernels in several changes of water for an hour and then soak in cold water for four or five days, changing the water on several occasions. Use the leached nuts immediately or dry them in a slow oven and store in screw-capped jars.

Coarsely Ground Acorns

These can be added to pottages, breads, stews or to recipes for confections. We prefer to serve them sautéed.

Sautéed Acorns

Take dried and leached (if necessary) acorns and sauté for 8 minutes in enough oil to cover the bottom of the pan. Remove from the pan, drain on brown paper, salt, cool, and serve. These nuts are delicious, tasting something like a cross between sunflower seeds and popcorn.

Finely Ground Acorns

Many tribes of Indians used acorn meal to thicken their venison broth or to make a soup. It was used as a flour to make cakes and breads and was often combined with cornmeal. Acorn meal can be substituted for conventional flour in a number of recipes. A favorite recipe of ours is acorn-corn bread.

Acorn-Corn Bread
(for 6)

1 cup yellow cornmeal	½ tsp salt
1 cup acorn meal	1 egg
1 tsp maple syrup	1 cup milk
4 tsp baking powder	¼ cup softened shortening

Sift together the dry ingredients. Add the maple syrup, milk, egg, and shortening. Beat until smooth. Bake in a greased cake pan in a preheated oven (425°F) 25 to 30 minutes.

Walnut

The Black Walnut or American Walnut
(*Juglans nigra*)
The Butternut or White Walnut
(*Juglans cinerea*)

Habitat and Range

There are about 20 species of walnuts found in the hardwood forests of North and South America, southern Europe, northern Africa and southern Asia. The cosmopolitan species, *Juglans regia* is extensively cultivated on the West Coast of the United States and its nut is sold as the "English or Persian Walnut" of commerce.

There are six species of walnut native to the United States, with the black walnut and the white walnut being the most important producers of lumber as well as good sources of nuts. Both these wild walnut trees can be found growing in the moist rich soil of the northeastern and southeastern forests. The butternut also grows well in drier areas, especially in soils of limestone origin.

Description

The walnuts are medium to large trees with a furrowed bark and dark brown wood. The leaves are alternate and compound with 9 to 23 egg-shaped to lance-shaped, saw-toothed leaflets. Male flowers are in drooping catkins which emerge from lateral buds on the past season's growth; the female flowers are borne in short spikes at the tip of the new growth. The fruit, which matures and falls in the Autumn, has a fleshy husk, hard shell, and an oily edible seed.

The black walnut and butternut can be easily distinguished from one another by certain characteristics of the bark and fruit. The black walnut has a dark brown bark divided by deep narrow furrows while that of the butternut is light gray and the fissures are shallow. The fruit of the black walnut is a globe-shaped structure about 2 inches in diameter covered by a thick hard husk while the butternut fruit is ellipsoid in shape averaging about 2 inches in length and covered with a greenish bronze sticky husk.

Collection and Preparation

Look for walnut trees in old farm yards and search for them throughout the eastern deciduous forest. They are seldom in pure stands and more often will be found scattered among other trees. The conspicuous fruit stays on the trees after the leaves fall and bumper crops are produced every two or three years.

Walnut trees will be a bit of a challenge to locate but once they are found, the highly nutritious fruits will justify your efforts. Black walnuts and butternuts contain a high amount of protein and fat as well as carbohydrate. In addition, the butternut is a good source of iron. The black walnut leads all our wild nuts in food value in that it is an excellent source of the minerals phosphorus, iron, and potassium, and it is rich in vitamin A and thiamine (B_1).

Because walnut trees grow rapidly, you might want to plant some for their beauty and fruit. Take care to place them a good distance from your garden as a toxin from the roots, fallen leaves, and husks can kill crop plants.

Walnuts should be used more as a table food. And

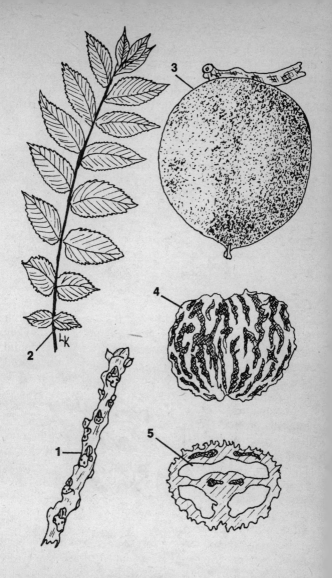

Black Walnut. 1, Stout twig. 2, Compound leaf with numerous, toothed leaflets. 3, Globose fruit with brown husk. 4, Shell of nut. 5, Kernel—a great variety of uses as fresh, dried or cooked nut.

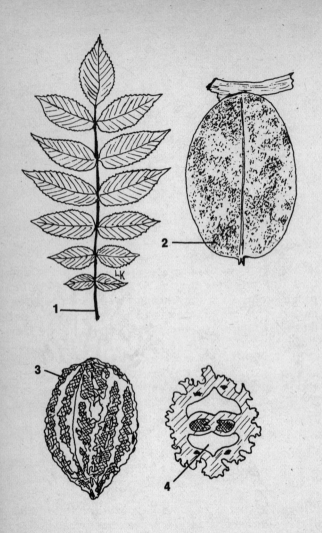

White Walnut. 1, Compound leaf with many-toothed leaflets. 2, Ellipsoid-shaped fruit with greenish-bronze husk. 3, Shell of nut. 4, Kernel—uses same as black walnut.

they are a must as a nutritious survival food. Our recipes for walnuts were designed to demonstrate their versatility as a foodstuff.

Black Walnut and Pumpkin Soup
(a highly nutritious American Indian dish, for 4)

1 cup chopped walnuts
1½ qt water
1 pumpkin (about 12"

in diameter)
salt and pepper to taste

Split the pumpkin and remove the seeds. (Put the seeds aside for use in the next recipe.) Cut pumpkin into smaller chunks, peel the rim, and dice into 1 to 2 inch chunks. Add to a quart of boiling water, cover, and cook over moderate heat for 20 minutes. In a separate pan, add the nuts to the remaining water and cook over moderate heat. When the pumpkin is soft, mash it and then add the nuts plus broth. Mix and simmer for 2 or 3 minutes. Serve.

Black walnut and pumpkin used in combination are a rich source of protein, carbohydrate, fat, phosphorus, iron, potassium, vitamin A, and thiamine, and also supply some calcium, riboflavin, niacin, and ascorbic acid. This dish is a must for vegetarians.

Toasted Pumpkin Seeds

Separate fiber from unwashed pumpkin seeds. Add to every 2 cups of seeds, 1½ tablespoons melted oil or butter and 1½ teaspoons salt. Spread in a shallow pan and cook at 250°F until crisp and brown. Cool and serve.

Walnut Butter

1 cup finely chopped walnuts

Grind the nuts to a paste between stones, with a mortar and pestle or in a blender.

Use as a topping for homemade bread, mix it with salad greens, or serve it with fresh fruit. Walnut butter is both delicious and nutritious.

We prefer to add a teaspoon or two of honey to our black walnut butter while the butternut butter is sweet enough plain.

Walnut and Corn Hot Cakes
(for 4)

1 cup ground walnuts
1 cup cornmeal
¾ cup milk

1 tbsp butter
1 egg (optional)

Mix together all the ingredients. Drop tablespoonfuls onto a heated, slightly greased skillet. Cook for 3 minutes on each side over moderate heat.

Walnut and Fresh Fruit Salad

any type of clean, fresh fruit
chopped walnuts

kirsch (optional)

Wash, slice, and arrange fruit on a platter. Garnish with the nuts and then top it all with some kirsh.

This can be served as a luncheon dish or as a dessert.

Walnut and Sour Cream Dressing
(for 2)

½ cup sour cream
½ cup chopped black
   walnuts

Mix the sour cream and nuts together and serve over salad greens or top your poached fish with it.

Sweet Walnut Bread
(1 loaf)

3 cups unbleached
   white flour
4½ tsp baking powder
1 tsp salt
1 cup maple sugar

2 eggs, well beaten
1 cup milk
1 cup chopped walnuts
¼ cup butter or shortening
   melted

Sift flour, baking powder, salt, and sugar together. Add eggs and milk to flour mixture. Stir in walnuts and cooled melted butter. Blend until smooth and pour into a well-greased 9 x 5 inch loaf pan and bake for 45 minutes in a moderate 350°F oven.

Walnut Strips

¼ cup butter
¾ cup maple sugar
1 egg
2 tbsp milk
½ tsp salt
½ tsp vanilla

½ tsp almond extract
1⅓ cups unbleached
   white flour
1 tsp baking powder
½ cup chopped walnuts

Cream butter and sugar, then add the egg and beat thoroughly. Add the milk and flavorings and beat. Sift flour, baking powder, and salt together and add to mixture. Blend well. Pour into a well-greased baking sheet, ⅛ inch thick. Sprinkle with chopped walnuts. Bake about 15 minutes at 375°F. When cool, cut into strips and serve.

Witloof

Witloof is the name given to chickory plants (*Cichorium intybus*)* which have been specially treated to produce heads of crisp, blanched leaves that are primarily used fresh in salads. It can be harvested indoors all winter and outdoors in early spring.

For a spring crop, locate a few dozen chicory plants in a relatively open area little used by people or vehicles. When the plants become dormant, hoe and rake around them and cover with 6 to 8 inches of soil. Early in spring, the buds will begin to grow under the soil and produce a compact head of crisp yellow leaves that should be harvested immediately, for once the leaves reach the surface, they will spread, become green and acquire a bitterness distasteful to some people. If you have a large crop of witloof, try braising some and serve as a hot vegetable.

To produce winter witloof at home, it will require a little more work. You will need a dark, cool room (60°F. is an optimal temperature for this crop), some soil, sand, and a wooden box 1 to 2 feet deep and as long and wide as you desire.

Dig out several dozen chicory roots with a pick and shovel. Pile them in a corner of an outbuilding to ensure that they are chilled, but cover with soil or hay to

* For additional information concerning this plant see pages 64–65.

prevent successive freezing and thawing. Witloof is forced by packing the roots closely together in a box and surrounding the roots with sand or sandy soil. The crowns should all be on the same level and covered with 6 inches of fine sand. Water every other day.

It takes about a dozen roots five weeks to produce sufficient witloof for a salad to feed 4 to 5 people. As needed, remove roots from the outbuilding and plant indoors.

Poor-man's-pepper

Poor-man's-pepper, Peppergrass
(*Lepidium*—several species)

History

Lepidium is a peppery flavored member of the mustard family (Cruciferae) represented by numerous humble weed species, which brighten dry and barren areas with their touch of green. Indians of Louisiana and some western tribes reportedly ate the leaves as greens and used the spicy seeds for flavoring foods or ground them for bread and mush.

Habitat and Range

These herbs of temperate and warm areas are nearly cosmopolitan in their distribution and are represented in the eastern United States by seven species, which thrive along roadsides, waste areas, and dry or moist open soil.

Description

In spring the leaves of *Lepidium* form a basal ro-

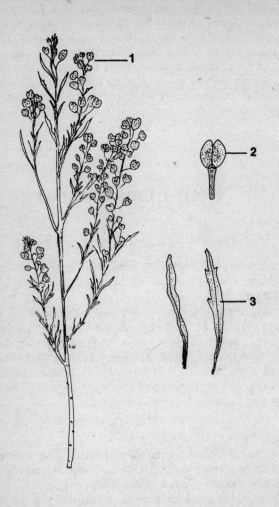

Poor-Man's-Pepper. 1, To illustrate the upright posture of the mature plant. 2, Scalelike fruit—fresh as pepper substitute. 3, Leaf—salad (when newly emerged).

sette but as the season advances, the plants take on a more upright aspect, often growing to a foot or more in height. The leaves are linear to elliptical in shape and can be deeply cut, toothed, or entire; the numerous minute, white, four-petaled flowers are borne in elongating spike-like clusters, and the nearly circular fruiting pods are flat and notched at the apex.

Collection and Preparation

These plants can be readily identified by the peppery taste of the abundant flattened pods, which resemble tiny stalked fish scales emerging from an elongate central stem. Indeed, the generic name *Lepidium,* is from the Greek, *lepidion,* which means "little scales."

The freshly gathered pods can be used as a pepper substitute and the young shoots produced in spring and autumn can serve as a salad green. *Lepidium virginicum* is a particularly useful plant to the forager because it continues to sprout well into November, providing greens long after the chilling frost has killed most greens.

Wild Autumn Salad Greens
(for 2)

1 cup chopped newly
  sprouted dock leaves

2 cups poor-man's-pepper
  leaves

Dressing

3 tsp poor-man's-pepper
  pods
½ tsp algal salt

¼ cup birch or maple
  vinegar
⅓ cup hickory nut oil

Wash and drain greens, toss with dressing.

Beach Plum

(*Prunus maritima*)

History

Indians along the northeast coast used beach plums as a fresh fruit, added them to porridges, and dried quantities to be used in their pemmican. It was among the first of our native fruits to be observed by the Europeans because it grew prominently displayed along the dunes of our north Atlantic coast, being particularly abundant in the area between what is now Massachusetts and southern New Jersey. One of the first accounts of the beach plum was that of Henry Hudson, who upon entering the river of his name, reported a fine harbor, an abundance of wild blue plums, and many tall oaks. Subsequent investigators believe that these plums were beach plums. The culinary virtues of this native plum were soon recognized by the settlers who used it for jelly, sauce, and pies. Today, beach plum jelly continues to be one of our best-known wild food products, particularly in parts of New England.

Habitat and Range

Beach plum bushes grow in sandy soils and dunes on the northeast coast from New Brunswick south to Delaware, but are most abundant between northern Massachusetts and southern New Jersey.

Description

This densely branched shrub can sometimes reach a height of 12 to 13 feet. The older limbs have a gray,

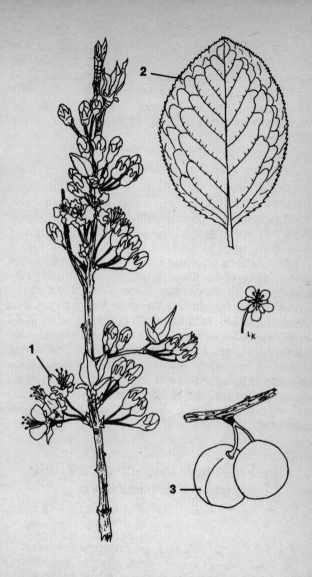

Beach Plum. 1, Flowering twig with pinkish, five-petaled blossoms. 2, Toothed, egg-shaped leaf. 3, Globose purple beach plums—jelly, sauce, pie.

rather scaly bark; the newer branches are maroon and marked with prominent gray, lens-shaped lenticels. The numerous flowers appear before the leaves and are in clusters of three (sometimes two); each flower has five white to pinkish petals. The egg-shaped leaves are simple, sharply toothed and hairy on the underside. Beach plum fruits are globose, purple structures about ½ inch in diameter. There is also a yellow form.

Collection and Preparation

Because the beach plum is one of our wild foods that has remained popular with a number of people, one must have several foraging spots selected to be sure of acquiring some of these fine fruits.

The best time to locate beach plum plants is in the spring, when the leafless shrubs are made quite prominent by their showy white flowers. On Cape Cod this display takes place during the latter part of May after the shadbush bloom has peaked. During summer it is a bit more difficult to find beach plum bushes because the ripening fruit are covered by the leaves. But toward the end of August, the plant once again becomes noticeable due to its abundance of rotund purple fruit, which can be picked throughout September. If the berries are not overripe, they will keep well and can be easily refrigerated or frozen.

Old-Fashioned Beach Plum Jelly
(about 6 medium glasses)

3 qt beach plums   raw sugar

Place the plums in a large pot, cover with water, add a lid, and bring to a boil. Then allow to simmer over low heat for about 30 minutes. Pour the fruit and juice into a jelly bag and squeeze. Take 1 cup of sugar for every cup of juice (3 quarts of plums should yield 4 to 5 cups of juice). Boil the juice alone for about 10 minutes, then stir in the sugar, and cook over medium heat until it sheets when dropped from a spoon. Skim the jelly and pour into washed and scalded jelly glasses. Seal with a thin layer of paraffin.

For best results, make jelly in small batches.

Wild Grapes

(*Vitis*—several species)

History

Grapes are plants of the north temperate zone which were first put under cultivation over 4,000 years ago. *Vitis vinifera,* the European grape, has been the main source of wine grapes since ancient times; the plant was widely spread throughout Europe by the Romans. It was introduced to the New World by Lord Baltimore; although it never thrived commercially in the east,* it is now extensively grown in California for its fruits, which are used for wines, table fruit, and raisins. However, because native American grape plants are more resistant to various insect and fungus pests than the European grape, vineyard owners have grafted thousands of European grape plants to the rootstalks of some American species to obtain resistant plants that produce a fine wine grape. In addition, native American grape species have been domesticated for their sweet fruit and sundry horticultural varieties are widely grown in the eastern states. The wild fox grape (*V. labrusca*) has given rise to such well-known cultivated varieties as the Concord, Catawba, and Delaware grape, while the wild muscadine grape (*V. rotundifolia*) has given rise to

---

* With the exception of some hybrids grown since World War II in New York State.

the Scuppernong which is popular in the southern Atlantic and Gulf states.

Like many other fruits and berries, grapes were popular with the Indians, who used them fresh or dried, while the sap of the frost grape (*V. vulpina*) and winter grape (*V. cinerea*) was also used as a beverage by some Indians of the east and midwest. Today, wild grapes are still harvested fairly extensively by people who prefer them to the cultivated varieties as jelly grapes.

Habitat and Range

In the eastern United States, several native species of wild grape and some domesticated varieties, which have gone wild, are commonly found along roadsides, in thickets, woods, and around old homesteads.

Description

Grape plants are usually high-climbing, thornless vines with naked, tipped tendrils, dark stems, and usually a shreddy bark. The leaves are simple, heart-shaped, toothed, and usually lobed. The green flowers are borne in clusters and are followed by the familiar round, usually purple- to black-colored fruits that contain four or less ovoid seeds. The tendrils and flower clusters grow opposite the leaves.

> *Note.* Canadian moonseed (*Menispermum canadense*) is similar in structure to the grape plants but it bears poisonous fruits which resemble grapes. To distinguish between this plant and the edible grapes, note that it has lobed leaves that are untoothed, while those of grape are toothed and usually lobed.

Collection and Preparation

The high-climbing woody vines of the grape can be easily located after leaf fall and conclusively identified

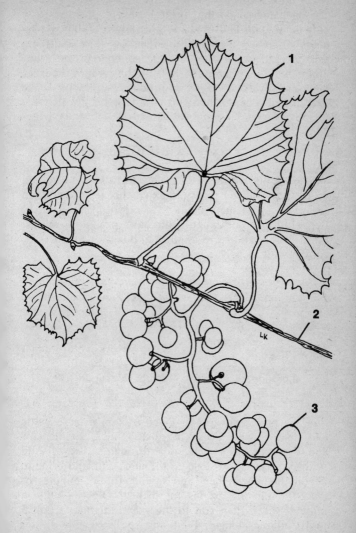

Wild Grape. 1, Heart-shaped, *toothed,* leaf—raw or cooked vegetable (when newly emerged). 2, Thornless, climbing stem. 3, Fruit—jelly, juice, raisin.

when the foliage and flowers apear. The young leaves can be gathered during spring, summer, and the early part of autumn and used for a variety of culinary purposes discussed in the Spring Section. The fruits are usually ready to harvest by late summer or early autumn; but "shop around" for suitable grapes, because there are several species that produce sweet fruit, while that of still others is not worth gathering.

Wild Raisins

Select only the largest, sweetest grapes and spread on trays in the sun to dry, making sure to screen them from insects. In the evening set the fruit in a dry room. Repeat this process until you have produced raisins. Pack loosely and store in covered boxes or tins. Use as cooking raisins.

Wild Grape Conserve
(about 6 medium glasses)

4 lb grapes
¾ cup raisins (seeded)
1 small orange (sliced thinly and quartered)
1 cup hickory nuts or walnuts (finely chopped)
8 cups raw sugar

Wash and stem grapes. Place fruit in a large kettle and heat slowly. Crush to release juice, simmer for about 5 minutes, then pour through a sieve. Add orange, raisins, and sugar to the juice. Stir and bring to a boil then lower heat and simmer for 30 minutes or until the mixture begins to thicken. Dip the nuts in boiling water, then add to the grape mixture. Cook 5 to 10 minutes longer. Pour into sterilized jelly glasses and seal with paraffin.

Wild Grape Juice
(about 1 quart)

2 cups grapes
boiling water

½ to 1 cup raw sugar
1 qt jar with lid

Wash the required number of jars and let stand in a hot (about 190°F) water bath. Meanwhile, wash grapes and remove stems. Place grapes in the jars, add sugar, and cover with the boiling water. Seal immediately and let stand in the water bath for 20 minutes more. Allow to cool. Store in a cool, dry room 3 to 4 months. Strain out the juice and, if desired, dilute before using.

Apple

(*Pyrus Malus*)

History

When the first colonists arrived on the eastern shores of the New World, they found no native apple trees except for the crab apple. The newcomers longed for the succulent familiar fruits of their homeland and subsequent waves of settlers began to bring in seed apples and apple trees from Europe. Soon the hillsides of colonial America were patched with apple orchards; by the time of the American Revolution even the eastern Indians were cultivating these popular imported fruits.

Habitat and Range

Apples are trees of the north temperate zone which originated from wild trees in southern Eurasia, presumably around the Black and Caspian seas.

Apple trees take well to cultivation and were first domesticated over 4,000 years ago. But once left to reproduce themselves, they easily revert to the wild state and develop thornlike branches and become scraggly and stunted. Once they escape from the orchard or garden, they begin to sprout along roadsides, on stream banks, and in damp hollows and fields. In this way, the European import has naturalized itself in most parts of this country.

Description

The apple is a low, sprawling tree with a stout, branching, gray-brown, scaly barked trunk. The egg-shaped, dark green, finely toothed leaves grow in irregular clusters and have a whitish fuzz on the underside and along the petiole. The flowers are characterized by five showy white petals and the fruit is a pome.

Note. Apple seeds are cyanogenic and should not be eaten in any quantity.

Collection and Preparation

In all likelihood, the apple is the most widely known and best-liked fruit in the north temperate zone. The aroma of fresh apples steaming on the stove recalls childhood memories of chill, sunny September days when after school we tramped through the woods behind our house to harvest the tart wild apples. Many were sampled, some were discarded and others were stuffed into pockets and wrapped in sweaters and jackets to be brought home, where mother converted them into fragrant applesauce or hot apple pie.

Storing Fresh Apples

Until the end of the last century, apples were one of the few fruits available from November until June. If apples are unbruised and packed properly, they can be easily kept over winter. An old method of storing apples or pears is to alternate layers of the fruit and dry peat (sphagnum) moss in earthenware vessels until the vessel is filled. The vessel is covered, the edges sealed with melted rosin and the whole container immersed about a foot in the dry sand of a deep cellar. A variation of this method is to alternate layers of sand rather than moss with the apples. The container is covered and stored in a cool cellar room.

A third method of storing apples requires tissue paper and a wooden egg crate with its cardboard dividers (or a suitable substitute). Wrap individual apples in tissue paper, place the cardboard in the crate, and layer the apples on it. Add another cardboard and continue packing and layering until the crate is full. Store in a cool, dry, airy, cellar room. Use as needed.

Dried Apples

In colonial days, a substantial portion of the autumn apple crop was converted into dried apples, applesauce, and apple butter, which were used throughout the year. At harvest time, farmhouse kitchens were filled with barrels of aromatic apples. The fruits were pared prior to drying or cooking. Apples to be used for drying were also cored, sliced thinly crosswise and strung on a cord which was often hung in the warm kitchen. When dry, they were packed into clean, covered containers and used by the children all winter as a sweet snack, while mothers and older daughters soaked the dried fruit overnight and used it for pies, tarts and sauce.

Applesauce

Core, peel, and quarter apples. Place in an enamel or glass pan with water. Cover, and cook over medium heat about 20 minutes. Mash, add cinnamon, and sweeten to taste with sugar. Serve hot or cold.

8 medium-size tart apples	maple sugar to taste
½ to 1 cup water	¼ tsp cinnamon

Days used to be spent in preparing the yearly supply of applesauce which was packed in barrels in the cold depths of the cellar and was always ready for use.

Apple Pancakes

Prepare a cup or so of your favorite pancake batter. Core, peel, and thinly slice apples. Dip the apple slices into batter and sauté slowly in a greased frying pan until golden brown. Serve hot or allow to cool and top with cranberry sauce as a relish for meat and poultry dishes.

Baked Apples

apples	raw sugar
nutmeg	margarine or butter
cinnamon	

Set oven at 375°F. and rub a baking dish with margarine.

Wash and core apples, place in the baking dish and sprinkle a little nutmeg and the cinnamon and sugar in the center of each apple. Top with a tablespoonful of butter. Pour a little boiling water in the bottom of the baking dish. Place in oven and cook for 30 minutes, basting occasionally. Serve hot or cold with cream.

Apples can also be filled with sweetened dry berries or cranberry sauce, then baked.

Apple Jelly

1 cup water to
  1 lb prepared apples

1 cup raw sugar to
  1 cup fruit juice

Scrub apples and remove blossom and stem ends. Quarter the apples and weigh. Place in a large pan, add the appropriate amount of water, bring to a boil, then simmer until the apples are soft. Remove from heat, mash and pour into a sieve lined with cheesecloth and catch the juice. Set the pulp aside for apple butter. Measure the juice into a large saucepan and bring to a boil. Slowly stir in the appropriate amount of sugar and boil rapidly until the syrup sheets when dropped from a spoon. Skim, pour into hot, sterilized jelly glasses, and seal with paraffin.

Apple Butter

1¼-1½ cups raw sugar to
  1 cup apple puree

¼ tsp cinnamon to
  1 cup puree

Mash the apple pulp through a sieve to hold back the skin, seeds, and core. Measure the puree into a saucepan, add sugar, and slowly bring to a boil. Cook 10 to 15 minutes, then remove from heat and skim. Ladle into hot, sterilized jars or glasses. Seal with paraffin.

Apple Butter and
Walnut Cake Filling

(for 2 layers or 2 dozen cupcakes)

½ cup chopped black or
    white walnuts

¾ cup apple butter
1 cup whipped cream

Stir nuts into the apple butter and fold this mixture
into the whipped cream.

Pickerelweed

(*Pontederia cordata*)

Introduction

In late summer, the edges of many ponds and quiet
streams are blanketed with the violet-blue flowers of
the common pickerelweed, one of our most striking
aquatic wild flower attractions. It can also serve as a
source of nutritious food. The aerial stem tips and
leaves as well as the fruits can be eaten fresh or
cooked.

Habitat and Range

Pickerelweed is found in southeastern Canada and
throughout the eastern United States, where it proliferates on shores and in the shallow waters of ponds,
streams, and marshes.

Description

These marsh or aquatic herbs consist of a thick,

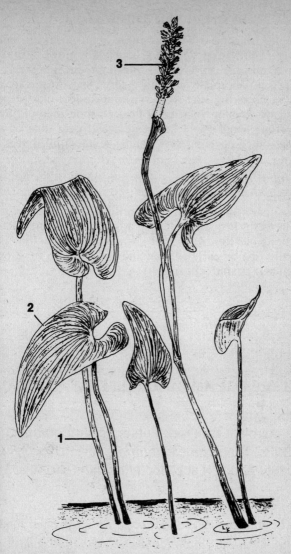

Pickerelweed. 1, Long petiole of leaf. 2, Leaf blade with characteristic venation (compare with that of Arrow Arum and Arrowhead)—raw or cooked vegetable (when newly emerged). 3, Cluster of fruit—raw or dried as cereal food. Flowers are purple.

creeping rhizome with erect, long petioled leaves and an erect flowering stem that commonly grows 1 or 2 feet above the surface and which produces a heart-shaped to lanceolate, untoothed aerial leaf. At the apex of the flowering stem is borne a spike-like cluster of small, violet-blue, ephemeral flowers, soon followed by the fruits about ⅓ inch in length and consisting of a loose, outer covering surrounding a starch-filled seed.

Collection and Preparation

Gather pickerelweed greens in the summer, when the aerial parts of the plant first arise. If they are to be eaten fresh, first wash them in a disinfectant rinse such as described for watercress on page 89. The fruit is usually ripe by early autumn and can be eaten fresh or dried and ground for cereal.

Arrowhead and Arrow Arum

Arrowhead, Duck Potato, Swan Potato,
Katniss, Wapatoo (*Sagittaria*—several species)
Arrow Arum, Tuckahoe (*Peltandra virginica*)

History

The starchy tubers of *Sagittaria* were a popular food with many tribes of Indians in the eastern and north-western United States. Early explorers recorded that each autumn the natives waded in the water and, with the feet, dug quantities of these walnut-size tubers; or they stole the stores of them hoarded by beavers and muskrats. They were served boiled or roasted; some tribes also sliced the boiled tubers, then strung them to dry for winter use.

Arrowhead tubers have also been long popular in the Orient. In China and Japan they are sometimes cultivated at the edges of rice fields.

For those of you willing to do a little digging in the chill of autumn, the arrowheads can provide a toothsome dish.

Habitat and Range

Sagittaria is represented by about 30 species of rooted aquatics which grow in temperate and tropical areas. In the northeastern United States, arrowheads are often found in pond and river margins, wet swamps, and in marshes.

Description

Within this genus and often within a single plant, there is a great variation in the shape of the leaf blade, ranging from those that resemble grass to those shaped like an arrowhead. Species easiest to recognize, however, are those that produce erect or sometimes floating, arrowhead-shaped leaves. The flowers are quite characteristic, usually arranged in whorls of three near the summit of the flower stalk and bearing broad, white petals; the seeds are borne in rounded heads. The plant is anchored in the soil by a small root and numerous stoloniferous rhizomes, which late in the season, bear tubers at their tip.

Note. Arrow arum (*Peltandra virginica*) is an edible look-alike of arrowhead and shares its predilection for moist habitats. It can be distinguished from arrowhead by its stout vertical root; beanlike seeds, which are borne in a pouch (spathe); and by the venation of its leaves (see illustration). Both the roots and seeds of arrow arum were eaten by some eastern Indians.

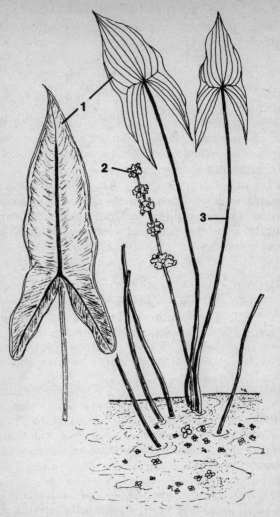

Arrow Arum and **Arrowhead.** 1, Leaf of arrow arum on left and that of arrowhead on right, to compare venation. 2, Typical flower stalk of arrowhead with white, three-petaled flowers. 3, Elongate petiole. Arrow arum roots and seeds when dried and stored for a while— soups and ground for meal, respectively. Arrowhead tubers—cooked vegetable.

Collection and Preparation

Arrowheads can be readily located in summer when their green foliage and white flowers blanket the margins of many ponds, marshes, and streams. However, the tubers are not ready to be harvested until late autumn. To gather them, take an iron rake or claw and trace the underground runners from the main plant out to the swollen tubers which can be snipped off, washed, and cooked in the same way as potatoes.

The root and seeds of arrow arum can also be gathered at this time but because these plants are so peppery, we suggest they be dried and held over winter before being used. The seeds can be ground for meal and the starchy roots added to soups.

Phragmites

The Common Reed (*Phragmites communis*)

History

Phragmites communis is a widespread plant that belongs to the economically important grass family (Gramineae) from which are obtained our cereal grains, most of our forage crops, and a good part of our sugar. *Phragmites* has played an important role in the lives of primitive people on nearly every continent. American Indians living south of the extensive northern wild rice fields used the seeds of *Pharagmites* as a source of grain, and the rhizome, shoots, and young leaves were cooked as vegetables. In addition, the aerial parts of *Phragmites* plants were used for weaving, thatching, and for arrow shafts.

Habitat and Range

Phragmites communis is very nearly cosmopolitan in its distribution. In North America it is found from Nova Scotia to British Columbia, south to Mexico, and throughout most of the United States. It is also found in South America, Africa, Eurasia, and Australia. It grows profusely in brackish water at the borders of salt marshes and is also found in freshwater areas, such as at pond borders and in ditches, marshes, and wet bogs.

Description

This is a conspicuously tall grass growing in colonies in moist areas. Perhaps its most distinctive characteristic is its graceful plume of flowers which grows at the tip end of tall (8 to 12 feet), cylindrical, jointed stems. In late summer and early fall these clusters are a rich purple; in winter they take on a light tan hue. The dark brown seeds are tiny.

Collection and Preparation

Phragmites is a very common plant in the northeast and does not seem hampered by the encroachment of civilization. For example, it can be readily observed growing in dense stands as one drives between New York City and New England, being especially evident in eastern Connecticut. All across northern New Jersey there are vast tracts of *Phragmites*. We have found good stands of this plant in marshy areas along the Connecticut River in southern Vermont and have found it to be very common on Cape Cod where it borders brackish marshes.

A number of wholesome and interesting dishes can be prepared from *Phragmites* but it best qualifies as a fine emergency food plant. Once you have located a stand of *Phragmites,* you have a good potential year

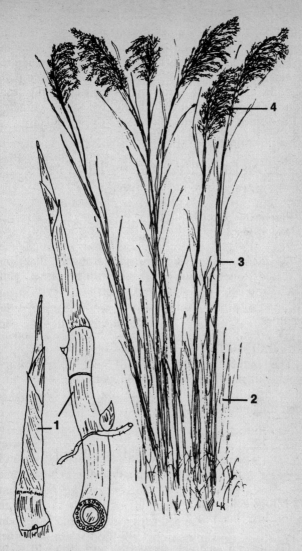

Common Reed. 1, Shoot with new leaves—peeled shoot, raw or added to soup; leaves—cooked greens. 2, Grasslike leaves. 3, Elongate, jointed stem. 4, Plume-like fruit clusters. Seeds—gruel. Rhizome—boiled or roasted vegetable.

round food supply. The shoots are a sweetly pleasant spring green and if you really search in winter you will find some of these shoots already emerged and ready to be eaten. The new young leaves are a good spring pot-herb; in autumn the seeds can be collected and used to make a nutritious gruel. Finally, the white, cylindrical rhizomes can be dug and roasted year-round.

Roasted Phragmites Rhizomes
(a year-round camp recipe, for 2)

12 *Phragmites* rhizomes
   (6 to 8" long)

Dig the rhizomes out and wash thoroughly. Place on a heated stone in your fire, cover with hot ashes, and bake 20 minutes or until brown and crisp.

These rhizomes taste like the "jackets" of baked potatoes.

Phragmites rhizomes can also be baked in a moderate oven (350°F) 25 to 30 minutes.

The Indians reportedly boiled and served *Phragmites* rhizomes much as we do potatoes. We found these to be sweet, but impossible to chew because of their toughness.

Boiled Phragmites Shoots
(a springtime camp recipe, for 2)

14 *Phragmites* shoots
   (about 6" long)

Gather the emerging shoots as they begin to elongate in the spring, or dig out the tiny winter shoots if you are really hungry and have plenty of time. Peel off the covering layer until you reach the sweet center of the stalk. Add these to a small amount of boiling water. Cover, lower heat, and cook 10 minutes or until tender.

These provide a sweet vegetable that can be eaten as is or served buttered or with hollandaise sauce as recommended for fern fiddleheads.

Phragmites Greens
(a vegetable or potherb)

1 cup young, unfolded
  Phragmites leaves
  per person

Collect, wash, and add the greens to a small amount of boiling water. Cover and cook over low heat for 10 minutes. Serve plain or with butter and salt and pepper.

These leaves can be also added to a fish or meat stew.

Phragmites Gruel
(an autumn camp recipe)

½ cup seeds of *Phragmites*   2 cups boiling water

Collect the heads of a dozen or so *Phragmites* plants. Remove the seeds by hand but do not bother to hull them, for they are so tiny. Crush the seeds between stones and then add to the boiling water. Cover and cook slowly until a thin, red-colored gruel is formed. Cool a bit and eat this nutritious, whole grain cereal. Maple syrup and milk go well with this.

Candleberries

Bayberry or Candleberry
(*Myrica pensylvanica*)
Wax Myrtle or Candleberry (*Myrica cerifera*)

History

Since colonial days, the fruits of the bayberry and wax myrtle have been utilized in the east for making candles, soaps, and dyes. In early autumn, bushels of the globose, gray, waxy fruits were gathered and stored in a dry area until ready for use. The wax was extracted by bruising a large quantity of the berry-like fruit and boiling in water for several hours. The wax rose to the surface and was skimmed off or was allowed to cool and then removed. The berries were removed and new fruit and water were added to the pot until all the fruit had been spent. The brittle, green wax was added to about one-third tallow for candle-making or it was employed in soapmaking in which only four pounds of wax could yield forty pounds of soap. The water in which the berries had been repeatedly boiled was used as a blue dye or some walnut husks, leaves or bark were added to produce a black dye. *Myrica* leaves were used in tanning leather and were also dried and employed as a spice.

Habitat and Range

Myrica pensylvanica is found growing on dunes, dry hills, and near shores along the coast from Quebec to Louisiana. It is also found in a few places inland as well as around the shores of Lake Erie; *M. cerifera* grows

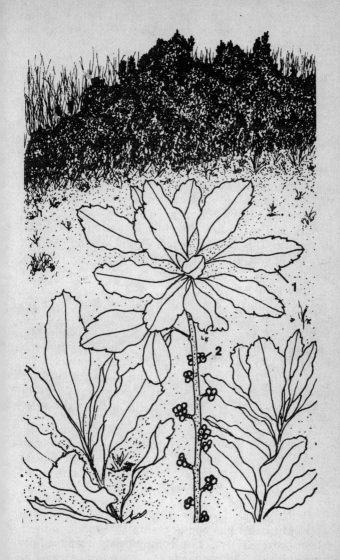

Bayberry. 1, Aromatic leaves—condiment. 2, Gray, aromatic bayberries, located below leaves—candles, soap, dye.

in damp sandy soil on the coast from southern New
Jersey to Florida and Texas and ranges inland to
Arkansas.

Description

The bayberry plant is a shrub with stiff branches that
tend to radiate upward and outward from the apical
end of the main stem; the flowers are borne in catkins
below the stem tips.

The bark of the older limbs is gray; it is an orange-
brown on some of the younger twigs. Leaves are only on
the stem tips and are deciduous. They grow to a length
of 1 to 3 inches, are elliptical in shape, sparsely toothed
(or untoothed) and have a fine down on the upper
surface and many tiny dots of wax are visible on the
underside. The flowers appear in midspring just before the leaves. By autumn, the waxy, gray, bayberries
are ready to harvest. The berries and crushed leaves
are highly aromatic.

The wax myrtle can be distinguished from the bayberry in that it can grow to the size of a small tree (up
to 30 feet or so in height), has narrow evergreen leaves,
and a smaller fruit. Where their range overlaps, the
bayberry and wax myrtle often interbreed, producing a
plant with the broad leaves of the bayberry and the
small fruits of the wax myrtle. This creates no problems because all the plants can be used in the same
way.

Candleberry Leaves
(a condiment)

Gather a quart or so of leaves. Wash, drain and
spread on a flat pan and dry in an attic room. Store in
clean, covered jars. Just before using, crumble into
small pieces with your hands.

These leaves are a fine seasoning for spaghetti sauce,
soups and chowders.

Candles

It takes a large amount of fruit to yield sufficient wax for candlemaking. Rather than gathering bushels of berries, try collecting a smaller amount and mix the fragrant green wax with paraffin.

1 gal candleberries   2 wicks
2 bars paraffin   4 6-oz cold drink cups

Gather berries in late summer or autumn and pick through them to remove any debris. Place in a large pan and cover with boiling water. Let the water cool a bit, then bruise the berries slightly with a potato masher, stir, and bring to a boil. Continue to boil over low heat for 3 or 4 hours. Stir occasionally and add boiling water to replace that which has evaporated. Turn off heat and allow to cool. The wax will rise to the surface and harden. If the berry wax has debris in it, reheat it in a little water and strain it through a cheese cloth. Pour boiling water through the cloth to remove the final bits of wax. Allow to cool and add this wax to the paraffin and melt over low heat.

The cold drink cups or any other suitable container can serve as molds. Double up the cups so that you have two reasonably leak-proof molds. Tie each wick onto a pencil and let this rest over each cup. Pour melted wax into the cups until they are almost full. Allow to cool a bit until a depression forms on top of the wax. Refill the depression with hard wax. When the candle is firm, peel away the cup.

Cranberry

The American Cranberry
(*Vaccinium macrocarpon*)
The Dwarf Cranberry (*Vaccinium oxycoccos*)

History

The Indians of the northeast were familiar with both the large, tart American cranberry and the smaller dwarf cranberry and collected quantities of them from September until snowfall. They were eaten as a raw or cooked fruit, added to pemmican and used to dye garments a colorful red. The nearly ripe berries were also made into a poultice for wounds. When the first settlers arrived in Massachusetts, they found an abundance of wild cranberries growing about them and with the help of the friendly Indians learned some of their varied uses. Reports from these early settlers tell that the Indians often added cooked cranberries as a relish for venison. The colonists began to serve cranberries with game and soon cranberry tarts, conserve, and pies were also being produced in colonial kitchens.

Attesting to the early popularity of this fruit is an account concerning King Charles II. He was enraged at the Massachusetts Bay Colony for coining "Pine Tree" shillings. To appease his wrath, the colonial authorities in 1677 sent him some of the prized foods of the New World: 3000 codfish, 2 hogs-heads of Indian corn, and 10 barrels of cranberries packed in water (a standard way of packing cranberries for distant markets).

Some reasons for the popularity of cranberries are their sharp, tart taste, their exceptional keeping qualities—we can vouch for this feature because we have made fine sauce from cranberries that were on the vine for one year—and their antiscorbutic properties. New England shipowners as well as Wisconsin lumbermen took note of this last quality and stores of cranberries were set aside and used on long voyages and in winter to ward off and treat the scourge of scurvy.

Eventually, the American cranberry became the cranberry of commerce and has been cultivated from the early part of the nineteenth century until the present. It has been used as a domestic fruit as well as for exportation. According to Dr. Porcher, during the Civil War, a bushel of American cranberries was bringing $8.00 on the London market. He also wrote that cranberry juice can be used to dye paper or linen purple.

Today, most cranberry production is still centered in Massachusetts, particularly in the area of Cape Cod, which is liberally supplied with ponds and lakes which are needed to flood the bogs during the winter and spring. The berries are also widely grown in Wisconsin, New Jersey, Washington, and Oregon.*

Habitat and Range

The American cranberry grows wild from Newfoundland to Manitoba and is found in the northeastern United States south to the mountains of Tennessee and North Carolina. The dwarf cranberry has a wider and more northerly distribution than the American cranberry, being found in northern Eurasia, Greenland, Newfoundland to Alaska, south from Alaska to California, and in the northeastern United States, south to the mountains of Virginia. Both types of cranberry favor the wet, acidic environment of bogs. The American cranberry is also found in swamps and along the wet shores of ponds and lakes.

---

* For additional information on the history and uses of cranberries write to Ocean Spray Inc., Main Street, Hanson, Massachusetts 02341. This company has a number of interesting, free pamphlets and recipes.

Description

The American cranberry is a low-growing, evergreen shrub with thin stems and tiny, egg-shaped leaves that grow up to ½ inch in length. The dainty flowers are borne at the tip of thin, elongate stalks and consist of a pink corona of four elongate petals that are turned back, thus exposing the yellow central floral parts. The fruit is a tart, red berry that grows up to ½ inch or more in diameter and remains on the plant all winter. The dwarf cranberry plant is a miniature version of the American cranberry but its leaves tend to be pointed at the apical end (tip) and are whitened beneath; the berry is pink to red in color and is extremely tart.

Collection and Preparation

Only a few generations ago, just as most Vermont farms had their own stand of sugar maples, many Cape Cod homesteads came replete with a cranberry bog or two. Unfortunately, progress and a dense human population have encroached upon these lovely, colorful areas and many cranberry bogs have been abandoned, filled in, or made part of "model communities." The happy side of this situation is that these former commercial bogs can be a good source of free cranberries and are available to those who seek them out in cranberry-producing states. In other areas, it is best to search for the wild berries in bogs, swamps, and on the spongy margins of lakes and ponds.

Cranberries are usually gathered in the autumn after a frost or two. Because they overwinter well and cling to the plant, they can also be collected in the winter or spring as long as they are not hidden by the snow. Firm, ripe cranberries keep exceptionally well and can be easily preserved without refrigeration or cooking. They can be kept for several months if they are picked on a clear, dry day and either loosely packed into burlap bags or placed into barrels of water and stored in a cool, dry area. They can be kept for several years if

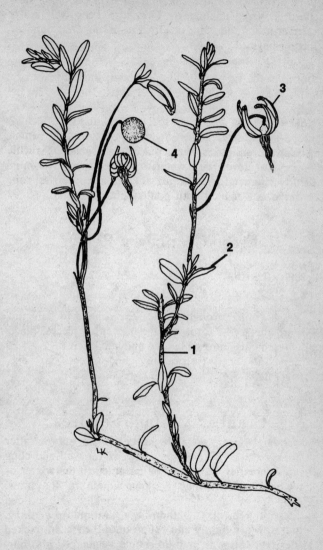

American Cranberry. 1, Thin stem. 2, Evergreen leaf. 3, Pink, graceful flower. 4, Red cranberry fruit—sauce, relish, pastry, beverage, dye.

they are dried in the sun and then placed into sterilized, covered containers. They also keep well under refrigeration and can be frozen in covered jars or freezer bags.

Cranberry Sauce

1 qt cranberries   2 cups raw sugar

Wash cranberries then place in a saucepan with sugar. Just cover with water, stir, and bring to a boil. Gently simmer for 5 minutes or until the berries pop.

Serve hot or cold with poultry and fish.

Fresh Cranberry Relish

2 cups cranberries   ½ cup honey
1 orange

Wash fruit thoroughly. Slice the orange in half and discard the seeds. Chop orange into small pieces. Place all ingredients into a blender and mix well.

Serve at once or store in clean, covered jars and refrigerate.

Cranberry-Apple Squares
(a rich pastry)

1 cup cranberries   1½ cups maple sugar
1 cup apples (sliced thinly)   1 cup water

Stew ingredients together in a saucepan 12 to 15 minutes. Mash lightly and spoon onto the baked pastry. If desired, top with a little maple sugar.

Dough

2 cups unbleached white
   flour
1 tbsp raw sugar
½ tsp baking powder

3 eggs (well beaten)
2 tbsp oil
¼ cup walnuts or hickory
   nuts (ground)

Preheat oven at 375°F. Sift flour, sugar and baking powder together, mix in remaining ingredients to make a soft dough. Roll out on a well floured board until the dough is about ¼ of an inch in thickness. Cut into small squares, place on a floured cookie sheet and bake until brown (about 10 minutes).

Winter

ICE FISHING

Introduction

Throughout the northeastern coastal plain and inland, one can find a wide assortment of fine winter ice fishing in lakes, ponds, and rivers. Under the layers of ice swim an abundance of delicious, edible fish, such as walleyes, yellow perch, northern pike, and pickerel. Ice fishing is a very chilly but pleasant and calming activity. The solitude and cold quiet beauty out on the ice is a fine winter tranquilizer, while sudden bursts of excitement occur when a flag goes up indicating that you have a fish on the line. To avoid the disappointment of losing your catch, you must remain calm and slowly play with the line. Your patience will be rewarded. Once you have pulled in your catch, you can more realistically dream of a succulent fresh fish dinner and see for yourself that winter foraging has its rewards.

Tips for the Novice Ice Fisherman

If you are new to ice fishing, take a look around your own area until you find some ice fishermen. Any winter weekend you can find these happy stalwarts out on the ice watching their traps and talking about their favorite subject—fishing. Go out onto the ice and observe the fishing techniques and get acquainted with the fishermen. Ice fishermen are an open and friendly group of individuals and most will be happy to share their knowledge.

If you decide to pursue ice fishing yourself, you will have to become more knowledgeable about the fishing areas and laws in your region. Inquire at your local fish and game department or at your chamber of commerce. These organizations were formed to serve the public and can supply you with enough information to keep you fishing for years.

Ice Fishing Bait and Gear

Live minnows are the most commonly used bait for ice fishing. Gear needed includes tip ups, hooks, nylon line, a minnow bucket, a sounder, and an ice chopper or ice auger. We suggest you use a sled to transport your gear to and from the ice.

When to Fish

Ice fishing can be pursued throughout most of the winter in the northeast, but the fishing is best from midwinter to ice out. What time of day to fish depends on the fish you are seeking, because some species bite most readily at sunrise or sunset and others are most active during the day.

Common Fish Caught Through the Ice

Many fish are not recommended for ice fishing because they are illegal to take in winter or they are in deeper water in a quiescent state.

In general, we have chosen fish more likely to be pulled through the ice, although the basses, particularly the smallmouth, are less commonly caught this way.

Perch

The Perch Family (Percidae)

Introduction

This is a common group of tasty freshwater game fish. The perches are characterized by a dorsal fin that is separated into an anterior spiny section and a posterior soft portion. All the perches are predaceous, feeding upon aquatic insect larvae, crayfish, and small fish, with the larger species being especially piscivorous.

Some of the Percidae more popular with the ice fishermen are the walleye, sauger, and yellow perch which are abundant and still active at very cold water temperatures. Some experimental data is available indicating that the yellow perch is most active during the day and hence most likely to be caught in the daylight hours, while the walleye begins to move about and actively feeds in the evening. Our ice-fishing experience correlates fairly closely with these more scientific studies in that we seem to catch most of our perch in the early afternoon, while the walleye start to bite heavily around dusk.

Range, Habitat, and Description

The Yellow Perch (*Perca flavescens*)

The yellow perch is a medium-size fish that grows to a length of about 1 foot. It can be easily recognized by its golden body color, red to orange ventral and anal fins and by the prominent blackish vertical bars that line its sides. However, young perch are more silvery in color and the vertical crossbars are less evident.

This species is widely distributed in ponds, lakes, rivers, and larger streams throughout the northeastern United States and southeastern Canada. It has also been widely introduced into other areas.

The Walleye (*Stizostedion vitreum*)

Walleyes are darker colored, larger, and more elongate than the yellow perch. They grow to a length of 3 feet, have many sharp, pointed teeth, and the lower lobe of the tail fin tends to be white. They do not have vertical bars on their body. There is usually a black spot of color at the posterior end of the spinous dorsal fin.

These large, delicious-tasting fish are most common in lakes, streams, and rivers throughout the northeast and are distributed in the northwest to British Columbia.

The Sauger (*Stizostedion canadense*)

Saugers look much like the walleye but they grow only to about 15 inches in length and are a more slender fish. They can be readily distinguished from their larger relative in that the lower lobe of their tail fin is not whitish, but it is a mottled black throughout. Also, there is no black spot on the basal part of the spinous dorsal fin, but there is one at the base of the pectoral fins.

Saugers have the same general range and habitat as the walleye and they have been introduced into a variety of other locations.

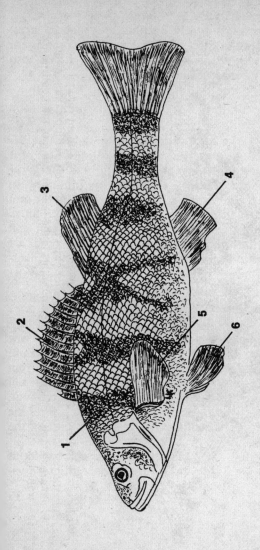

Yellow Perch. 1, Rather elongate yellow-gold body with prominent blackish, vertical bars. 2, Spinous portion separated from 3, soft portion of dorsal fin. 4, Anal fin. 5, Pectoral fin. 6, Pelvic fin. 4, 5, and 6 are red to orange. Excellent sautéed.

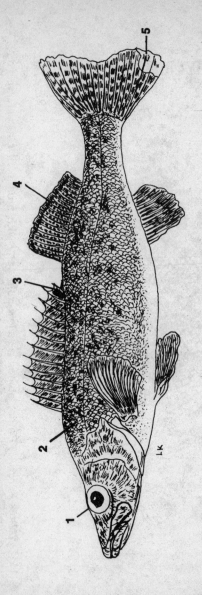

Walleye. 1, Large eye. 2, Elongate, usually dark olive colored body without vertical bars. 3, Spinous portion of dorsal fin with dark spot at its base. 4, Soft portion of dorsal fin. 5, White area at base of tail fin. In our opinion this is the finest tasting of the freshwater fish—trout included.

Preparation

Sautéed Yellow Perch with Capers
(for 4)

4 medium-size perch	1 lemon
½ cup unbleached white flour	½ lb butter
½ tsp salt	4 tbsp capers
	½ cup lard

Clean and wash perch. Lightly sprinkle salt on the inside of fish and dip into flour. Sear in hot lard, then reduce heat to medium and sauté slowly on both sides until golden brown. Place the fish on brown paper to drain. Pour the lard from the fish skillet, and place the butter and capers in the pan. Sauté over medium heat for 2 minutes, squeeze lemon into the mixture, and stir. Pour the caper sauce over the fish and serve at once.

Broiled Yellow Perch Filets
(for 4)

4 medium-size perch fileted	3 tbsp corn oil
1 lemon	¼ lb butter

Place the filets on a sheet pan. Squeeze lemon juice and a few drops of oil over the fish. Place under broiler and cook for about 10 minutes. Serve with lemon wedges and drawn butter.

Walleye and Sauger

The walleye and sauger are among the finest white meat fish, whose taste can be compared favorably with any trout.

Sautéed Walleye with Nut Sauce
(for 2)

1 large walleye
1 tsp salt
½ cup unbleached white
   flour

1 lemon
¼ lb butter
¼ cup wild nuts

Clean and wash fish, salt lightly on the inside. Dip in flour and sauté in skillet on medium heat, cooking slowly until golden brown on both sides. While the fish is cooking, sauté the wild nuts in butter over medium heat for 3 to 4 minutes. When the fish is done, place it on a platter, squeeze the lemon over it, and top with the nut sauce.

Baked Walleye
(for 2)

1 large fish
1 lemon
¼ lb butter

1 tsp thyme
salt and pepper to taste

Preheat oven to 350°F. Clean and wash fish and place in a deep baking dish. Squeeze the lemon over the fish and place chunks of butter on the fish. Sprinkle on the thyme, salt and pepper. Cover and bake for 20 minutes. Just before serving, remove cover and brown fish in the broiler for a couple of minutes.

Pike

The Pike Family (Esocidae)

Introduction

This is a highly predaceous family whose members feed primarily on smaller fish, and crayfish, but which have also been known to consume amphibians, birds, and even mammals. They are characterized by their long, narrow bodies, with the soft rayed dorsal fin located well towards the posterior and by the elongate, flattened, beaklike jaws containing many sharp teeth.

The members of this family, such as the northern pike, muskellunge, and various species of pickerels, are all popular with ice fishermen, although they are a bit bony for eating. Observers have noted that the northern pike and pickerel are most active during the day. Our ice-fishing experiences confirm this, as our best catches were made during the early afternoon.

Range, Habitat, and Description

The Eastern Chain Pickerel (*Esox niger*)

This fish grows to about 2 feet in length and can be recognized by the chain-like pattern of dark markings on its back and sides.

The members of this family are further distinguished from one another by the scalation of the cheek and gill cover; the pickerels have both fully scaled.

The chain pickerel is commonly found in lakes,

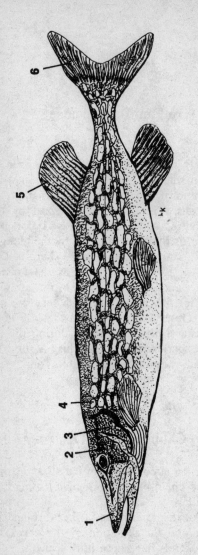

Eastern Chain Pickerel. 1, Flat, beaklike jaws. 2, Scale-covered cheek. 3, Scale-covered operculum. 4, Elongate body with chainlike markings. 5, Soft portion of dorsal fin. 6, Deeply forked tail fin. Rather bony, but fine for chowder.

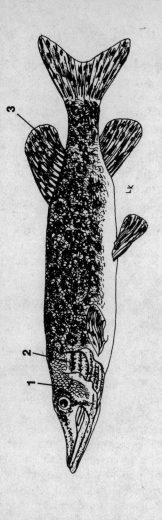

Northern Pike. Similar in general structure to the pickerels. However, note that cheek (1) is fully scaled, but only the top half of the operculum (2) is scaled—in the pickerels both structures are fully scaled. Also, all the fins are usually spotted as shown in the dorsal fin (3). We prefer to serve this fish poached.

ponds, and shallow streams east of the Appalachians from Canada south to Florida and west to Texas.

The Northern Pike (*Esox lucius*)

This rugged species grows to about 3½ feet in length and can be distinguished from the chain pickerel by its body color, which consists of light spots on a darker background, and by its scalation, the cheek cover being completely scaled but only the upper portion of the gill cover is scaled

The northern pike is a very important game fish of northern streams and lakes and is found in the eastern United States north of the Ohio River, ranging in the northwest to Alaska. It is also found in Asia and in Europe.

Preparation

Pickerel Corn Chowder
(for 4)

1 large pickerel	1 large onion (minced)
salt and pepper to taste	2 large potatoes (diced)
¼ lb butter	1 lb can of corn
1 clove garlic (minced)	1 cup milk or cream

Wash and clean pickerel. Place the fish in a wire basket or on top of a rack and set into a deep pan. Add enough salted water to cover the fish and simmer over medium heat until tender. When cooked, pick the pickerel meat away from the bone and set aside. Sauté the garlic and onions in butter until they are light brown and then add to the fish broth. Stir in the diced potatoes and boil for 15 minutes. Add the corn, milk, and pickerel meat, and simmer for 15 more minutes.

Poached Northern Pike
with Hollandaise Sauce
(for 4)

1 medium-sized northern pike	1 qt salted water

Clean and wash fish and slice crosswise into 4 or so pieces. Place the pieces of fish into a wire basket or on top of a rack and set this into a deep pan. Cover the fish with salted water and simmer until tender. Remove fish, place on platter, pour the hollandaise sauce (see page 45 for the recipe) over the fish and serve at once.

Sunfish

The Sunfish Family (Centrarchidae)

Introduction

This family* is characterized by fish that have rather compressed bodies and a single dorsal fin typically formed by the fusion of the spinous anterior dorsal fin with the soft, rayed posterior dorsal. Members of the sunfish family include the common panfish, such as the bluegills and pumpkinseeds, as well as the more popular and crafty game fish, the basses. Most of the species in the sunfish family prefer warmer lakes and streams and are found throughout southeastern Canada and the eastern United States. Many members of this family

* For additional information concerning this family see pages 47–51.

have been introduced into various parts of the world. Farm ponds in the southeast are commonly stocked with bluegills and largemouth bass. The bluegills feed upon microscopic plants and animals and the bass eat a variety of foods as well as consuming the bluegills.

Most of the Centrachidae are known as easy species to catch and are quite active in spring, early summer, and in autumn when they are readily hooked even by novice anglers. But as winter sets in, most members of this family go into deeper water and remain in a relatively quiescent state until after ice out when they move again to the shallows and start to feed actively.

This seasonal activity would lead one to expect that pulling in a member of the sunfish family through the ice would be a rare occasion. This is often true, but sometimes one gets lucky and pulls in a fine largemouth or smallmouth bass; once a group is located you might come home with several. Even more common types to catch through the ice are the black crappie and white crappie which are the largest of the sunfish (excluding the bass) and are the two species in this family that are very active all winter. They can be most readily caught in the evening or at sunrise and sunset.

Range, Habitat, and Description

The Black Crappie (*Pomoxis nigromaculatus*)

The black crappie grows up to 1 foot in length and is silvery mottled with dark green and black. Its vertical fins are spotted and its short snout is turned up.

These fish prefer clear lakes, ponds, and rivers and are common throughout the upper Mississippi valley and the Great Lakes south to Florida and Texas. Due to their popularity with fishermen, the black and white crappies have been transplanted to waters throughout the United States.

The White Crappie (*Pomoxis annularis*)

The white crappie grows up to 1 foot in length, has vertical stripes on its sides, and has about the same body coloration as the black crappie.

This species favors the more turbid lakes, ponds, sloughs and rivers and occupies about the same range as the black crappie.

The Largemouth Bass (*Micropterus salmoides*)

These fish grow up to 2 feet or more in length and can be distinguished by their body coloration and their mouth size. The back and sides of the body are green; the ventral surface is silvery. A longitudinal black band runs along the sides of the body, but tends to fade away as the fish ages. The upper jaw extends beyond the eye. Also note, a deep notch almost separates the spinous and soft portions of the dorsal fin.

Largemouth bass are common in eastern streams, rivers, lakes, and ponds and they range in the southwest as far as Mexico. They have also been widely introduced into many areas west of the Mississippi.

The Smallmouth Bass (*Micropterus dolomieu*)

The smallmouth bass grows to about 1½ feet in length and can usually be distinguished from the largemouth bass by its upper jaw, which extends to, but not beyond, the eye and by its more bronze body color with vertical bars on its sides.

This species prefers cooler and deeper waters than the largemouth bass and does not range quite as far south. It is absent from the Gulf coast streams.

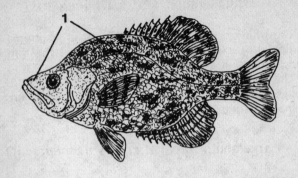

Black Crappie (1), with short turned-up snout; silvery body marked with splotches of dark green and black.

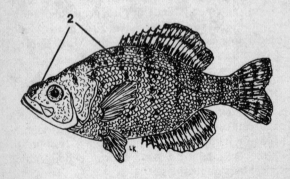

White Crappie (2), with straighter snout and has dark vertical bars on the body. Serve sautéed.

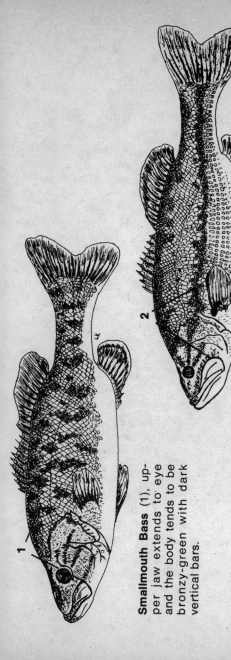

Smallmouth Bass (1), upper jaw extends to eye and the body tends to be bronzy-green with dark vertical bars.

Largemouth Bass (2), upper jaw extends beyond eye, and in young fish greenish body has a longitudinal dark band running its length—band disappears in older animals. Delicious broiled, baked or sautéed.

Preparation

Sautéed Crappies with Cucumber Sauce
(for 2)

4 medium-size fish
1 cup unbleached
   white flour
¼ cup corn oil

¼ lb butter
1 cucumber (sliced thinly)
1 lemon

Clean and wash fish, salt on the inside. Dip in flour and sauté in oil on both sides until golden brown. While the fish is cooking, sauté the cucumber slices in butter for 3 to 4 minutes on a high flame. Squeeze the lemon into the cucumber and stir. Pour the hot cucumber sauce over the cooked fish and serve.

Sautéed Bass with Beer Batter
(for 4)

2 large bass
2 tbsp flour
2 cups Bisquick
12 oz beer

1 tsp salt
½ tsp pepper
3 tbsp butter

Clean and filet the fish. Combine Bisquick, condiments and beer in a bowl, mix well. Flour the fish filets and then dip into the Bisquick batter. Sauté the filets in butter until they are a deep golden brown.

Broiled Bass
(for 4)

2 medium-size bass   corn oil
salt

Clean and wash the fish. Lightly salt the inside of
the fish, sprinkle oil on the outside, and place on a
grill. Broil the fish, turning it over a couple of times
until it is tender.

Serve with lemon and butter.

Fish Shashlik
(for 6)

When ice fishing, the catch usually will consist of a
variety of edible species. Therefore, you can cook a
delightful dinner with the assorted catch mixed together.

3 lbs of cleaned fish   1 lb bacon
2 large peppers (chopped)   ½ lb drawn butter
3 firm tomatoes cut in halves 3 cloves garlic (chopped)
1 large onion (sliced)   salt and pepper to taste
½ lb mushrooms

Clean, bone, and wash fish. Cut into 3 inch squares.
Roll the fish chunks in the strips of bacon. Alternate the
chunks of fish, green peppers, tomatoes, onions, and
mushrooms on a skewer. *Repeat until skewer is full.*
Arrange on sheet and sprinkle the top with chopped
garlic, salt and pepper. Broil for 15 minutes or until
cooked. Serve with drawn butter, and enjoy.

Conifers

History

The conifers have a long history of usage by peoples of northern latitudes as sources of emergency foods during times of famine. Perhaps the most common food prepared from these plants is a flour that was obtained by drying and grinding the inner bark, which was usually collected in the spring. This flour was used for breads and to thicken soups.

Another vital role of the conifers was the use of their foliage and bark by some northern tribes of Indians as the main ingredient in their antiscorbutic winter drinks. It is recorded that decoctions made from hemlock, northern white cedar, spruce or white pine were used by several tribes as scurvy preventives as well as to treat this vitamin-C deficiency disease. Indeed, the men of Jacques Cartier's party, who discovered the St. Lawrence River, were scurvy-ridden until the Laurentian Iroquois gave them a decoction of the bark and leaves of what most scholars agree to have been hemlock, which greatly alleviated their symptoms. It was the year 1536 and Cartier had already lost 25 of his men, who had slowly died from the ravages of scurvy. A more detailed account of their hardships, taken from Biggar (1924, pp. 212–213), is given below.

"One day our captain, seeing the disease so general and his men so striken by it, * * * caught sight of a band of Indians approaching from Stadadona (Quebec), and among them was Dom Agaya whom he had seen 10 or 12 days previous to this, extremely ill with the very disease his own men were suffering from; for one of his legs above the knee had swollen to the size of a

2-year-old baby, and the sinews had become con-
tracted. His teeth had gone bad and decayed, and the
gums had rotted and become tainted. The captain, seeing Dom Agaya well * * * was delighted, hoping to
learn what had healed him, in order to cure his own
men. And when the Indians had come near the fort,
the captain inquired of him, what had cured him of his
sickness. Dom Agaya replied that he had been healed
by the juice of the leaves of a tree and the dregs of
these, and that this was the only way to cure sickness.
Upon this the captain asked him if there was not some
of it thereabouts, and to show it to him that he might
heal his servant who (in his opinion) had caught the
disease when staying in Chief Donnacona's wigwam at
Canada, being unwilling that he should know how many
sailors were ill. Thereupon Dom Agaya sent two squaws
with our captain to gather some of it; and they brought
back 9 or 10 branches. They showed us how to grind
the bark and the leaves and to boil the whole in water.
Of this one should drink every 2 days, and place the
dregs on the legs where they were swollen and af-
fected. According to them this tree cured every kind of
disease. They call it in their language Annedda."

Some other foods that have been obtained from the
conifers of the northeast are juniper berries, which are
used in flavoring gin and are a tasty nibble; the roasted
seeds of the white pine, which are nutritious; the new
shoots of larch and spruce, which can be eaten fresh
or added to woodland pottages; and, finally, the pitch
of the balsam fir, which can be eaten as is for a concentrated emergency food.

TABLE 11

Habitat, Range, and Description of the Conifers

Species	Habitat	Range
Balsam Fir (*Abies balsamea*)	Woods	Labrador and eastern Canada to the northeastern states and in the mountains to Virginia
Eastern Hemlock (*Tsuga canadensis*)	Hilly and open woods	Eastern Canada and eastern states to Minnesota and along the mountains to Georgia and Alabama
Dwarf Juniper Common Juniper (*Juniperus communis*)	Dry, open pastures and slopes	Labrador to Alaska northern states and in the mountains to Georgia. Also Eurasia
Larch (*Larix laricina*)	Swamps in southern part of its range, farther north it is in the uplands	Transcontinental Canada and the northeastern states
Northern White Cedar Eastern Arbor Vitae (*Thuja occidentalis*)	Swamps and woods	Southeastern Canada, northeastern states and along the mountains to North Carolina and Tennessee
Spruce (several species) (*Picea*)	Woods and uplands	Canada and northeastern states. Also Eurasia
White Pine (*Pinus Strobus*)	Woods	Southern Canada, Lake states, northeastern states to the mountains of Georgia and Tennessee

Description

Profile: Medium, 40–60' tall, steeple shaped, branches ascending

Leaves: Flat, short about 1¼" long, underside silvery, leaves have a circular base

Cones: About 3" long, erect

Profile: Medium, 60–70' tall, tip more rounded than fir, loose irregular branching

Leaves: Flat, short, about ½" long, attached by slender *stalks,* underside has 2 white bands running along its length

Cones: About ¾" long, borne at the tips of twigs

Profile: Shrubs or small trees

Leaves: About ¾" long, sharp, occur in whorls of 3

Cones: Blue-black, edible berry-like cone

Profile: Small to medium, 40–50' tall, pyramidal shape

Leaves: Deciduous about 1" long, most are arranged in bundles, some single

Cones: ½–¾" long, erect

Profile: Small to medium, 40–50' tall, conical-shaped

Leaves: Yellow green, on leading tips almost ½" long, on lateral branchlets are flat and scale-like

Cone: Small, ⅓–½" long, bell-shaped

Profile: Small to large, 30–90' tall, sharply steeple shaped

Leaves: Short, about ½" long, stiff, sharp, 4-sided, extend from all sides of the twig

Cones: Small, about 2" long, hanging

Profile: Large, 80–200' tall, horizontal branches

Leaves: Large, 3–5", in bundles of 5

Cones: Oblong, 4–8" long

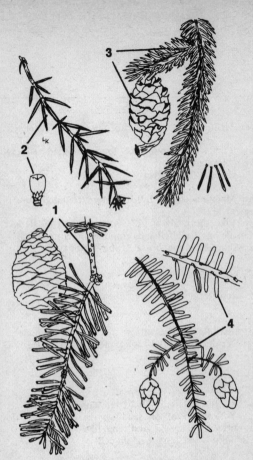

Balsam Fir (1), with erect cone and flattened leaves which have a circular base. Pitch—emergency food. **Dwarf Juniper** (2), illustrating the elongate, sharply tipped leaves arranged in whorls of three. Also, blue-to-black cone (juniper berry)—flavoring or nibble. **Spruce** (3), twig with cone and stiff, sharply pointed, four-sided leaves which extend from all sides of the twig. Leaves —tea; leaves and twigs—beer. **Eastern Hemlock** (4), with cones hanging from the end of a twig; flattened leaves attached to twig by a slender stalk—tea and "gravy." Underside of leaf has two white bands running along its length.

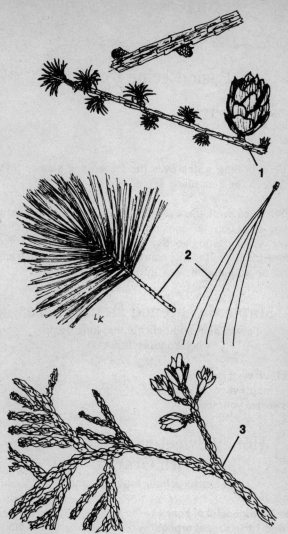

Larch (1), twig with bundles of deciduous leaves and erect cone—seeds within, used as a nibble. Top twig illustrates leaf buds. **White Pine** (2), with elongate leaves arranged in groups of five—tea. Also seeds of cone as nibble. **Northern White Cedar** (3), with cones and flattened, scalelike leaves—tea.

Conifer Teas

Basic Recipe for Tea

¼ cup freshly picked stem
   tips with leaves per cup
   of water

Pour boiling water over the leaves and stems, cover and steep for 5 minutes. Serve.

While each of the evergreen teas has its own unique flavor and can be consumed without additives, their taste is a bit too woodsy for most palates. We recommend the following combinations which can transform an unpalatable tea into a tasty one.

Maple Sweetened Hemlock Tea
(a soothing and delicate tea, long used by the Iroquois Indians)

Add sufficient maple syrup
   or maple sugar to slightly
   sweeten your tea

Honey Sweetened Spruce Tea with Orange
(a tea to delight most gourmets)

Use 1 teaspoonful of honey
   and 1 thin slice of orange
   per cup of tea

Squeeze the oil from the rind and the juice from the pulp into the tea. Stir in the honey until it dissolves. Serve.

White Pine with Sugar Tea

The flavor of this mild-tasting tea is enhanced by the addition of raw sugar. Add 1 to 2 teaspoonfuls of sugar per cup of pine tea.

White Cedar Tea with Maple Syrup
(a palatable drink when prepared as described below)

Plain cedar tea has a very medicinal taste and is rather bitter especially if it is strong. A dilute tea can be made by steeping about ¾ of a teaspoon of the leaves per cup of water and adding 1 teaspoonful of maple syrup. This tea is said to be helpful for those who suffer from rheumatism.

Antiscorbutic Winter Beverages

Spruce and Maple Beer
(an enjoyable late winter drink)

10 qt water
2 qt maple syrup
3 qt spruce stem tips
   with leaves

1 pkg dry yeast

Mix the water and maple syrup in a large pan and bring to a boil. Remove from heat, add the spruce, cover and let steep for 2 hours. Mix the yeast with a little bit of the liquid in a dish and then stir this into the mixture. Cover the pan with a clean cloth and place it in a cool room (about 60°F). After 24 hours, remove the spruce and pour the liquid through a sieve into a clean container. Cover with a cloth and let it "work" for 10 to 12 days. Strain the liquid, cool, and serve.

Maple Sweetened Hemlock Gravy
(an old Iroquois recipe)

½ cup hemlock leaves   2 tsp maple sugar
   per cup of water   per cup of water

Add enough boiling water to cover the leaves, cover the pan, and steep for 10 minutes. Sweeten with maple sugar. Serve as a dunk for corn bread.

White Pine Chew
(an emergency source of sugar and starch)

You can gather the inner bark of this evergreen year-round, but it is easier to peel it away from the trunk in the spring. We recommend the white pine because it is sweeter and less astringent than the other evergreens discussed here. Choose large trees with few side branches because they are less resinous than smaller, more branched trees. Separate the pliable inner bark from the hard outer bark and eat it fresh. It is chewy and sweet and after a few minutes you can spit out the more fibrous part. It is a good source of carbohydrate if you are stranded in the woods. Needless to say, in the interest of conservation, this foodstuff should only be used in times of great need.

Larch Stem Tips and Seeds
(a reasonably tasty winter source of emergency food)

If you are in larch territory and in need of nutriment, gather the cones and young orange-brown twig tips of the larch tree. The twig tips can be eaten as is and you can pick the seeds out of the cones and eat them fresh.

Sumac

(*Rhus*—several species)

History

Several species of sumac with red berry-like fruits are found throughout the United States. These plants were used by the Indians as a source of leaves to smoke alone or with tobacco, and for the red fruit which was used to make a tart drink. An interesting nonculinary use of the sumac fruit was reported by Bartram (1940). He tells how the Creek and Cherokee Indians rubbed the furry covering of the sumac fruits into their hair then tightly tied it up with a handkerchief for overnight. In the morning the hair was combed out and clear bear's oil was used as a dressing. Presumably this treatmeat helped preserve the rich black color and splendor of the hair.

Habitat and Range

There are three common edible red sumacs in the northeast: the staghorn sumac (*Rhus typhina*), the smooth sumac (*R. glabra*), and the dwarf sumac (*R. copàllinum*). All inhabit open, dry, rocky or gravelly soil.

Description

The edible sumacs are small trees or shrubs with stout, soft branches, feathery compound leaves, and terminal clusters of red berry-like fruit which are pyramidal in shape. The three edible types can be distinguished from one another by the amount of hair on

337

Staghorn Sumac. 1, Profile of plant in winter to illustrate the pyramidal shaped fruit clusters—tea, soup, cooling drink, sauce. 2, Compound leaf with 19 rather elongate, toothed leaflets.

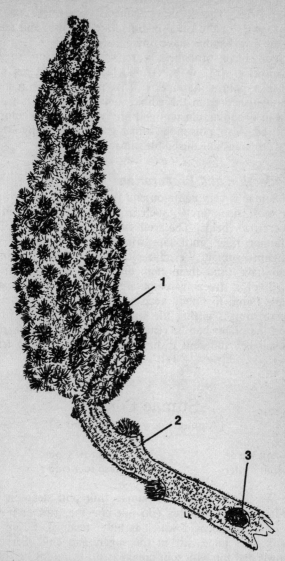

Staghorn Sumac, Close-up. Twig bearing (1), the hairy, red fruit clusters—tea, soup, cooling drink, sauce. 2, Densely hairy twig. 3, Bud.

their twigs. The staghorn sumac has a thick coat of hair; twigs of the smooth sumac are hairless; and those of the dwarf sumac have tiny hairs.

You have probably heard of the poison sumac (*Rhus Vernix*), whose fruits, leaves, and stems can cause a painful dermatitis. This plant can be readily distinguished from the edible sumacs because its fruits are in drooping clusters and are ivory white in color—not red. Also, poisonous sumac grows in swampy areas, not dry areas like the edible sumacs.

Collection and Preparation

Sumac is very common and should be found growing in most open areas, such as along roadsides and in overgrown fields. The fruit can be gathered from late summer right until late winter. Our favorite is the staghorn sumac. We have picked these fruits in winter and have used them immediately, or stored them at 70°F or at freezing temperatures for three weeks and have found that they keep well. The biggest virtues of these sumacs is that the fruits are available all winter and the plants can be readily located. We devised some deliciously different dishes employing the sumac fruit.

Sumac Borscht
(A unique new cold soup, for 2)

2 cups water	2 tbsp raw sugar
2 fruit clusters	4 tbsp sour cream

Wash and crush the sumac fruit and steep in hot water for 15 minutes (do not boil the fruit or it will release tannic acid which is bitter tasting). Strain the pink, tart juice, stir in the sugar, and chill. Serve in bowls and top with sour cream.

We highly recommend this light and delicious new soup.

Sumac Cream Sauce
(A delicious new topping for poached eggs,
fish or green vegetables, for 2)

4 tbsp butter
3 tbsp unbleached
 white flour
1½ cups sumac juice
 (prepared as described

above, omitting the
 sour cream)
2 tbsp grated Parmesan
 cheese (optional)

Melt the butter in a frying pan over low heat and
gradually stir in the flour. Then slowly stir in the sumac
juice until you have a smooth cream sauce.

Top poached eggs with this sauce and serve. For
fish and vegetable dishes, add the cream sauce to the
cooked preparation, sprinkle on Parmesan cheese, and
then place the preparation under a broiler for 3 or 4
minutes. Serve and enjoy.

Sumac Tea
(an old Indian drink)

1 fruit cluster per 2 cups
 of water

maple sugar, to taste

Prepare the juice as described in borscht recipe, add
sugar to taste and serve hot or cold.

Wintergreen and Partridgeberry

Wintergreen, "Petit Thé des Bois,"
Checkerberry, Teaberry, Mountain Tea
(*Gaultheria procumbens*)
Partridgeberry (*Mitchella repens*)

History

The use of the wintergreen plant for tea was said to be discovered by Dr. Jean-François Gaultier (1708?–1756), who was a naturalist and court physician in Quebec. This *thé du Canada* was so popular that the generic name, *Gaultheria,* was named after him. We do have a reference citing the use of wintergreen tea by some Iroquois tribes but have not ascertained whether this use predated Gaultier's discovery. Whatever the case may be, the wintergreen plant provides a tasty berry that can be found from fall to spring and leaves that can be collected year-round and used for teas or flavoring.

Habitat and Range

The genus *Gaultheria* is represented by herbs and shrubs found in North and South America, Australia and Asia; *G. procumbens* is found in clearings around bogs and ponds and in open woodlands from Newfoundland south to Georgia and Alabama and northwest to Manitoba.

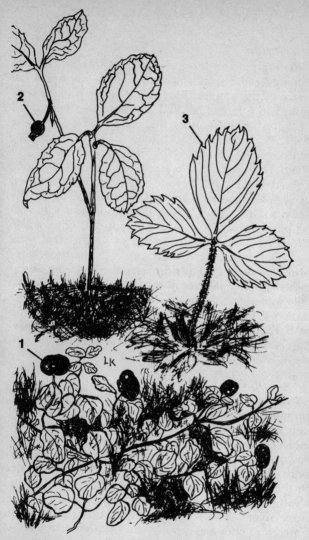

Partridgeberry (1). Note the creeping stems and rather rounded leaves with their whitish veins and red fruit—nibble and flavoring. **Wintergreen** (2), with red fruit—nibble, flavoring; firm, evergreen leaves—nibble, tea, flavoring, syrup. **Wild Strawberry** (3), leaf—nibble, tea.

Description

Wintergreen is a low-growing plant with an elongate creeping slender stem which grows on or just below the surface of the ground. The upright fertile branches are about 3 to 6 inches tall and in midsummer bear small urn-shaped white flowers that hang down under the leaves. The flowers are soon followed by the bright red berrylike edible fruits which cling to the plant over winter. The alternate, evergreen leaves grow to a length of about 1½ inches; they are soft when newly emerged but soon become hard and rather rigid. The upper surface is a dark, shiny green sometimes flecked with reddish-purple areas; the underside is a dull olive green.

Another low-growing evergreen plant that you might find in wintergreen territory is the partridgeberry (*Mitchella repens*). Partridgeberry can be easily distinguished from wintergreen as it grows in dense carpets, while wintergreen growth is more patchy. In addition, its leaves are faintly marked with white veins and they do not have a wintergreen aroma. However, the red partridgeberries are edible.

Collection and Preparation

When searching for wintergreen during the winter, you must look under evergreens, where the snow is not deep, or on the sunnier woodland slopes and clearings, where the snow has melted, thus revealing these low-growing plants. The tiny evergreen plants are quite obvious as they stand erect in the cold. Pick one of the hard, dark green or reddish leaves, crush it and smell. It will have a distinct wintergreen odor if you have the correct plant. The red berries have an even stronger wintergreen odor and taste.

The leaves can be used fresh or they can be dried in a slow oven (200°F) for 20 minutes and then stored in clean, dry screw-capped jars.

Wintergreen Tea
(a year-round woodland drink, for 1)

¼ cup wintergreen leaves   1½ cups boiling water

Add the wintergreen leaves to the boiling water, cover, and simmer over low heat for 30 minutes or more. If desired, serve with honey or sugar.

Wintergreen Syrup
(¾ cup yield)

1 cup wintergreen leaves   2 cups water
2 cups raw sugar

Combine ingredients and boil over medium heat for 20 minutes or until the mixture thickens.

Use this aromatic wintergreen syrup on French toast, pancakes, crepes, waffles, or ice cream.

Wintergreen Milk Tea
(a soothing drink for winter colds, for 1)

¼ cup wintergreen leaves   1¼ cups milk
1 tsp honey

Simmer the leaves and milk together for 10 minutes. Strain out the liquid. Stir in the honey and serve. The milk quickly captures the wintergreen flavor and aroma. A delicious drink even if you do not have a cold.

Wintergreen Butter

¼ lb butter (unsalted)   ¼ cup finely chopped dried
1 tsp honey   wintergreen leaves

Remove the center vein from the wintergreen leaves
and crush the remaining part into tiny pieces. Pick out
any other fibers that remain. Soften the butter and combine all ingredients. Mold into a ball and refrigerate
until ready to use.

This is a mildly aromatic topping for toast.

Wintergreen Berry Cocktail
(for 2)

½ cup wintergreen berries   4 oz gin
2 tsp raw sugar   1 cup shaved ice

Crush the berries and mix with sugar. Add the gin
and shaved ice and mix in a shaking glass or in a
blender.

This is a refreshing reward for those who forage in
winter.

Note. If you do go foraging for wintergreen
and come up with only partridgeberry plants, you
can try the red fruits as a nibble or add them to a
fruit cup as a garnish. Or, you might like to take
a few of these berry plants home—if you can get
to the roots. The partridgeberry plant can be easily
grown indoors; many people gather it and place it
in transparent bowls with moss so as to be afforded
the beauty of its glossy green leaves and bright red
berries throughout the winter.

Winter Cress

(*Barbarea*—several species)

History

Winter cress has been used as a foodstuff by Europeans for years and was called the Herb of St. Barbara as the seeds of *Barbarea verna* were customarily sown in the middle of December near St. Barbara's day. The generic name, *Barbarea,* resulted either from this tradition or from the fact that the new young leaves could be gathered on St. Barbara's day. In North America, winter cress is used as a salad plant by French-Canadians and is utilized both as a cooked vegetable and as a salad plant by many people in our southeastern states. In the northeast it is relished mainly by country people and by European immigrants who have continued the warm tradition of gathering and eating wild vegetables.

Habitat and Range

Barbarea is represented by several species of biennials and perennials found in Europe, Asia and North America. The two most common species of winter cress found in the northeast, (*B. vulgaris* and *B. verna*), are weed plants introduced from Europe and now naturalized here. They both like moisture and are found in fields, waste areas, damp woods, roadsides, and meadows.

Description

During winter, these plants tend to form low-growing

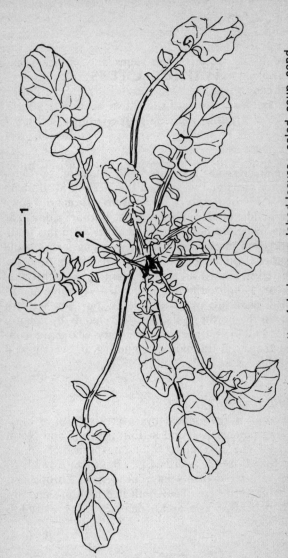

Winter Cress. 1, Low-growing rosette of dark green, lobed leaves—salad, soup, sandwiches. Region from which the stem will emerge. Flowering stems—fritters.

rosettes of dark green leaves that hug the ground, but
when the snow is dispelled and the stem emerges, they
take on a more upright posture. The sturdy stems rapidly grow to a height of 1 to 2 feet and tend to branch
above in *B. vulgaris*. The stems and branches have
leaves along most of their length, but are leafless at the
distal end, which bears the spike-like cluster of flowers.
The basal leaves grow to a length of about 6 to 8 inches
and have a rather rounded terminal lobe and one to
several pairs of smaller lateral lobes; the upper leaves
are smaller and bear fewer lateral lobes. The flowers
are yellow with the four petals characteristic of the
mustard family (Cruciferae) and the elongate seed pods
grow to 1 to 2 inches in length.

Collection and Preparation

Winter cress is a favorite vegetable for the forager
because it produces new leaves during winter thaws.
Both the young leaves and the newly emerged flower
stalks are edible.

During winter the leaves of this plant can be gathered and eaten, but as the weather becomes warmer
they become too bitter for most palates. However, by
midspring the countryside is dotted with the golden
blossoms of winter cress. Gather the flowering branches
and use as a vegetable. We recommend that they be
sautéed or used for flower fritters.

Cream of Winter Cress Soup
(for 4)

¼ lb butter	1 qt milk
1 medium-size onion (chopped)	2 cups winter cress leaves
1 cup unbleached white flour	4 vegetable bouillon cubes
	salt and pepper to taste

Sauté the onions lightly in butter, add the flour, and

make smooth by stirring. Slowly pour in the milk, stirring constantly. Now add winter cress and bouillon
cubes. Season to taste and let simmer on low heat until
greens are tender. Stir occasionally to prevent the con-
tents from burning.

Winter Cress Salad
(for 2)

¾ lb winter cress leaves   raw onion
½ cup wine vinegar   salt and papper to taste
⅓ cup olive oil

Wash the leaves thoroughly. Beat the oil and vinegar,
and season to taste. Pour over greens and serve.

Note. Winter cress has a sharp and bitter taste
for the average palate, but it can be substituted
half-and-half with other greens for a milder salad.

Winter Cress Flower Fritters

Winter cress flowering stalks can be collected when
they emerge in spring and prepared in the same way
described for elder flower fritters on page 000 but omit
the brandy and the berry sauce. Serve as a vegetable
with salt and pepper.

Winter Apples

(*Pyrus*—several species)

Collection and Preparation

During the winter you might encounter apple trees still holding their fruit. These apples are favorites with winter birds, such as chickadees and grosbeaks and, although unappetizing in appearance, can also serve as human fare. Apples that mature late in the fall and then are frozen before much decomposition takes place can be boiled and prepared into a delicious slightly fermented tasting applesauce.

Select the best-looking fruit and use immediately. Wash the apples thoroughly, place into a saucepan and just cover with water. Boil slowly until the whole apples can be easily mashed. Place in a collander and with a flat wooden spoon force the applesauce and juice through. Discard the skins, seeds, and other inedible parts. Remember apple seeds are poisonous any time of the year. Sweeten the applesauce with honey.

Apple Garnish

Prepare the applesauce as described above and serve a tablespoonful or two with each serving of pork or chicken.

Frozen Apples. Profile of tree in winter to illustrate 1, fruit—crêpe filling.

Apple Crepes
(a gourmet dish made with frozen apples)
Crepes
(prepare an hour before eating)

4 tbsp unbleached
   white flour
1 egg yolk
1 whole egg

¼ tsp salt and pepper
2 tbsp cool melted butter
1 cup milk

Place the flour in a bowl and make a well in the center. Place the eggs, condiments, butter and 4 tablespoonsful of milk into the well. Beat ingredients with a wire whisk until smooth. Slowly add the remaining milk until the mixture is of a creamy consistency. Store in the refrigerator for an hour.

Grease a small frying pan, heat, cover the bottom with a thin layer of batter and brown on both sides. Cook the rest of the batter in the same way.

Crepe Filling and Topping

1 cup of applesauce
   prepared as described
   above

½ cup wintergreen syrup
   or maple syrup
¾ cup Cointreau (optional)

Place the applesauce in the center of each crepe and then spread it thinly. Roll up the crepes tightly, place in a Pyrex serving dish, pour the wintergreen sauce over them and serve. If you want a flaming dish, pour Cointreau over the sweetened crepes, ignite the liquor and serve.

Strawberry Leaves

Wild Strawberries (*Fragaria*—several species)

Collection and Preparation

Strawberries continue to produce their characteristic three leaflets throughout the winter. Look for the vitamin-C-rich leaves in clearings, fields, slopes and in rocky woods where the snow has melted thus revealing these hardy low-growing plants.

Vitamin C Rich Strawberry Leaf Tea
(an old English recipe)

¼ cup strawberry leaves   1¼ cups boiling water

Bruise the leaves and pour the boiling water over them. Cover and let simmer over low heat for 20 minutes.

Serve as is or sweeten with honey.

Maple

(*Acer*—several species)

History

Maple syrup and maple sugar are original American wild food products steeped in the history and lore of this country. When the first explorers arrived here, they found two main linguistic groups among the Indians of the northeast. These were the prominent Algonquians and the Iroquois whose people long followed the custom of tapping maples for the sweet sap. They consumed the newly drawn sap as a refreshing drink and food sweetener and they produced and relished maple syrup and maple sugar as tasty food sweeteners. Soon written reports filtered back to Europe describing the curious, hard, yellow Indian sugar made from the juice of "wounded maples." The white man readily saw the merits of this palatable and wholesome new food product and even today commercial maple syrup production is pursued in southeastern Canada and in the northeastern United States from Maine to Minnesota, south to Indiana and West Virginia. A tribute to the sugar maple (*Acer saccharum*) is the fact that long ago the people of Vermont, New York, and Wisconsin declared it their state tree and the Canadians chose its leaf as their national emblem.

The northeastern Indians tapped several species of maple and among the most popular were the sugar maple (*A. saccharum*), the black maple (*A. nigrum*), the silver maple (*A. saccharinum*), and the red maple (*A. rubrum*). Farther south, the southern sugar maple (*A. barbatum*) was sometimes used as a source of sugar and Indians of the north and west utilized the widely distributed box elder, or ash-leafed maple (*A. negundo*). In the early spring, the Indians made a V-shaped slash in the trees and then placed a reed or curved piece of bark at the point of the incision to convey the sap into large troughs made of elm bark or basswood. To make syrup from the sap they usually threw hot stones into the large troughs and then repeatedly let the mixture freeze. They cast off the ice leaving the thickened syrup at the bottom of the troughs. Sugar was made by repeating the freezing process until the syrup crystallized.

Many legends and myths involving the maple tree developed among the maple-sugar-eating Indians. The Mohicans believed that that melting snow in the spring furnished the maple trees with their sap. The snow itself was believed to be the dripping oil of the celestial bear that had been slain by the hunters in wintertime.

Several myths evolved which served to explain the dilute nature of the maple sap and, incidentally, revealed the Indians' awareness of human foibles. One from the Chippewa and Ottawa tribes tells how the devilish Ne-naw-bo-zhoo tasted the sweet sap and then diluted it until the sweet taste disappeared. He wanted there to be hard labor involved in making sugar from the sap, to ensure that the sugar would be more valued by his people. Another form of this myth was reported in 1891 from a Menomini Indian.

"One day Nokomis, the grandmother of Manabush, was in the forest and accidently cut the bark of a tree. Seeing that a thick syrup exuded from the cut, she put her finger to the substance, and upon tasting it found it to be very sweet and agreeable. She then gave some of it to her grandson, Manabush, who liked it very much, but thought that if the syrup ran from the trees in such a state it would cause idleness among the women. He then told Nokomis that in order to give his aunts employment and keep them from idleness he would dilute the thick sap. Whereupon he took up a vessel of water and poured it over the tops of the trees, and thus reduced the sap to its present consistency. This is why the women have to boil down the sap to make syrup." (Chamberlain 1891, p. 41).

Habitat, Range, and Description

The genus *Acer* is composed of approximately 148 species of trees and shrubs, which are mainly distributed in the temperate regions of the northern hemisphere. There are over a dozen species of maple in the United States today, eight of which are native; the others have been introduced and planted as shade trees. The sap of all the maples contains sugar in solution; in times of scarcity, all species could probably be tapped for their sugar. However, for commercial purposes, only the sugar maple and black maple produce sap of a fine enough quality to make it a profitable venture. The sap of these species can range from 1 to 9 percent sucrose with 2 to 3 percent being the average yield from a sugar lot.

The maples can be most easily identified by their usually simple, fan-shaped, lobed, opposite leaves. The box-elder is the only maple discussed here that has compound leaves. Another distinguishing characteristic is the paired, terminally winged fruits commonly referred to as "keys." Additional characteristics of 5 of our most common eastern maples are listed in Table 12.

Tapping Maples*

Maples should be tapped in late winter or early spring when the sap begins to "run." In Vermont the sap usually begins to flow around the middle of March and continues for a month or so with the best flow occurring when there are warm sunny days that have

* For more details concerning the production of maple products consult Department of Agriculture Extension Service in maple-producing states and they will furnish you with help and literature. Among the most informative of their publications is *Maple Sirup Producers Manual* (USDA Handbook 134). It is for sale (70¢) by the U.S. Government Printing Office, Washington, D.C. 20402.

TABLE 12

Habitat, Range, and Description of
Five Common Eastern Maples

Species	Habitat	Range
Sugar maple (*Acer saccharum*)	Rich, mostly hilly woods	New Brunswick to Northern Georgia, west to northeast Texas and north to southeastern Manitoba. Not on the south Atlantic or Gulf Coastal Plains
Black maple (*A. nigrum*) Note: Some botanists consider this species to be a subspecies of *A. saccharum*	Rich, moist woods	Southern Quebec and western New England to Kentucky and Missouri and north to southern Minnesota. Not on the Atlantic coast
Silver maple (*A. saccharinum*)	Riverbanks and bottomlands	New Bruswick to north-western Florida west to Oklahoma and north to Minnesota. Sparsely distributed along the Atlantic coast
Red maple (*A. rubrum*)	Swamps, low-lands, moist uplands	New Brunswick to Florida, west to east Texas and north to southern Ontario. Present along the Atlantic and Gulf coasts
Box-elder (*A. Negundo*)	Riverbanks	New Hampshire to northern Florida, west to Arizona and Nevada, north to Alberta. Rare on the coast except on the southeast Atlantic and the East Gulf

Description

Leaves: Mostly 5 lobed about
5" wide
Bark: Gray, gets deeply
furrowed with age

Flowers: Appear with leaves,
bright yellow
Fruit: U-shaped, mature in
autumn

Leaves: Mostly 3 lobed about
5" wide, hairy below
Bark: Dark gray, deeply
furrowed

Flowers: Same as sugar maple
Fruit: Same as sugar maple

Leaves: Deeply 5 lobed,
about 6" wide, silvery
below
Bark: Young trees silvery
gray, older trees have thin,
gray, scaly plates

Flowers: Appear before
leaves, green or red
Fruit: Wings very divergent,
mature in late spring

Leaves: 3 lobed, about 4"
wide
Bark: Young trees smooth
and gray, older trees have
scaly plates

Flowers: Appear before
leaves, reddish or yellow
Fruit: Wings slightly divergent, mature in late spring

Leaves: Compound with 3–7
leaflets, variable in shape
Bark: Thin, light brown,
fissured. Gets more
furrowed with age

Flowers: Appear just before
leaves, greenish
Fruit: V-shaped, mature in
late spring

Sugaring. Sap buckets on sugar maples.

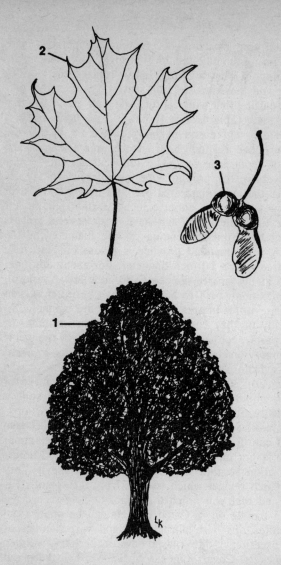

Sugar Maple. 1, Profile of tree grown in the open. 2, Broad leaf with five lobes. 3, U-shaped fruit. Sap of this tree and black maple used commercially for syrup, sugar, and confections.

followed cold frosty nights. Optimal temperatures are 55°F during the day and 25°F at night. In Vermont the beginning of the sugaring season marks the end of winter and the start of "mud season."

To ensure that you capture the first run, bore tap holes, insert spigots (or "spiles") and hang buckets just before sap season begins. Using a ⅜ inch wood drill bit, bore a 3 inch hole into the tree at an upward pitch of about 5 degrees. The hole is usually made 2 or 3 feet above the ground. One cannot reuse old holes because the immediate area becomes necrotic, but drill new ones each year about 6 inches to the right or left of the old hole. You can have 1 to several spigots circling the trunk depending on the diameter of the tree. A recommended practice is to use one tap hole on a tree with a 10 inch diameter. For each additional 4 to 6 inches in tree diameter add another tap hole up to a maximum of 4 to 5. Spigots can be purchased in hardware stores in areas where maples are tapped commercially or they can be fashioned from a number of plant parts, such as bark, basswood chips, or the stems of sumac, horsetail, elder or reeds. We prefer to carve spigots from the easily obtainable branches of the sumac. For each spigot, take a 7 inch long piece of branch about ¾ of an inch in diameter and split it lengthwise. Remove the pith (the soft central portion), thus creating a channel, and whittle down one end so that it can fit snugly into the tap hole. Gently hammer in the spigot until it is in the full 3 inches and adjust its position so that the sap can flow by gravity into your catch bucket which is hung from the spigot. It is suggested that you notch the spigot to help secure the bucket handle on it. Catch buckets can be made from old coffee tins with plastic tops and wire handles or from used heavy-duty plastic bags or, perhaps, wooden sap buckets. Cover your sap buckets to help keep out rainwater and plant or animal debris that might be blown or washed in.

Because standing sap has a tendency to spoil and can spoil fresh sap that might be mixed with it, collect

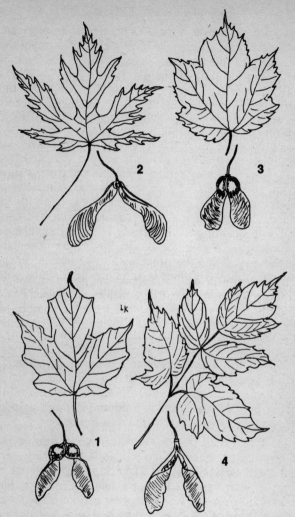

Black Maple (1), with three-lobed leaf and U-shaped fruit. **Silver Maple** (2), with delicate deeply five-lobed leaf and fruit with widely divergent wings. **Red Maple** (3), with three-lobed leaf, and fruit with wings slightly divergent. **Box Elder** (4), compound leaf with five-toothed leaflets and U-shaped fruit. Sap of all these species can be used for syrup and sugar.

your sap daily and refrigerate it or boil it down immediately.

Boiling Down Maple Sap to Syrup and Sugar

These procedures for boiling down maple sap are designed for the homeowner who is tapping one to several trees and is using a home range. The commercial production of maple products must of necessity follow more strictly prescribed methods.

A large old maple in a good season can produce about 100 gallons of sap. It takes approximately 40 gallons of sap to produce 1 gallon of sprup or 20 pounds of sugar. These figures indicate that one must deal with quantities of liquid not ordinarily handled in the kitchen. To ease the burden of boiling down, we suggest you divide the process into two phases. In the first phase, boil 3 gallons of sap down to a quart; pour this liquid into a clean screw-capped jar and store in the refrigerator. This phase takes 2 to 4 hours. When you have 4 or so quarts of partially boiled down sap, you can begin phase two of boiling down which is described under syrup and sugarmaking.

If your freshly collected sap has debris in it, filter it before you boil it down. When boiling sap, keep a high flame under the pot to ensure that you have a full rolling boil. Much steam is produced during this process and an exhaust fan is almost a necessity.

Making Maple Syrup
(time —about 1 hour)

4 qt partly boiled down sap (as described above)	1 clean cloth (felt, if possible)
1 candy thermometer	1 funnel
1 qt fruit jar or wine bottle (sterilized)	

You must determine the boiling point of water because it varies according to altitude. Bring water to a rolling boil in a saucepan and insert the candy thermometer into the water; the temperature at which the needle rests is the boiling point of water. At sea level, water boils at about 212°F.

We take our gallon of partially boiled down sap and place it into 2 saucepans and boil down under high heat. When the volume is halved, all the sap is poured into a single pan into which a candy thermometer has been placed. When the temperature reads 7°F above the boiling point of water, the syrup is done. Remove it from the heat, cool slightly, and filter through the cloth into the bottle. Cap and store in the refrigerator.

Making Granulated Maple Sugar and Sugar Candy
(time —about 1 hour)

4 qt partly boiled down sap (as described above)	1 bowl and 1 fork containers for sugar and
1 candy thermometer	candy

Determine the boiling point of water as described above. Bring the liquid 40 to 45°F above the boiling point of water (after the sap reaches the syrup stage, the temperature will rise very rapidly). Pour the thick liquid into the stirring bowl and stir rapidly with a fork until crystallization is completed. In about 5 minutes you will have a mixture of fine granulated sugar and some balls about half the size of marbles. We particularly enjoy the sugar on hot, whole-grained cereal and the balls are used as candy.

Maple Sap

These recipes using maple sap should be useful to people who might have only one tree to tap or who might not have sufficient amounts of sap to make boiling down to syrup worthwhile.

Maple Sap as a Cooling Drink
(a sweet survival food during sap season
and a great favorite with children)

Early missionaries in this country spoke of the Indians' use of the sweet maple sap as a refreshing drink. To obtain this sweet sap, the Iroquois either made a rough incision in the bark or ripped off the end of an overhanging limb and caught the sap with a bark or wooden container.

These procedures for obtaining sap are not good for the trees and boring a hole as described earlier in this section is recommended unless you are stranded.

Serve freshly collected sap as a light beverage with your meals or drink it as a snack.

Partially Boiled Down Maple Sap
(a fragrant and mildly sweet topping)

**3 qt maple sap to a
cup of syrup**

Boil down the sap over a medium high flame until you have a cup of liquid.

Serve plain as a hot or cold drink, mix half and half with milk, or use on hotcakes and other dishes. Some people prefer this syrup over regular maple syrup because the latter is so sweet.

Maple Sap Popsicles
(a mildly sweet ice)

Take freshly collected sap and pour into molds, such as muffin tins, and place in the freezer until firm. Stand the tins at room temperature for a few minutes and remove the ice from them. Eat immediately.

To make a sweeter ice, boil down the sap until it is one half or one third its original volume and then freeze.

Sap Beer
(a warming beverage to help you welcome the spring)

4 gal sap   ½ lb raisins

Boil down the sap over medium high heat until you have half the original volume. Remove from heat, allow to cool, and mix in the raisins. Cover the crock with a clean cloth, store in a cool part of the house, and let ferment for a week to 10 days. When the beer is ready, cool and serve.

Sap Vinegar

6 gal sap   1 yeast cake

Boil down the sap until it is one half to one third its original volume. Remove from heat, allow to cool, and pour into a crock. Dissolve the yeast in a little of the liquid and add it to the crock. Cover the crock with a towel and store in a cool room for 6 weeks or until it stops bubbling. Filter and pour into clean bottles. Place bottles in a water bath and bring vinegar to 150°F for 30 minutes. Cork before cooling.

This homemade white vinegar can be used in the same ways as the store-bought product.

Maple Sugar as Seasoning

An interesting custom developed by the Menomini Indians was their practice of not using salt, but instead, employing maple syrup and maple sugar as seasonings during meals and in their baking and cooking. The wisdom of this aboriginal custom has been confirmed by modern chemical analyses of these maple products, which have been found to be rich in minerals and carbohydrates. Like brown cane or beet sugar, maple sugar and maple syrup contain the nutritionally important minerals calcium, iron, phosphorus, sodium, and potassium, being especially rich in calcium and potassium. Why not add these nutritious native sweeteners to your diet?

To those of you who do not make your own maple syrup and sugar but still want to try some maple recipes, stand forewarned that maple sources of sweets are relatively more expensive than cane sugar products; but the rich and unique maple flavor helps compensate for the cost differential.

Maple Sweetened Parched Corn
(an Iroquois traveling food)

cornmeal (parched)   dried berries or nuts
maple sugar to taste   (optional)

Dry the cornmeal in a skillet over the fire or on medium heat on your stove. Add the maple sugar and dried berries or nuts if desired. Pour the ingredients into dry, covered containers and store in a moderately cool place.

When ready to eat, add sufficient hot or cold water to make a loose mush. This mixture swells upon addition of the water and can provide a filling, nutritious, and easy-to-transport woodland food. The Iroquois carried this concentrated dried food with them in times of war and when on hunting trips, away from home.

If mush is not to your taste, try the next two recipes in which the ingredients used here are prepared into different products that can be readily prepared in the wild.

Boiled Corn Bread
(an easy-to-prepare woodland bread)

Use the same ingredients as for the previous recipe. Mix together the sugar and cornmeal and add enough boiling water to make a paste. Knead and add the dried berries or nuts if desired. Break off lumps of the paste and mold them into balls about 2 inches in diameter. Place the balls into a pan of boiling water and cook until they float to the surface. Once the bread has begun to float, remove it from the water immediately lest it fall apart. When first removed from the water the bread will be rather soft but upon cooling, it will become firmer and easier to handle. Serve as is or add honey and butter.

Do not discard the water you used for this recipe, because it can be employed in the recipes described below.

Corn Bread Liquor Soup or Drink
(an interesting way to stretch your food supply
—from the Iroquois Indians)

liquor used for boiling   maple sugar (to taste)
    corn bread

Sweeten the liquor with the maple sugar. Heat and serve as a soup or cool and serve as a sweet drink.

Maple Syrup

Along with its wide use as a topping for hot cakes, cereals, ice cream and pudding, maple syrup can be used to make nutritious relishes, glazes and sweet drinks. Some of our favorite maple syrup recipes are given below.

Maple Mustard
(a delicious topping for vegetables and cold cuts)

2 tbsp prepared mustard
  to each tbsp maple syrup

Blend ingredients until smooth and serve with hot or cold dishes.

Maple Relish
(a unique relish for fish or fowl)

juice of two oranges   (diced fine)
juice of 1 lemon   ½ cup maple syrup
2 cups chopped apples

Combine all ingredients, chill, and serve as a garnish for poultry or fish.

Maple Glazed Ham

1 ham (4 to 5 lb)   ½ cup maple syrup

Bake ham according to your method until half done. Remove from oven and pour off the drippings. Baste the ham with half of the syrup and return to oven. Every 15 minutes baste with the remaining syrup and new drippings.

Maple Egg Nog
(a nutritious, natural food drink)

1 cup milk   1 egg
1 tbsp maple syrup

Combine all ingredients in a blender and beat 1 minute. If you do not have a blender, beat the egg with a fork until foamy, mix in the syrup, add the milk, and stir. Serve cold.

Maple Baked Beans
(for 4)

1 lb dried navy beans	¼ tsp dry mustard
3 tbsp vinegar	1 tsp salt
½ cup maple syrup	½ lb salt pork

Wash the beans, cover with water, and soak overnight. Simmer over low heat for an hour or until the beans are tender and then ladle them into a bean pot or casserole with just enough water to cover them.

Set the oven at 300°F. Dice the salt pork into 1 inch pieces and brown in a frying pan over medium heat. Remove from pan and place on brown paper. Set aside.

Mix the maple syrup, vinegar, mustard, and salt. Stir this mixture plus the salt pork into the beans, and bake for 4 hours. Cover during the first 2 hours then uncover and continue to cook for the remaining 2 hours.

Serve hot or cold.

Glossary of General Terms

Algae—Simple plants that undergo photosynthesis. They have no vascular tissue, or true roots, stems, or leaves. They are found mainly in aquatic environments (see p. xxiii).

Annual—A plant that completes its life cycle in a single year.

Biennial—A plant that takes two years to complete its life cycle. Food is stored in the first year and flowers and fruit are produced in the second.

Bivalve—A mollusk having a shell of two parts joined by a hinge. The pelecypods (see p. xxi).

Conifer—A cone-bearing plant.

Family—Taxonomic category consisting of similar genera. In animals, the family name ends in *idae;* in plants usually in *ceae*.

Fern—A perennial, usually with roots, stems, and large leaves. Reproduction by spores, not seeds (see p. xv).

Gastropod—One of the six classes of mollusks. Representatives are snails and slugs (see p. xxi).

Genus—A taxonomic category including one or more species. Genus is capitalized and printed in italics.

Habitat—The natural and normal place an animal or plant lives and grows.

Herb—A plant with no persistent woody parts above ground as distinct from shrubs and trees.

Intertidal—Pertaining to the part of the sea bottom between the high- and low-tide marks.

Mollusk—Any invertebrate, such as a squid, snail or clam, having a soft body typically enclosed in a calcareous shell. Broadly known as shellfish (see p. xxi).

Naturalized—Pertaining to an organism not native to a region, but established and reproducing as though a native.

Perennial—A plant that has a life cycle of more than two years.

Range—An area over which an organism lives or grows.

Seaweed—Any, usually large, marine alga, as kelp (see p. xxiii).

Seed—The part of a flowering plant that contains an embryo capable of germinating, and having a protective cover and usually some food.

Shrub—Any woody perennial having several stems and usually less than 30 feet high.

Species—Usually the smallest unit of taxonomic category. In sexually reproducing organisms it is a group that can interbreed. Species is printed in italics and usually begins with a lowercase letter.

Spore—An asexual reproductive body, usually produced by plants.

Subtidal—Below the low-tide mark.

Tree—Any perennial woody plant with a trunk.

Weed—Any plant that grows without cultivation (particularly on cultivated land) and is considered valueless by (most) people.

Bibliography

Aiken, G. D. *Pioneering with Wild Flowers*. Englewood Cliffs, N.J.: Prentice-Hall, 1968.

Anderson, E. *Plants, Man and Life*. Berkeley, Calif.: Univ. of Calif. Press, 1967.

Baker, H. G. *Plants and Civilization*. Belmont, Calif.: Wadsworth Pub., 1970.

Barnes, R. D. *Invertebrate Zoology*. Philadelphia: W. B. Saunders Co., 1968.

Bartram, W. *Travels through North and South Carolina, Georgia, East and West Florida, the Cherokee Country, the Extensive Territories of the Muscogulges or Creek Confederacy and the Country of the Choctaws*. London, 1772. New York: Columbia Univ. Press, Facsimile Library Text, 1940.

————. "Observations on the Creek and Cherokee Indians." *Transactions of the American Ethnological Society* 3, Pt. 1 (1909).

Biggar, H. P., ed. *The Voyages of Jacques Cartier*. Ottawa: F. A. Actland Press, 1924.

Buchsbaum, R., and Milne, L. J. *The Lower Animals*. New York: Doubleday & Co., 1966.

Chamberlain, A. F. "The Maple Amongst the Algonkian Tribes." *American Anthropologist* 4 (1891): 39–43.

————. "Maple Sugar and the Indians." *American Anthropologist* 4 (1891): 381–84.

Chamberlain, L. S., "Plants Used by the Indians of North America." *American Naturalist* 35 (1901):

Classen, P. W. "A Possible New Source of Food Supply." *New York State Museum Bulletin 144* (1919): 179–85.

Crowder, W. C. *Between the Tides*. New York: Dodd, Mead & Co., 1931.

Dale, B. "The Water Harvesters." *Field and Stream,* no. 4 (1906): 319–24.

Dawson, E. Y. *Marine Botany.* New York: Holt, Rinehart & Winston, 1966.

Earle, A. M. *Home Life in Colonial Days.* New York: The Macmillan Co., 1898.

Eastwood, B. *Complete Manual for the Cultivation of the Cranberry.* New York: C. M. Saxton, Barker & Co., 1857.

Eddy, S. *How to Know the Freshwater Fishes.* Dubuque, Iowa: Wm. C. Brown Co., 1970.

Fenton, W. N. "Contacts Between Iroquois Herbalism and Colonial Medicine." *Annual Report of Smithsonian Institution* (1942): 503–26.

Fernald, M. L. *Gray's Manual of Botany.* New York: American Book Co., 1950.

Fernald, M. L.; Kinsey, A. C.; and Rollins, R. C. *Edible Plants of Eastern North America.* New York: Harper & Row, 1958.

Gleason, H. A. *The New Britton and Brown Illustrated Flora of the Northeastern United States and Adjacent Canada.* 3 vols. New York: Hafner Press, 1958.

———, and Cronquist, A. *The Natural Geography of Plants.* New York: Columbia Univ. Press, 1964.

Gookin, D. *Historical Collections of the Indians in New England.* New York: Arno Press, 1972.

Grieve, M. *A Modern Herbal.* 2 vols. New York: Dover Publications, 1971.

Guberlet, M. L. *Seaweeds at Ebb Tide.* Seattle: Univ. of Wash. Press, 1956.

Hariot, T. *Narrative of the First English Plantation of Virginia.* London: Bernard Quaritch, 1893.

Havard, V. "Food Plants of the North American Indians." *Torrey Botanical Club Bulletin 22* (1893): 98–123.

———. "Drink Plants of the North American Indians." *Torrey Botanical Club Bulletin 23* (1896): 36–46.

Hay, J. *The Run.* New York: Ballantine Books, 1971.

Hedrick, U. P. *A History of Horticulture in America to 1860.* New York: Oxford Univ. Press, 1950.

Herald, E. S. *Living Fishes of the World.* New York: Doubleday & Co., 1961.

Hill, A. F. *Economic Botany*. New York: McGraw-Hill Book Co., 1952.

Hopkins, M. "Wild Plants Used in Cooking." *Journal of the New York Botanical Garden 43* (1942): 71–76.

Kingsbury, J. M. *Poisonous Plants of the United States and Canada*. Englewood Cliffs, N.J.: Prentice-Hall, 1964.

Kroeber, T. *Ishi in Two Worlds*. Berkeley, Calif.: Univ. of Calif. Press, 1961.

Lawson, J. *Lawson's History of North Carolina*. Richmond, Va.: Garrett and Massie, 1937.

Lucas, R. *Nature's Medicines*. Englewood Cliffs, N.J.: Parker Publishing Co., 1966.

MacGintrie, G. E., and N. *Natural History of Marine Animals*. New York: McGraw-Hill Book Co., 1968.

Meehan, T. "Historical Notes on the Arbor Vitae." *Proceedings of the Academy of Natural Sciences of Philadelphia 34* (1882): 110–11.

Miner, R. W. *Field Book of Seashore Life*. New York: G. P. Putnam's Sons, 1950.

Morris, P. A. *A Field Guide to the Shells*. Boston: Houghton Mifflin Co., 1951.

Mugford, P. S. *Illustrated Manual of Massachusetts Freshwater Fishes*. Boston: Massachusetts Division of Fisheries and Game, 1969.

Odum, E. P. *Fundamentals of Ecology*. Philadelphia: W. B. Saunders, 1971.

Osal, A.; Pratt, R.; and Altschule, M. *The United States Dispensatory* 26th ed. Philadelphia: J. B. Lippincott Co., 1967.

Peterson, R. T. and M. McKenny. *A Field Guide to Wild Flowers*. Boston: Houghton Mifflin Co., 1968.

Petrides, G. A. *A Field Guide to the Trees and Shrubs*. Boston: Houghton Mifflin Co., 1958.

Porcher, F. P. *Resources of the Southern Fields and Forests*. New York: Arno Press, 1970.

Pratt, H. S. *Manual of the Common Invertebrate Animals*. New York: McGraw-Hill Book Co., 1935.

Ray, C., and Ciampi, E. *The Underwater Guide to Marine Life*. Cranbury, N.J.: A. S. Barnes & Co., 1956.

Rohde, E. S. *A Garden of Herbs*. Boston: Hale, Cushman & Flint, 1936.

Smith, H. H. "Ethnobotany of the Menomini Indians." *Bulletin of the Public Museum of the City of Milwaukee* 4, no. 1 (1923): 1–174.

Smith, R. L. *Ecology and Field Biology*. New York: Harper & Row, 1966.

Solbrig, O. T. "The Population Biology of Dandelions." *American Scientist* 59 (1971): 686–94.

Swanton, J. R. *The Indians of the Southeastern United States*. Westport, Conn.: Greenwood Press, 1969.

Symonds, G. W. D., and Chelminski, S. V. *The Tree Identification Book*. New York: M. Barrows, 1958.

Taylor, W. R. *Marine Algae of the Northeastern Coast of North America*. Ann Arbor, Mich.: Univ. of Mich. Press, 1957.

Teal, J., and M. *Life and Death of the Salt Marsh*. Boston: Atlantic Monthly Press, 1969.

Thorson, G. *Life in the Sea*. New York: McGraw-Hill Book Co., 1971.

Tiedjens, V. A. *The Vegetable Encyclopedia and Gardeners Guide*. Philadelphia: Blakiston New Home Library, 1943.

Tilden, J. E. *The Algae and Their Life Relations*. Minneapolis: Univ. of Minn. Press, 1935.

Trautman, M. B. *The Fishes of Ohio*. Athens, Ohio: Ohio Univ. Press, 1957.

Trigger, B. G. *The Huron: Farmers of the North*. New York: Holt, Rinehart & Winston, 1969.

Underhill, R. M. *Red Man's America*. Chicago: Univ. of Chicago Press, 1953.

United States Government Printing Office. *After a Hundred Years*. Washington, D.C.: Government Printing Office, 1962.

———. *Composition of Foods*. Washington, D.C.: Government Printing Office, 1963.

———. *Food*. Washington, D.C.: Government Printing Office, 1959.

———. *Food and Life*. Washington, D.C.: Government Printing Office, 1939.

————. *Food Plants of the North American Indians.* Washington, D.C.: Government Printing Office, 1936.

————. *Maple Sirup Producers Manual.* Washington, D.C.: Government Printing Office, 1965.

————. *Silvics of Forest Trees of the United States.* Washington, D.C.: Government Printing Office, 1965.

————. *Trees.* Washington, D.C.: Government Printing Office, 1949.

Waugh, F. W. *Iroquois Foods and Food Preparation.* Ottawa: Government Printing Bureau, 1916.

Werthner, W. B. *Some American Trees.* New York: The Macmillan Co., 1935.

Wherry, E. T. "Go Slow on Eating Fern Fiddleheads." *American Fern Journal 32* (1942): 108–09.

Williams, S.C., ed. *Adair's History of the American Indians.* Johnson City, Tennessee: Watauga Press, 1930.

Wittrock, M. A. and G. L. "Food Plants of the Indians." *Journal of the New York Botanical Garden 43* (1942): 57–71.

Index